THE ELUSIVE HUMAN SUBJECT

020 7 487 7449

THE ELUSIVE HUMAN SUBJECT

A Psychoanalytical Theory of Subject Relations

ROGER KENNEDY

FREE ASSOCIATION BOOKS / LONDON / NEW YORK

Published in 1998 by
Free Association Books Ltd
57 Warren Street, London W1P 5PA
and 70 Washington Square South,
New York, NY 10012–1091

© Roger Kennedy 1998

The right of Roger Kennedy to be identified as the author
of this work has been asserted by him in accordance with
the Copyright, Designs and Patents Act 1988.

ISBN 1 85343 394 2 hardback; 1 85343 396 9 paperback.

A CIP catalogue record for this book is available from
the British Library.

Produced for Free Association Books Ltd by
Chase Production Services, Chadlington, OX7 3LN
Printed in the EC by J. W. Arrowsmith Ltd, Bristol

CONTENTS

ACKNOWLEDGEMENTS

Chapter 2 appeared in an earlier version in *Psychoanalytic Dialogues* (1995) 6:73–96. An outline of the theme of the book appeared in *Psychoanalytic Dialogues* (1997) 7:553–81.

I would like to thank the following for permission to quote from published material: Macmillan Press Ltd for permission to quote from *The Division of Labour* by E. Durkheim, translated by W.D. Halls; The Free Press for permission to quote from *The Elementary Forms of Religious Life* by E. Durkheim, translated by K. Fields; and the University of Chicago Press for permission to quote from *Mind, Self and Society* by G. Mead, edited by C. Morris.

AUTHOR'S NOTE

In the interests of clarity and simplicity, I use masculine pronouns throughout the book, so that complex theories are not further complicated by the awkwardness of writing 'he or she' / 'him- or herself'. I hope this will not cause offence.

TO JENNY

1 INTRODUCTION: WHERE IS THE HUMAN SUBJECT?

THE CENTRELESS SUBJECT

I begin with a question about the location of human subjectivity which seems to be vital to the psychoanalytic experience, but which is full of difficulties and ambiguities. I shall suggest that there is something essentially elusive about our subjective life, which makes it difficult to capture. I shall nevertheless attempt to examine something about the nature of our subjective life, from a theoretical and clinical point of view. In the *Interpretation of Dreams*, Freud came up with an image of the mental apparatus that highlighted this very issue. In order to capture the way that the mental apparatus functioned, he disregarded any notion of anatomical locality; instead, he pictured the apparatus to be like a compound microscope or a photographic instrument. 'On that basis, psychical locality will correspond to a point inside the apparatus at which one of the preliminary stages of an image comes into being. In the microscope and telescope, as we know, these occur in part at ideal points, regions in which no tangible component of the apparatus is situated' (Freud, 1900, p.536).

I shall explore how we can have access to the human subject not only through what we experience as individuals, 'inside the apparatus' as it were, but also through multiple and complex interactions between individuals in the social field. Indeed, one of my main points is that it is in the social field, through these interactions, that we find some degree of coherence. These interactions may be experienced as events, but I will suggest that it is still difficult to say where the subject is located; except perhaps, to adapt Freud's analogy, at various 'ideal' points of contact between subjects.

The issue of where and how subjectivity is located is not only of theoretical interest but is, I would suggest, of clinical relevance. The clinical setting provides a unique opportunity for understanding the enigmas of subjectivity. Psychoanalysts deal with human suffering and we have privileged access to the most intimate and complex aspects of human reality. Yet it is not uncommon to discover that it may be very difficult for the patient to be in contact with his subjective life; indeed, he may actively avoid it. Through the intimate encounter between analyst and patient there may gradually arise a sense that the patient can locate something more subjective. We may describe these moments in terms of something 'alive' happening in the session, or patient and analyst having 'live contact', the patient being more 'in touch'; the patient having 'insight', or the patient having some increased sense of himself, more sense of an 'internal' space. Though these practical descriptions are useful and may serve their purpose in the day-to-day work of analysis, I would suggest that human subjectivity, or the nature of what one might call our 'subjective world', is far more complex than they imply. I would also suggest that it is worthwhile to examine the nature of subjectivity, using a number of different disciplines, not only out of theoretical interest, but also because ultimately this will help us understand more about what we do with our patients in the clinical setting. Though my own investigation will follow a number of different disciplines, I aim to keep the clinical encounter as my base, even though it may appear to drift out of sight on occasions.

I shall propose that the term 'subject' as a functioning structure is certainly not one that can only be applied to 'internal' states belonging to a single individual, but that it merges with what has been traditionally called the 'social', a point of view I take from Freud. His own position was that social psychology and individual psychology merged into one another, with individual psychology concerned with the satisfaction of instincts, and social psychology with the relations between individuals. As he put it in *Group Psychology and the Analysis of the Ego*:

> The contrast between individual psychology and social or group psychology, which at first glance may seem to be full of significance, loses a great deal of its sharpness when it is examined closely. It is true that individual psychology is concerned with the individual man and explores the paths by which he seeks to find satisfaction for his instinctual impulses; but only rarely and under certain exceptional conditions is individual psychology in a position to disregard the relations of this individual to others. In the individual's mental life someone else is invariably involved, as a model, as an object, as a helper, as an opponent; and so from the very first individual psychology, in this extended but entirely justifiable sense of the words, is at the same time social psychology as well. (Freud, 1921, p.69)

My own inquiry starts from a similar position, extending so-called individual psychology into the territory of social psychology with which it is, in my view, inextricably linked. This assumption will have a number of theoretical and clinical ramifications, not the least of which is concerned with the problem of psychical locality and subjectivity; for example, whether or not it makes sense to locate the subject in the individual, in the social field, somewhere between, or, as I shall propose, at some shifting position, involving both individual and social fields. My overall emphasis is that in trying to make sense of the complex issue of human subjectivity it is necessary to have a pluralistic model, one which takes account of multiple streams or processes, consisting of many elements with varying degrees of connectedness. Though there is complexity in this way of thinking, I also propose to consider how the many elements may cohere by means of various amounts of organization.

An image comes to mind which may begin to illustrate what I mean. Think of a field in the country, perhaps recently ploughed. The farmer may or may not be visible at the moment you come across the field; certainly he has left traces of his work. Around the field there are a number of paths, some of them cross one another, not necessarily in any order. The field can be used to cultivate a number of different crops; it may be dug up, left fallow, used in a variety of ways, for leisure or for economic activity. If you use special techniques it may be possible to have a picture of how the field was used in the past, where previous paths were made and old crops were sewn. The field is like the human subject, with criss-crossing paths and furrows, available for multiple use, and with the farmer, the owner of the field, coming and going in order to attend to it. There is no centre in the field as such, at least not in a functional sense; it has a different kind of structure, a network of traces of activity, with varying degrees of organization.

The philosopher Thomas Nagel has a similar description of the world, which he also considers as centreless, full of many different points of view:

> when we conceive of the world as centerless we are conceiving of it as it is. Not being a solipsist, I do not believe that the point of view from which I see the world is the perspective of reality. Mine is only one of the many points of view from which the world is seen. The centerless conception of the world must include all the innumerable subjects of consciousness on a roughly equal footing – even if some see the world more clearly than others. (Nagel, 1986, p.57)

Nagel graphically captures this view of the world in the title of the book from which I have quoted, *The View from Nowhere*. That is, the centre is nowhere to be found, and we have to view the world from that position.

The old quest for the human 'centre' is perhaps reminiscent of the search for the location of the 'soul', or for the place where consciousness resides or where memory or language is centrally organized by the brain. As I shall discuss in due course, these quests have proved fruitless until the search for a centre has been abandoned in favour of an 'interactional' model, where a function is produced as a result of interaction between many elements, many paths as it were. Such a model was, I believe, an integral part of Freud's thinking, at least since his early work on speech disorders – *On Aphasia* (Freud, 1891) – where he saw language as a property of the whole language system in the brain rather than as only a property of individual areas. As I shall explore in Chapter 2, Freud continued to use this interactional approach in his psychoanalytical thinking. I would suggest that such an approach to the nature of the human psyche is fundamentally different from that which starts out from the individual mind isolated from other minds, on the lines begun by Descartes, where, in the French philosopher Paul Ricoeur's words, 'The subjectivity that posits itself through reflection on its own doubt, a doubt radicalized by the fable of the great deceiver, is a free-floating subjectivity' (Ricoeur, 1990, p.7). That is, this form of subjectivity first described by Descartes and still central to so much philosophical and psychoanalytic thought, is free-floating in the sense of being cut off from the social world; for only that kind of knowledge formed by the solitary Cartesian ego is certain. Freud's thought at times adheres to the traditional Cartesian world; but there is often a pull towards another kind of thinking, which takes account of the fleeting and ambiguous nature of our subjective life as it exists in relation to a world of other subjects, and which cannot be tied down to the centralized and solitary ego.

However, Freud does have some place for the notion of a 'soul', though not as an entity located in some centre. As Bettelheim has reminded us, Freud considered that psychoanalysis was ultimately the treatment of man's soul (German *Seele*). Freud was not precise about what the soul was, which is perhaps ironic, considering how important it was for him. Bettelheim suggested that he chose the term '*because* of its inexactitude, its emotional resonance. Its ambiguity speaks for the ambiguity of the psyche itself, which reflects many different, warring levels of consciousness simultaneously. By "soul" or "psyche" Freud means that which is most valuable in man while he is alive ... it is intangible, but it nevertheless exercises a powerful influence on our lives. It is what makes us human' (Bettelheim, 1983, pp.77–8).

Indeed, the notion of a soul does seem to capture the human aspects of psychoanalysis in an emotionally convincing way; in that psychoanalysts treat human souls, and we have to respect the uniqueness of each individual soul, as I shall explore in Chapter 4. But that does not imply that this entity is isolated from others or is located at some specific and identifiably objective place.

Different ways of conceiving human subjectivity are not only of theoretical or clinical interest but may concretely affect our daily life and the political structures which surround us. Thus thought which strives to find a centre rather than accept multiple paths seems more common in dictatorships. Vaclav Havel (1986) describes eloquently in his essay 'The power of the powerless' how in the modern totalitarian state the centre of power is identical with the centre of truth; only the centralized state has the truth. The way that power is structured in this way affects every individual; by insisting that truth is in the centre, the individual lives within a lie rather than in the truth. Havel describes how this occurs with the manager of a fruit and vegetable shop, when he places a communist slogan in his window, in order to ingratiate himself with the authorities, whether or not he actually agrees with what the slogan says. Havel describes in detail how multiple similar acts bolster up and bind together the entire totalitarian power structure, with the 'glue' of a lying ideology focused around the notion of some central site where truth can be found. However, Havel also and prophetically imagined what would happen if one day the greengrocer were to snap and stop putting up the slogans merely to ingratiate himself. If this act were repeated all over, then he suggested that the 'entire pyramid of totalitarian power, deprived of the element that binds it together, would collapse in upon itself, as it were, in a kind of material implosion' (Havel, 1986, p.46). This would be a revolution of the powerless, as of course occurred in Eastern Europe in 1989.

Havel also pointed out that living a lie is unfortunately part of the human condition, that human beings can be compelled to live within a lie only because they are in fact capable of living in this way. We are easily seduced by the offer of clear answers and the wish for certainty, psychoanalysts no less than anyone else. Living in the truth on the contrary is difficult perhaps because it 'covers a vast territory whose outer limits are vague and difficult to map, a territory full of modest expressions of human volition' (ibid., p.85).

One could perhaps apply some of Havel's thinking directly to the clinical setting, not only by providing a restraining influence on those psychoanalysts and patients who have difficulty in tolerating uncertainty, but also more directly in the understanding of how some patients may wish to hold on to the notion of a centre in order to avoid the truth. This is more obvious with psychotic patients whose life may be organized around a central delusion; but also relevant to less ill patients, where a symptom can become the central focus of conflicts.

A brief clinical example may highlight what I mean. This is from a rather depressed and borderline patient who had great difficulty in simply having feelings located anywhere within himself. This caused him a considerable amount of frustration and despair. Almost the only time that he was aware of having a positive emotion was when he recalled some songs his otherwise depressed mother sang to him as a boy. On the other hand, he could become very angry about the political situation in this country. He was particularly angry when there was any issue concerned with the increasing centralization of power and the loss of local autonomy. This became almost an obsession with him; the obsession seemed to organize much of his life and had become the central focus of his waking thoughts. In the early part of treatment most of the sessions were concerned with my pointing out where his fierce political views were reflections of his own state of mind. This did free his thoughts a little to begin to focus around other matters. They certainly had become very fixed and limited in scope; there were, as it were, few paths for them to take. His political thoughts, though intellectually turned against centralized authority, became in themselves, in the ruthless way they dominated him, a kind of authoritarian organization of his subjective life.

Much of his childhood was spent in isolated play where he would build complicated city landscapes, escaping into a kind of safe citadel under his own control. His mother had been generally unresponsive to him as a child, and his father came across as an uncaring and ruthless figure.

Treatment was quite difficult and progress slow. Whenever there was some slight shift in him, he was deeply sceptical about his own capacity to hold on to anything positive. He did not present many dreams, but the following one became quite useful.

Neil Kinnock was with various figures from the Labour Party's National Executive, which my patient named. Kinnock turned his back on the others so that he was 150 degrees to them. He became ruthless as a chairman. Whenever the others began to speak with any hesitation, he would not allow them a moment's parenthesis or doubt. The patient at this point talked with great relish about this.

His associations led to the following themes: he never had a sense of coherence, particularly where feelings were concerned. He was plagued by a ruthless sense of constantly being taken to pieces, with no feeling of rest. He despaired about ever being able to stop this from happening.

We spent some time looking again at how he took himself to pieces. The very fact that he had had a dream was for him a particularly positive step, and yet he was already trying to dismiss it as having no value. In fact, attention to his self-critical side was fairly helpful; he did become more aware of his destructive impulses. At some point in the session I had the thought that the angle between my chair and the analytic couch was roughly 150 degrees, the angle in the dream, and so clearly this was some implied reference to me. He was somewhat startled by my observation. He was amazed and fairly sceptical about a dream having any reference to me at all. But my observation led to his thinking that he did wish for order, for someone like myself to chair his 'executive'; but until now this was only possible with a ruthless chairman who demanded absolute accuracy, even absolute certainty, really a dictator – more like the Prime Minister of that time than the Leader of the Opposition, he added wryly. This led him to realize that for most of the time he felt that he had no chairman in his mind, that there was no centre and hence constant anarchy. He was not sure if he wanted any central authority, after all this would conflict with his political beliefs, but its absence was a problem. He was reminded of his childhood, where he had created a solitary and precarious world of isolated play, which had also been full of anxiety and despair, because there were no other children, and because he would build and build but was never satisfied with what he had created. He had hoped for some kind of order but in fact there was only a feeling of emptiness.

Thus my patient highlights in his very being the whole issue of whether or not there is or should be a central organizing psychic structure and its significance. Is the quest for the centre doomed to fail, and hence a symptom in itself? Is the desire for a centre in fact a reflection of chaos, so that with my patient his feeling of emptiness was a result of a desire for a 'central executive', not the result of its absence? My patient thus raises some fundamental issues which inform some of the following arguments.

Freud's overturning of the central place of conscious reason in the life of the subject in favour of the unconscious, or the so-called 'decentering' of the subject, has often been compared to the revolution produced by Copernicus when he proposed that the earth revolved round the sun and not the other way round. But there is a further development of this 'Copernican' revolution; the individual is no longer even the centre of his own world; instead, the individual subject belongs to a wider structure, one which involves the network of other subjects. As I shall discuss in detail later, there is no one centre in this network; rather I would conceive of a series of 'contact points', where subjects meet one another. As I shall argue, the organization that involves the subject, what I shall call the 'subjective organization', goes beyond that of the individual as such and includes the realm of the social, and thus cuts into what can be seen mistakenly as two rather separate realms, the individual and the social. The advantage of using a psychoanalytic perspective is that it can provide a detailed description of subjective states; however, I think that this approach needs insights gained by other disciplines such as sociology in order to fill in the wider social perspective.

In order to illustrate my general viewpoint in a brief but perhaps vivid way, I would like to quote part of an essay by the distinguished art critic David Sylvester on the artist Paul Klee. Sylvester is trying to capture what makes Klee's forms so different from the traditional means of representation. I feel that what he says echoes some of the ways that we can now begin more fully to understand subjectivity with its many aspects, compared to the more limited view of ourselves as focused around a single and isolated point. As Sylvester writes:

The last works of Klee undermine your perceptual habits ...

These are pictures without a focal point. They cannot be seen by a static eye, for to look at the whole surface simultaneously, arranged about its centre – or any other point which at first seems a possible focal point – is to encounter an attractive chaos. The eye must not rest, it must allow itself to be forced away from the centre to find a point at which it can enter the composition – there are usually many such points, most of them near the edge – and so journey through the picture ...

Even the most diffuse compositions in the Renaissance tradition lead the eye to a single, usually central, point of focus, a point at which all formal and spatial relations are concentrated. If any points in a Klee are outstanding, they are not points of arrival but points of departure. Their predominance is therefore ephemeral. In the long run, all points are of equal importance. Indeed, they are of no individual importance because they are only stages, fixed by an arbitrary choice, in the journey which is the reality ...

In a late Klee, every point of arrival at once becomes a point of departure. The journey is unending. (Sylvester, 1996, pp.35–6)

Thus Klee's work, like many modernist artists, moves away from the traditional, central point of focus towards many-faceted and unending points of departure. (I think that this kind of open-ended process was something that the patient I described above found very difficult indeed.) This description could equally apply to those occasions when we try and look intimately into our own and other people's subjective lives. When the life of the subject is looked at, it is inevitable that another subject comes into view. As Ricoeur described from a philosophical viewpoint, 'Oneself as another [the title of his book] suggests from the outset that the selfhood of oneself implies otherness to such an intimate degree that one cannot be thought about without the other, that instead one passes into the other' (Ricoeur, 1990, p.3).

My own exploration of this field will proceed along a number of different paths, or points of departure, borrowing from, and making excursions into, philosophy, sociology, neurophysiology, social psychology and social anthropology, while keeping psychoanalysis as my home base. The Russian thinker Bakhtin, to whom I shall refer on a number of occasions, wrote that ideas begin to take shape, come to life and develop only when entering into genuine dialogue with other ideas and with the ideas of others (Bakhtin, 1963, p.88). In order to develop my own thinking I have always felt the need to take account of a number of other disciplines and the many different vantage points which each discipline has to offer. Though I may run the risk of being too eclectic, I would suggest that the topic of human subjectivity is so vast that it is only though encountering multiple contact points between disciplines that one can begin to do justice to it. However, I shall also endeavour to carve out the psychoanalytic contribution to the topic, and on some occasions to illustrate my points with clinical material.

SUBJECT RELATIONS

I will specifically aim to develop for a discussion a number of speculations and proposals about a 'subject relations' theory of psychoanalysis, focusing on how subjects interact with other subjects. Much of what I will suggest merges with, and overlaps, the field of the object relations theory of psychoanalysis. Yet I hope that I am pointing towards possible new areas of clinical theory as well as a shift in our conceptual horizon. I am not aiming to replace object relations theory, especially as it has become such a rich source of clinical and theoretical thinking; rather, I am aiming to add another dimension to the field it covers. At the very least, I feel that there is still not enough attention paid in object relations theory to the subjective side of the analytic encounter. There are also, as I shall endeavour to tackle in due course, certain theoretical difficulties about the theory, particularly when it comes to considering the nature of 'internal objects', which I consider an interesting fiction, but a fiction none the less.

Self psychologists and intersubjectivists have made significant inroads into the area I am considering, but, as I shall argue, do not yet provide a comprehensive theoretical model which can both incorporate the experience of subjectivity and put forward a rigorous theoretical framework which takes account of the complexity of the human subject, particularly in relation to social structure. But I would agree with Irwin Hoffman (1991) that we are witnessing the evolution of a new paradigm for understanding the psychoanalytic situation. Very much influenced by the work of Berger and Luckmann (1966) on the sociology of knowledge, he calls it the 'social-constructivist' paradigm. Berger and Luckmann emphasize how reality is socially constructed. It is neither already given nor just created by individual endeavours, but arises out of constant interaction between subjects. This social reality can be looked at as both an independent objective reality created by interaction, and as a subjective reality because society is built up by activity that expresses subjective meaning. Hoffman takes account of the analyst's constant participation in the analytic process, which is created out of the interaction of analyst and patient; how there is a need to take account of the mutual influence of analyst and patient, and how meaning is constructed out of the analytic situation. He argues for the interdependence of the social and individual aspects of experience, a point of view which has influenced my own consideration of the role of social structure in the life of the subject.

I have also been influenced by the work of the French psychoanalyst Jacques Lacan, who put forward a rigorous concept of the human subject, but did not, in my view, address clinical issues as convincingly as, say, Bion, Klein and Winnicott, whom I have also found essential to my arguments. Some of what I have to contribute overlaps concerns of intersubjective thinkers such as Aron (1991), Bromberg (1993), Mitchell (1991,1993), Ogden (1992a, b; 1994) and Stolorow et al. (1994), to whom I shall refer, though I think that I am approaching similar territory from a different angle. Where I tend to disagree with their approach, as I shall explore in detail later, is that I think we need to distinguish what is individual, personal or human from the subjective state of mind induced in the analyst by the patient, or the patient's view of the analyst's subjectivity, or what one might call the general methodology of analysis. That is, there is a difference between considering the subject as an individual and a systematic study of the nature of analytic subjectivity which, as it were, examines the individual as a subject.

The term 'subject relations' theory seems to have been first used by Christopher Bollas in his book *Forces of Destiny* (1989) to cover the interplay between the subjectivities of analyst and patient:

The patient free associates. So does the psychoanalyst. Analysis is an interplay of two subjectivities, although the psychoanalyst has an established area of self and mind devoted to the psychic processing and interpretive knowing of the analysand. But any psychoanalytic session is a dialectic between two subjectivities, and although they will form and project internal mental representations of one another, the understanding of which we term object relations theory, they will also act in a successional interplay of idiom elements, which I think we should say is more of a subject relations theory. If object relations theory attends to the formation and projection of self and object representations, subject relations theory attends to the interplay of two human sensibilities, who together create environments unique to their cohabitation. The concepts of interplay, interrelating, intersubjectivity, have as much use in a subject relations theory as in an object relations theory. (Bollas, 1989, pp.108–9)

Bollas thus defines two basic areas with which analysis deals, that of object relations and that of subject relations. While he, and of course many other analytic thinkers, have continued to develop the realm of object relations, Bollas does not develop his notion of subject relations theory in a theoretically comprehensive way, although I think it is implicit in much of what he writes, for example in his notion of 'idiom'. This refers to the unique nucleus of each individual, the defining essence of each subject, a 'figuration of being that is like a kernel that can, under favourable circumstances, evolve and articulate' (ibid., p.212). And he graphically and at times almost poetically articulates the way that the sensibilities of patient and analyst interconnect. My aim will be to continue and develop a line of thought which Bollas began, examining in detail the nature of analytic subjectivity and how the subject may be looked at in terms of what I have called for convenience 'subjective organizations'. This is intentionally rather a loose and open term which aims to cover a fairly wide field of subjective phenomena, ranging from what could be considered as the merely individual to what takes place between subjects in the social field, where subjects meet others in the network of other subjects. In essence, I consider that whatever we have individually in our minds or brains is effectively organized in interaction in the social field, and that we need to examine in detail the nature of this organization. I would add that we do also need to examine how what takes place in the individual may modify and distort what is received from others in various ways, but this is rather well-trodden ground, and is particularly the territory of object relations theory. I shall look at how focusing on subject relations may add an important dimension to object relations theory, and how it may be useful clinically to look at the way that various subjective positions of patient and analyst interact. I shall also look, in due course, at various transference states where subjectivity is sustained or eliminated to varying degrees.

It is perhaps worth emphasizing here that analytic subjectivity, with its openness to the unconscious, incorporating ambiguity, paradox and uncertainty, is a particular form of subjectivity. It may have links with other descriptions and experiences of subjective life, but it has its own status and structure. Indeed, the term 'subject' has many shades of meaning. For example, it refers to the subject of the sentence, the one who speaks, the subject of a story or narrative; and, in the traditional Cartesian model of the mind (whose status I shall later question), the subject who relates to an object. The term has philosophical and political resonances. Traditionally the philosophical subject usually refers to the conscious, thinking subject, the subject of conscious reason. The political subject is a citizen with certain fundamental rights, such as that of belonging to civil society and having the right to vote, though the term can also imply being subject to a higher authority. The Freudian subject, a unique construct, incorporates a number of ambiguities, uncertainties and paradoxes, which follow from the existence of an unconscious. At the heart of our subjectivity, as seen through the psychoanalytic perspective, is an obvious and fundamental paradox – the fact that psychoanalysis has shown that much of our most human aspects, which make us passionate, vulnerable and problematic beings, reside in our unconscious, and often appear to us as if they came from somewhere else, from an 'It', Freud's *Das Es*. We may experience this core of our being, as Freud described the unconscious wishful impulses embedded in the unconscious (Freud, 1900, p.603), as a place outside ourselves in some way, in some objective place, certainly in some other location. Even when we begin to discuss in a formal way the nature of this subjectivity, something becomes lost. We fall too readily into an objective way of thinking, where we may lose the heart of who we are. At the same time, this dilemma highlights what Husserl (1954, p.178) called the paradox of human subjectivity, the fact that the human being is both a subject for the world and at the same time an object in the world.

SUBJECTIVE AND OBJECTIVE

The issue of objective as opposed to subjective understanding is a complex one, and to explore fully the differences and similarities between these two approaches requires a full description of my own views about subjectivity, which will gradually unfold. However, I think it worth making a view general points about this issue as the backdrop for a fuller investigation. In addition, some of the points raised by considering a selection of the relevant thinkers will, I hope, provide useful signposts along the winding path of my investigation.

There seem to be many different views of what we mean by an objective as opposed to a subjective understanding of humans. I would suggest that there have been at least three ways of seeing this dichotomy: first, to eliminate the distinction, as, for example, Husserl and Dewey attempted; second, to focus more on the subjective understanding, as, for example, Kierkegaard and Sartre proposed; and third, to attempt to find a place for both the subjective and the objective realms, as the philosopher Thomas Nagel has suggested.

First of all, the objective view often seems to be more linked with the scientific view of reality as having a physical existence, with certain observable and measurable phenomena. This observable world, first fully described by Galileo, is encapsulated in precise mathematical terms. As Husserl described (1954, p.60), Galileo abstracted from human subjects as persons leading a personal and cultural life, with the result that the world is split into two, nature as scientifically objective and the vague psychic world of human beings. What characterizes the objective view is 'that it moves upon the ground of the world which is pregiven, taken for granted through experience, seeks the "objective truth" of this world, seeks what, in this world, is unconditionally valid for every rational being, what it is in itself' (ibid., p.68). Husserl contrasts this objective view of man with a subjective view which studies the subjectivity of man by paying attention to the meaning of the pregiven life-world, the world that is actually experienced by human subjects as opposed to the theoretically constructed objective world. His whole investigation in his last and unfinished work, *The Crisis of European Sciences* (1954), was focused on the attempt to make the pregivenness of the life-world a universal subject of investigation in its own right. Science simply 'presupposes as its point of departure the intuitive surrounding world, pregiven as existing for all in common' (ibid., p.121). Husserl in contrast investigates this very pregiven world, the world where human beings interact socially and culturally with others.

In addition, he points out that although science may disdain the validity of the life-world to be considered as a subject of investigation, the whole edifice of objective science is built up through the collaborative work of scientists, a concrete world of everyday interactions. This everyday, concrete life-world provides the grounding for the 'scientifically true' world. Thus for Husserl straightforward experience 'in which the life-world is given, is the ultimate foundation of all objective knowledge' (ibid., p.226). Furthermore, psychology is uniquely placed to tackle the nature of the life-world. Its specific subject matter concerns what is essentially proper to persons as such, as subjects with an intentional life, and in relation to other subjects (ibid., p.238).

There are similarities between Husserl's and John Dewey's critique of the scientific objective viewpoint, but the latter goes back even further than Galileo to the Ancient Greeks. For Dewey, the split between everyday man and the world arose when the Greeks made the distinction between the everyday world of activity and the 'higher' world where 'true' being was placed.

> Although this Greek formulation was made long ago and much of it is now strange in its specific terms, certain features of it are relevant to present thought as they were significant in their original formulation. For in spite of the great, the enormous changes in the subject-matter and method of the sciences and the tremendous expansion of practical activities by means of arts and technologies, the main tradition of western culture has retained intact this framework of ideas. Perfect certainty is what man wants. It cannot be found by practical doing or making; these take effect in an uncertain future, and involve peril, the risk of misadventure, frustration and failure. Knowledge, on the other hand, is thought to be concerned with a region of being which is fixed in itself. (Dewey, 1929, p.368)

One could say that science later took over this split between the world of the everyday and the true world of being when it proposed that it dealt with the true, objective world as opposed to the fleeting, uncertain and unmeasurable world of human subjects. Dewey emphasized how the scientific view has, since the seventeenth century, wrought havoc to philosophy by setting the subjective private consciousness against the physical world of nature. 'It is responsible for the feeling ... that "nature" and "experience" are names for things which have nothing to do with each other' (ibid., p.13).

Since then, there has been a tendency to 'set up a hard and fast wall between the experiencing subject and that nature which is experienced' (ibid., p.24). This results on the one hand on undue emphasis either on the world as 'out there', an objective realm cut off from the human subject, or to focus (like much psychoanalytic theory) on a subjective world as separate and isolated, self-sufficient and self-enclosed, an 'inner world' remote from the world of nature. There is a tendency either to resort to 'an objectivism which ignores initiating and reorganizing desire and imagination' (ibid., p.197) or to a subjectivism which 'consists in escape to the enjoyment of inward landscape' (ibid.). Dewey, on the other hand, proposes 'to do justice to the inclusive integrity of "experience" ' (ibid., p.11). Again, eliminating the ancient split between doing and being, he asserts that 'things are objects to be treated, used, acted upon and with, enjoyed and endured, even more than things to be known. They are things *had* before they are things cognized' (ibid., p.21). Rather like Husserl, Dewey proposes that we return to examine concrete everyday human experience, the world of social interaction and human communication. Human cooperation, discourse, shared experience and sociability are the cornerstones of his thinking, not the isolated knowing subject looking out at the separate objective world of things. This way of thinking links with that of his fellow American, the social psychologist George Mead and even with that of the later Wittgenstein, both of whom I shall subsequently refer to on a number of occasions, both when tackling the issue of so-called 'internal representations' and the role of social structure in the constitution of the human subject.

Kierkegaard is an example of a thinker who aimed to appropriate the realm of the subjective from that of the objective. His book *Concluding Unscientific Postscript* (1846), aims to carve out the realm of the subjectivity of the individual as a fundamental human task. It involves the realm of the inward; moments of choice and decisiveness, and ethical considerations. In order to become subjective, the individual has to reflect on his own existence rather than become lost in an objective way of thinking which submerges subjectivity. The objective and subjective points of view are constantly presented as opposites. The truly existing individual has to throw off the weight of objectivity. Thus, in a section which could well be used as the motto of my book, he writes:

> Objectively we consider only the matter at issue, subjectively we have regard to the subject and his subjectivity; and behold, precisely this subjectivity is the matter at issue. This must constantly be borne in mind, namely, that the subjective problem is not something about an objective issue, but is the subjectivity itself. For since the problem in question poses a decision, and since all decisiveness ... inheres in subjectivity, it is essential that every trace of an objective issue should be eliminated. If any such trace remains, it is at once a sign that the subject seeks to shirk something of the pain and crisis of the decision; that is, he seeks to make the problem to some degree objective. (Kierkegaard, 1846, p. 115)

Objectivity is thus seen as a turning away from subjectivity. The subject has two ways of existing open to him – to forget he is an existing individual and become submerged in the objective realm, or to strive to become an existing individual, to aim to become subjective. The objective tendency, which proposes to make everyone an observer can turn the observer almost into a ghost (ibid., p.118). Objective reflection 'makes the subject accidental, and thereby transforms existence into something indifferent, something vanishing ... The way of objective reflection leads to abstract thought, to mathematics ... and always leads away from the subject, whose existence or non-existence, and from the objective point of view quite rightly, becomes infinitely indifferent' (ibid., p.173).

The true realm of the subjective for Kierkegaard is not that of knowing or cognition, but that of existing. The existing subject is engaged in the process of becoming essentially subjective, moving away from objectivity and objective truth towards inwardness and subjective truth. Kierkegaard's philosophy, as a precursor of the existentialist movement, has deeply influenced a number of clinicians – existential psychiatrists such as Binswanger, Boss and May, as well as Laing. But by focusing on the issue of existence in his thought they may have missed his more formal examination of the nature of subjectivity.

Jean-Paul Sartre's monumental book *Being and Nothingness* (1943) charts, among other things, a subtle interplay between subjective and objective stances in the relation of the self to the other, to which I shall return at various points in my argument. One could say that Sartre develops and extends Kierkegaard's existential project, although he does not much use the term objective as such; instead he usually refers to Objectité or Objectness, the quality or state of being an object, a fundamental dimension of relations between self and others.

Constitutive for the subject is his relation to the Other. The Other is a phenomenon of a particular kind. 'In the first place the appearance of the Other is manifested by the presence of organized forms such as gestures and expression, acts and conduct. These organized forms refer to an organizing unity which on principle is located outside of our experience' (Sartre, 1943, p.226). The Other consists of a group of phenomena outside of me, yet which have a fundamental role in organizing my own experience and in the formation of my being, like a skeletal framework, a whole system of meanings and experiences radically different from and yet constitutive of my own being. The Other appears as the one who is other than me, not only whom I see but the one who sees me. 'The Other ... is presented in a certain sense as the radical negation of my experience, since he is the one for whom I am not subject but object. Therefore as the subject of knowledge I strive to determine as object the subject who denies my character as subject and who himself determines me as object' (ibid., p.228).

Negativity plays a fundamental role for Sartre in his dialectic between self and Other, subject and object. For, 'At the origin of the problem of the existence of others, there is a fundamental presupposition: others are the Other, that is the self which is *not* myself. Therefore we grasp here a negation as the constitutive structure of the being-of-others ... Between the Other and myself there is a nothingness of separation. This nothingness does not derive its origin from myself nor from the other, nor is it a reciprocal relation between the Other and myself. On the contrary, as a primary absence of relation, it is originally the foundation of all relation between the Other and me' (ibid., p.230).

Negation and conflict are at the heart of relations between self and Other. 'While I attempt to free myself from the hold of the Other, the Other is trying to free himself from mine; while I seek to enslave the Other, the Other seeks to enslave me' (ibid., p.364). We are dealing with 'reciprocal and moving relations' (ibid.). The Other both steals my being from me and yet is the one who causes there to be a being which is mine to steal; there is a basic duality in the way that our being is structured.

Sartre also points out another duality, particularly relevant to my theme. The Other can be seen as an object, and the Other can see me as an object. This is an important element of the relation between self and Other, but I am denied as subject; my true being – for Sartre, my freedom – is denied, as I, in turn, deny his freedom. We have to take account of this situation, for it is inevitable in everyday interactions. Sartre has marvellous descriptions of how the Other can freeze the self with a look; how the self can become alienated by the act of being looked at. But at another level, the Other can be encountered as a subject; indeed, inherent even in all the patterns of conduct towards the Other-as-object, there is the possibility of experiencing the Other-as-subject, which for Sartre is ultimately the Other's freedom. He conceives of a constant interplay or movement between the Other-as-object and the Other-as-subject (ibid., p.408). Yet there is something unknowable about the Other-as-subject. With the Other-as-object:

nothing is hidden and in so far as objects refer to other objects, I can increase indefinitely my knowledge of the Other by indefinitely making explicit his relations with other instruments in the world.

The ideal of *knowledge* of the Other remains the exhaustive specification of the meaning of the flow of the world. The difference of principle between the Other-as-object and the Other-as-subject stems solely from this fact: that the Other-as-subject can in no way be known nor even conceived as such. (ibid., p.293)

Thus, one could say, perhaps extending Sartre's dialectic somewhat, that I as an object and the Other-as-object can be known in some sense as a totality; but that I as subject am in some sense unknowable and inexhaustible. We may try to know the Other, and we can as an object in one sense; yet the Other-as-object cannot be encountered in a full way. When we try fully to encounter the Other, we are taken away from the Other-as-subject to the Other-as-object; and we are perpetually moving between these two positions. Thus one could interpret Sartre as indicating a model of the human subject with no centre, rather as comprising an essential absence, a negativity, something unknown, within its structure; and that the subject is constantly moving between positions rather than being fixed in one position. I shall return to this sort of model of subjectivity on a number of occasions.

Freud, too, considered that there was always a point where we reached the unknown in the human subject. He was particularly referring to the interpretation of dreams, where we reach the dream's navel (Freud, 1900, p.525), the spot where it reaches down into the unknown, the 'core of our being', or *Kern Unsere Wesens*. One could, then, extend this notion to express the possibility that there is always something unknowable and irreducible in the human subject, and hence something about us essentially difficult to describe, even in clinical accounts which can at least attempt to capture some of the elusiveness of the subject in the reality of a human encounter. I do not have solutions to this dilemma; I still propose to attempt to examine what we mean by human subjectivity, but I can only point towards various ways of describing what is a difficult dilemma.

A third way of viewing the subjective and objective dimensions by attempting to reconcile them is illustrated by Thomas Nagel who, in his book *The View from Nowhere*, attempts to examine 'a single problem: how to combine the perspective of a particular person inside the world with an objective view of that same world, the person and his viewpoint combined. It is a problem that faces every creature with the impulse and capacity to transcend its particular point of view and to conceive of the world as a whole' (Nagel, 1986, p.3).

His inquiry into this field was most graphically illustrated by his seminal paper, 'What is it like to be a bat?' (1974), which aimed to examine the nature of consciousness. If he had been a psychoanalyst he might have called the paper 'What is it like to be a baby?', as there is perhaps a similar puzzle about what a baby experiences. Nagel sets out by suggesting that the most important and characteristic feature of conscious mental phenomena, that of their being subjective, is poorly understood. The subjective character of experience of an organism is what it is like to be that organism, whether it be a bat or a human. This points towards having a particular point of view: in order to understand another creature we have to take up its own particular point of view. Nagel makes the point that this is not a clear matter at all. The objective point of view as one which involves a physical explanation of facts does not help us that much; indeed, it can take us further away from the experience itself we are trying to comprehend. In the end, we may be left only with empathy and imagination to guide us. Indeed, in this paper, Nagel states that 'At present we are completely unequipped to think about the subjective character of experience without relying on the imagination – without taking up the point of view of the experiential subject' (Nagel, 1974, p.178). But he also, perhaps over-optimistically, regards this as 'a challenge to form new concepts and devise a new method – an objective phenomenology not dependent on empathy or the imagination' (ibid., p.179).

Nagel continues his search for such a methodology, combining the subjective and objective points of view, in *The View from Nowhere*. He aims to show how these different views interplay, can be unified at certain times and then are also irreconcilable. However, he also cautions that the distinction between more subjective and more objective views is really a matter of degree and covers a wide spectrum:

A view or form of thought is more objective than another if it relies less on the specifics of the individual's makeup and position in the world, or on the character of the particular type of creature he is. The wider the range of subjective types to which a form of understanding is accessible – the less it depends on specific subjective capacities – the more objective it is. A standpoint that is objective by comparison with the personal view of one individual may be subjective by comparison with a theoretical standpoint still farther out. The standpoint of morality is more objective than that of private life, but less objective than the standpoint of physics. We may think of reality as a set of concentric spheres, progressively revealed as we detach gradually from the contingencies of the self. (Nagel, 1986, p.5)

Thus what may be subjective from one point of view can be seen as objective from another. Yet he still defends retaining the distinction between the two viewpoints, providing their limits are understood. He argues that it is necessary to have an objective viewpoint if one is to understand the world as it is, but that we cannot understand life, ourselves and the world if we become so objectively detached that we lose the human, subjective perspective.

One could propose a similar distinction in psychoanalytic terms by looking at the Oedipal situation. The father's position is objective in relation to the mother's position, in that he is outside of the close mother–baby relationship. Yet in another sense he is no more or less objective than the mother and just as subjective. Lacan (1966) talked of the father's function as that of the third, the Other of the mother, the one who could take up a position other than that of the mother, or what Britton (1989) has called the 'third position'. In that sense again the father's position is more objective than that of the mother, but only in a relative sense. After all, one could also say that she was more objective, in the sense of being more aware of the child's emotional states.

Kenneth Wright, in his book *Vision and Separation* (1991), makes a similar point when he emphasizes how important it is to have a position from which one can see oneself, by for example imagining the position of the third person. Influenced very much by Sartre's dialectic of self and Other, Wright considers that such an attitude provides the basis for what he calls an objective self, the self that is objectified through the Other looking at it. This ability to see oneself though the eyes of the Other, however, does not imply that there is one privileged position from which all others follow, and that there is some truly objective position where absolute truth can be found.

> If we think for a moment in a structural or systems way, we can easily see that, *within* any social system, there is no such place as an 'objective' position – in other words, no position can describe the 'truth' of the system. No view is privileged or has preeminence over any other. All are relative and describe a limited perspective.
>
> Outside of the system concerned, however, there do exist one or more privileged positions. They are privileged *because* they are outside and therefore allow that particular system to be viewed as a whole ... If there is no truly objective position, all we can hope for is to realize this and to relativize our views as much as possible. (Wright, 1991, pp.231–2)

In the analytic encounter itself there is a need to have a place for an observing, critical and hence in this sense a more objective attitude; and the analyst often provides this function. This is different from being detached. Objectivity in the sense of observing from a viewpoint can fall into detachment, if taken too far. We may encounter this situation with schizoid patients who observe themselves so much that they cannot relate spontaneously. That is, they lose their subjectivity as they become increasingly objective. An important task of treatment is, as it were, to help the patient emerge into subjectivity away from objectivity, rather along the lines that Kierkegaard indicated from a philosophical viewpoint.

R.D. Laing, in his book *The Divided Self* (1960), provides many examples of how schizoid patients isolate themselves from others by setting up a defensive system whereby the self is detached both from their own body and from others. Interactions between self and others are not immediate but always at one remove. In a sense one could say that the schizoid person experiences the world as a detached observer, but for this reason does not feel alive. He feels increasingly isolated, impoverished and futile. One can see here that, paradoxically, the more the objective attitude is maintained the less real the world feels; thus emphasizing the need for the subjective element in order for a person to live in the world. At the same time, without some observing and objective attitude the self can become disembodied and unreal. As Laing describes, the self can then aim to avoid being 'grasped, pinpointed, trapped, possessed. Its aim is to be a pure subject, without any objective existence. Thus, except in certain possible safe moments, the individual seeks to regard the whole of his objective existence as the expression of a false self' (Laing, 1960, p.95). Having only a subjective identity, a person will not feel real.

THE SELF

Several authors I have cited have used the term 'self' when tackling subjective states. Indeed, the term does have the advantage of capturing something of the emotional quality of human life. We talk of self-awareness, self-expression, self-reflection and self-knowledge. The self in Kohut's self psychology, according to Ernest Wolf, is 'That part of the personality which confers the sense of selfhood and which is evoked and sustained by a constant supply of responsiveness from the functioning of selfobjects' (Wolf, 1988, p.38). However, Wolf also points out that the concept of a self is awkward to define precisely. Nor does he want to define it in such a way that its sense becomes too rigid. It can be defined as 'that psychological structure which makes its presence evident by providing one with a healthy sense of self, of self-esteem and well-being' (ibid., p.27). It refers to the 'core of the personality, which is made up of various constituents that emerge into a coherent and enduring configuration during the interplay of inherited and environmental factors ... the self is the center of initiative, recipient of impressions, and repository of that individual's particular constellation of nuclear ambitions, ideals, talents, and skills' (ibid., p.182). Self psychology 'recognizes as the most fundamental essence of human psychology the individual's need (1) to organize his or her psychological experience into a cohesive configuration, the self, and (2) to establish self-sustaining relationships between this self and its surround that have the function to evoke, maintain, and strengthen the structural coherence, energic vigour, and balanced harmony among the constituents of the self' (ibid., p.184).

In this view of the self, an important aim of treatment is to help achieve integration of the personality through strengthening of the self, by offering a responsive and sustaining analytic relationship. This may mean having to face moments of fragmentation, disruption to the analytic process and narcissistic rage, but a position of empathic responsiveness is vital for the analyst to help the patient achieve integration.

Stephen Mitchell, however, points out that 'the most striking thing about the concept of self within current psychoanalytic thought is precisely the striking contrast between the centrality of concern with the self and the enormous variability and lack of consensus about what the term even means' (Mitchell, 1991, p.124). None the less, he proposes an interesting model for understanding self-experience from different points of view or aspects. The self can be multiple and discontinuous, which refers to 'the multiple configurations of self patterned variability in different relational contexts' (ibid., p.139); or the self can be separate, integral and continuous, which refers to the 'subjective experience of the pattern making itself, activity that is experienced over time and across the different organizational schemes' (ibid.).

Philip Bromberg offers an alternative description of a similar view, when he suggests that 'Health is the ability to stand between realities without losing any of them. This is what I believe *self-acceptance* means and what *creativity* is really all about – the capacity to feel like one self while being many' (Bromberg, 1993, p.166).

Contemporary self psychology seems, then, to revolve around the issue of how much the self is a coherent central structure and how much it is made up of multiple elements. This is very much a redescription of what is an ancient philosophical problem – that of the 'One and the Many'. That is, the question, for example, of whether or not there are many realities or just one reality; is there one being or many beings, one God or many gods?

Though I find the clinical descriptions of self psychology match my own practice to some extent, I feel that we need to clarify more rigorously how single and/or multiple organizations are structured. I am also uncomfortable with self psychology's emphasis on the centre, on central integration and cohesiveness, which is linked to well-being. As I have already suggested, the notion of a psychical centre is a doubtful concept. However, whatever the limits and uncertainties of the term 'self', it does seem more responsive to ordinary human aspects of the person, while the term 'subject' does suffer in this regard from having philosophical resonances. Part of the point of what I am proposing is that there is no perfect solution to the dilemma of human subjectivity, for terms are always losing something essential in us. But I do feel that the term 'self' is too loose for theoretical purposes and does not capture enough of our complexity. However, I would like to keep the term 'self' somewhere, and I propose that it could be used primarily to describe the affective, responsive, experiencing side or element of the human subject, one aspect of the subjective organization, separate from other aspects which I will consider in due course, such as the place of social structure, desire and embodiment.

I think it is possible that there can be self-experiences with little subjectivity. What I have in mind is certain patients who report the day's experiences in the session over and over, yet it is very difficult to make sense of what has happened. There may be little sense of a subject of these experiences, little sense that experiences have psychical value. Things are reported but then not reflected on or put into any context; and it is difficult for the analyst to interpret what has been happening. The session is rather like a news bulletin; 'raw news from the self', but not 'commentary'.

There has recently been considerable interest in the psychoanalytic literature on the nature of the human subject. Thomas Ogden, for example, has recently written two review papers (Ogden 1992a, b) on the topic and a book, *Subjects of Analysis* (1994), in which he discusses in considerable detail the analytic conception of the subject. The latter for him is 'the cornerstone of the psychoanalytic project and is at the same time one of the least well-articulated psychoanalytic concepts' (Ogden 1992b, p.624). Intersubjectivity as a central concept has also been used by, for example, Stolorow and his colleagues (Stolorow et al., 1994) who use it as a framework for a theory of relatedness. For them, intersubjectivity provides the essential context for relating. There is an emphasis on the mutual and reciprocal interplay of subjective worlds, including that of the analyst in an intersubjective 'field'. Though I would not disagree with the need to look at the interactive dimension between people, I suspect that the intersubjective theory as currently put forward is essentially an interpersonal theory. The nature of the subject is rather loosely defined and owes much to self psychology; that is, the subject of the theory is really a self and the nature of the subject as such is not really 'well-articulated', to use Ogden's phrase. However, I will return in due course to consider intersubjective thinking in more detail.

– – –

The chapter began with a question about the location of the human subject, which has pushed this investigation in a number of directions, which will form the basis of the rest of the book. A picture of the subject has begun to be built up, one in which the subject is made up of inter-acting elements with no privileged place where the elements all come together, no central place where meaning and truth are located. This sort of picture is consistent with much recent neurophysiological work, which focuses on the complex nature of consciousness. The next chapter will consider, among other topics, some of this work and how it may be relevant to psychoanalysis; in particular how it may help to extend our understanding of human subjectivity. In order to do this, I first of all consider what is often neglected in psychoanalytic theory and practice, the nature of consciousness.

2 THE MANY VOICES OF CONSCIOUSNESS

Freud's 'Copernican' revolution consisted in reassessing the value previously attached to consciousness and emphasizing that the unconscious was the 'true psychical reality' (Freud, 1990, p.613); that one had to abandon the over-valuation of the property of being conscious; and that the unconscious was the larger sphere. Although emphasis was understandably placed on the significance of the unconscious, Freud did not necessarily imply that consciousness was of marginal importance. For example, he wrote that 'the attribute of being conscious forms the departure for all our psychoanalytical investigations and that the attribute of being conscious is the only characteristic of psychical processes that is directly presented to us' (Freud, 1940, p.192). He also wrote that consciousness is a fact without parallel, which defies all explanation or description. 'Nevertheless,' he wrote, 'if anyone speaks of consciousness we know immediately and from our most personal experience what is meant by it' (ibid., p.157).

While one may not wish to over-value the importance of consciousness, there has been perhaps, as Edward Joseph (1987) has pointed out, a tendency to go the other way and under-value its role and significance. Thus he writes:

> We have become so accustomed in our work to looking behind or through the conscious productions, that often we do not see them, but see through them as though they were screening the important mental content we really seek. That the form and nature of the conscious productions presented are determined by unconscious processes is beyond question, and that our work of determining what lies below the surface is of therapeutic benefit as well as scientific importance, is also beyond question. But in overlooking or looking through the outward form and outermost content of what Freud (1940) in the *Outline* called the 'periphery of the ego' (p.162), we have perhaps been doing ourselves, and certainly our knowledge of mental activity, an injustice. We may also have been restricting our total knowledge of mental activity. (Joseph, 1987, p.9)

Joseph tends to emphasize the 'higher' mental functions of consciousness, such as when it serves in the regulation, control and integration of mental activity. However, I would see its function as complex and multiple, and also as intimately bound up with unconscious processes.

Our reluctance to tackle the 'surface' provided by consciousness may have something to do with the fact that Freud's metapsychological paper on consciousness was lost or destroyed, thus making us hesitate to pursue uncharted territory. Perhaps our reluctance arises from having to tackle consciousness by way of its own protective shield, which enables it to divert us from our task, or perhaps it stems from Freud's warning that consciousness defies all explanation.

There are, none the less, various ways of tackling the phenomenon of consciousness – for example, from a natural science viewpoint, seeing it in the context of the brain's contents; from a philosophical viewpoint, such as linking it to the development of reason; from a social science perspective, linking it to social encounters; and from a historical horizon, emphasizing the sort of consciousness of the past which influences us. I shall look at a number of perspectives for their various contributions, in order to come up with a pluralistic and multilayered model of consciousness that I believe corresponds more fully to the experience of the analytic encounter. A fuller understanding of consciousness may help us to understand more about how we lose a sense of who we are, as well as to enable us to gain more of a subjective life. But in order not to lose my way through the maze of different approaches, I shall begin by tackling some of Freud's extant texts.

FREUD AND CONSCIOUSNESS

The Psychical System

The first theme that runs through many of Freud's descriptions of the psychical apparatus concerns, as has already been mentioned, how he saw the mental apparatus as a whole system with various interacting parts and functions. This approach was already in evidence in his monograph *On Aphasia* (1891), or speech disorders, where he saw language as a property of the whole language system in the brain rather than as only a property of individual areas. As he wrote:

We have rejected the assumptions that the speech apparatus consists of distinct centres separated by functionless areas, and that ideas (memories) serving speech are stored in certain parts of the cortex called centres while their association is provided exclusively by subcortical fibre tracts. It only remains for us to state the view that the speech area is a continuous cortical region within which the associations and transmissions underlying the speech functions are taking place; they are of a complexity beyond comprehension. (Freud, 1891, p.62)

Freud also put forward the notion that the idea or concept could not be separated from that of association, as 'We cannot have a perception without immediately associating it; however sharply we may separate the two concepts, in reality they belong to one single process which, starting from one point, spreads over the whole cortex' (ibid., p.57). Once again, the model is one involving a whole organization; a representation is not localized in one place as it always immediately involves associations, links with other places. Different forms of aphasia are caused by disruptions to associations between areas of the brain. 'All aphasias originate in interruption of associations, i.e. of conduction. Aphasia through destruction or lesion of a centre is no more and no less than aphasia through lesion of those association fibres which meet in that nodal point called a centre' (ibid., pp.67–8). Thus, so-called centres are essentially meeting places for associations.

In the *Aphasia* monograph, Freud comments on the relation between the physical and psychological realms, which also remains the basis for much of his subsequent work, and is of particular relevance to understanding the nature of consciousness. His approach to this, as well as to that of aphasia, was very much influenced by the neurologist Hughlings Jackson,* for whom the physical and psychological were parallel processes. As Freud put it, 'The relationship between the chain of physiological events in the nervous system and the mental processes is probably not one of cause and effect. The former do not cease when the latter set in; they tend to continue; but from a certain moment, a mental phenomenon corresponds to each part of the chain, or to several parts. The psychic is, therefore, a process parallel to the physiological, "a dependent concomitant"' (ibid., p.55).

Of course it is difficult to know quite when the 'certain moment' arises and the mental phenomenon occurs. Later, Freud hovered between concentrating only on the mental process per se; but there were also times when he tried to examine where the physical side came into the picture. For example, with drive theory (Freud, 1915a,

---

* See Solms and Saling (1986) and Goldstein (1995) for detailed discussion of this influence.

p.122), a drive is on the border of the physical and the mental; we can only know the drive from the mental representation of it, and yet it is also a biological process. Perhaps it would be better here to think of a duality rather than a parallel process. The drive, for example, in its effects is both biological and psychical; its dual structure is what is significant. I shall examine later how the subject and the drive may be interrelated when I offer one interpretation of Freud's paper 'Instincts and their vicissitudes' (1915a). Rather than eliminate drive theory completely, as a number of recent thinkers have done, I would propose that one considers a dual structure whereby one can conceive of a drive as a force transforming the subject, while drives are themselves transformed by different subjective positions. Similarly, one can think of a dual structure with regard to the processes involved in consciousness; and hence it may be useful to examine both psychological and physiological evidence when considering the nature of consciousness.

This contrasts with the traditional scientific view that all mental events are directly caused by physical brain events, as put forward, for example, by Francis Crick, who asserts that, '"You" your joys and your sorrows, your memories and your ambitions, your sense of personal identity and free will, are in fact no more than the behaviour of a vast assembly of nerve cells and their associated molecules' (Crick, 1994, p.3). It also contrasts, to some extent, with the subtle thought of the philosopher Donald Davidson who separates the world of mental events from those of physical events. For him, mental events are in a class of their own which cannot be explained by physical science, certainly not in the sense in which psychoanalysts are interested:

> Mental events as a class cannot be explained by physical science; particular mental events can when we know particular identities. But the explanation of mental events in which we are typically interested relate them to other mental events and conditions. We explain a man's free actions, for example, by appeal to his desires, habits, knowledge and perceptions. Such accounts of intentional behaviour operate in a conceptual framework removed from the direct reach of physical law by describing both cause and effect, reason and action, as aspects of a portrait of a human agent. (Davidson, 1980, p. 225)

I would go along for the most part with this latter view of mental events; except where the drives come into the picture, on the border between what we distinguish perhaps unsatisfactorily, as the physical and mental.

To return to the issue of the functioning of the mental apparatus, in *The Interpretation of Dreams* (Freud, 1900, p.511) Freud also emphasized the need to look at interactions of functioning parts and not to look at a single mental function in isolation. In the paper 'The unconscious' (Freud, 1915b), I think that one can see how Freud provided a flexible model of interacting functions in which consciousness cannot be isolated from the other parts of the system. Indeed, the justification and legitimation of his notion of the unconscious comes through a constant comparison with the role and function of consciousness.

In the first section of the paper, 'Justification for the Concept of the Unconscious', what seems to come across is how rough and ready is the whole concept of the unconscious. Freud considered that the assumption of the existence of the unconscious as 'necessary and legitimate'; and yet he emphasized that it was not easy to arrive at a knowledge of the unconscious except by a process of 'translation' into something conscious. He argued that the concept of the unconscious was necessary because the data of consciousness had so many gaps in them, and because many psychical acts, such as dreams, neurotic symptoms and jokes, occurred in healthy and ill people alike and could be explained only by presupposing other acts of which consciousness afforded us no evidence (Freud, 1915b, pp. 166–7). All such acts remain disconnected and unintelligible until we interpolate unconscious acts.

The next argument concerned how one could infer the existence of the unconscious in the same way that one could infer the existence of consciousness in others. But, being an inference, such an assumption of existence does not have the same immediate certainty that we have of our own consciousness. He added, however, that the process of inference does not lead at first to the disclosure of an unconscious but instead to another, second consciousness united in the self with the consciousness that one knows. Yet, regardless of this logic, psychoanalytic experience reveals that the unconscious follows laws different from those of consciousness, leading us to conclude that there exists not a second consciousness but psychical acts that lacked consciousness.

The next section of the paper tackles the first Freudian topography. Preconscious contents differ from those of the unconscious in that they are in principle available to consciousness. The conscious is closely linked to the organs of perception. Although consciousness provides us with a sketchy picture of our mental processes, it is of great importance whether or not a psychical phenomenon can be recognized consciously. Freud was, in fact, at pains to emphasize the temporary and pragmatic use of the terms of his first topography. Indeed, he even went so far as to state that there is really no clear-cut distinction between the systems:

> the unconscious is alive and capable of development and maintains a number of ... relations with the preconscious, amongst them that of cooperation. In brief, it must be said that the unconscious is continued into ... derivatives, that it is accessible to the impressions of life, that it constantly influences the preconscious, and is even, for its part, subjected to influences from the preconscious.
>
> Study of the derivatives of the unconscious will completely disappoint our expectations of a schematically clear-cut distinction between the two psychical systems. (ibid., p.190)

Freud justified this finding by denying that he was under no obligation to provide a well-rounded theory. He also warned that we must be prepared to find situations when the systems 'alter or even exchange both their contents and their characteristics' (ibid., p.189).

The place of unconscious emotions is particularly ambiguous, for he wrote that the antithesis of conscious and unconscious does not apply to them. He emphasized that the exact nature of affects and emotions remains unclear but seems to correspond to processes of discharge, the final manifestations of which are perceived as feelings. But the control over ideation and affects by the conscious and unconscious appears to be different, and there is a constant struggle for primacy over affects between the conscious and the unconscious.

Thus Freud in this paper revealed a complex and dynamic notion of the unconscious and its relation to other parts of the psyche, that was flexible and covered a wide field of psychical phenomena.

The Elements of the Psychical System

Another theme linked to that of a system of flexibly interacting parts is that of the issue of the localization of the psychical structure. In *The Interpretation of Dreams* where Freud discussed the psychical apparatus as essentially involving a dynamic play of forces between two systems – the unconscious and preconscious/conscious – he dismissed any notion of anatomical localization, as I have already indicated in Chapter 1. When unconscious thoughts come into consciousness, Freud was not thinking of the formation of a 'second thought situated in a new place, like a transcription which continues to exist alongside the original' (Freud, 1900, p.610). There was no idea of a change of locality. Instead, he thought that particular mental groupings can have cathexes of energy attached to them or withdrawn from them under the sway of a particular agency. What is mobile is not the psychical structure but its connections, or associations, to use the language of the *Aphasia* monograph. Instead of thoughts and feelings being located in organic elements of he nervous system, they arise between them. That is, thoughts and feelings take place in facilitations and resistances between the elements.* In other words, the psychical apparatus, and with it the property of consciousness, is made up of a system of relations between elements. Once again, Freud's thinking involves elimination of the old notion of a particular centre where the functioning of the psychical apparatus takes place; instead he proposes a radical model of interacting elements.

Receptivity and Retention

A theme that runs from the 'Project' to the late Freud concerns how the mental apparatus can be receptive of new impressions and also retain permanent traces of impressions. In *The Interpretation of Dreams*, Freud pointed out the difficulty that 'one and the same system can accurately retain modifications in its elements and yet remain perpetually open to the reception of fresh occasions for modification' (Freud, 1900, p.558). He proposed that a dual system with separate elements needs to be present – one that allows consciousness of impressions to take place and the other to register memory of impressions. Freud (1920, pp. 28–9) put forward the notion that the perceptual apparatus consists of two layers – an outer protective shield against stimuli whose function is to decrease the strength of incoming excitations – and a surface behind it – the system Pcpt-Cs – which receive the stimuli.

Freud (1924) used the analogy of a toy pad for the psychical apparatus. The pad has a thin protective sheath and also a receptive surface that can be used repeatedly, while permanent traces are left on the underlying wax slab. The problem of receptivity and retention was solved by dividing the two functions between two separate but interrelated component parts. Freud compared the appearance and disappearance of the writing on the pad 'with the flickering-up and passing away of consciousness in the process of perception' (Freud, 1924, p.231). Once again, one can see how the

* This was a concept first put forward by Freud in his 'Project for a scientific psychology' (1895a, p.360).

functions of the psychical apparatus take place as a result of interactions between parts or systems. From this supposition, one could also speculate that this predisposes the apparatus to be particularly susceptible to problems when the links between parts of the system are interfered with, whether this be for physical reasons, as in the case of aphasia, or for psychological reasons, as with severe psychotic states.

The treatment of psychotic or near-psychotic children can reveal in rather a basic way some of the ways that these links can be understood. I have in mind as a clinical example the treatment of a confused seven-year-old, 'James', whom I saw for therapy. He had great difficulties separating from his anxious, rather depressed mother, and great problems in learning. He had poor concept development, poor memory and concentration. He showed psychotic features in that he had poor social relations with a lack of awareness of others, great difficulty in symbolization, and confusion between self and Other. He was a timid boy who could not relate to other children, remained very immature, still used a potty, and would climb into his mother's bed to sleep, where he would stay. She herself admitted that she did not want him to grow up. In a special school setting, he had little confidence, would cling to the teachers and could hardly do any activities except cooking, during which he was, however, in a constant state of anxiety. He had had a disrupted early life, in that his mother had left him for hours on end in the basement, with only a dummy full of orange juice as comfort, while she worked upstairs as a receptionist. Since then, he had never really shown much evidence of normal development.

The early part of therapy with James was exceedingly difficult. He was at first fearful of me, had difficulty in speaking and needed the comfort of a cup of orange juice in the room. He gradually began to trust me and, perhaps most significantly, he began to fold some paper into little books, sellotaping the pages while vigorously biting off pieces of sellotape. This activity seemed to convey that he already knew the therapy was going to be about trying to link things up in his mind. He would paint simple pictures in these books which seemed to convey his state of mind. For example, to begin with, while he was anxious, he painted a number of black squares, with the occasional bits of red, and then made more and more of a mess. But then he gradually drew more structured, if simple, pictures, such as small flowers.

When I brought up with him the coming Christmas break, the therapy became increasingly fraught, as he became more and more agitated about coming to the therapy room. Yet he also drew four mountains, each joined to the other at the base, with flags on the rounded tops. He said there were people on the tops. A 'bridge' – a straight line – connected the peaks just below each flag. He asked me several times about the time and when we would go, and whether other children would be there when he returned to his class, a frequent preoccupation. I gave a few brief interpretations which, summarized, ran: Maybe he wanted me to be a bridge for him. The people won't be alone at Christmas and between sessions, and he wouldn't be without me if he drew a bridge. He agreed shyly, and then drew some hills in the distance, some birds and sky beyond the hills.

With the approaching Christmas break, the sessions became more difficult and occasionally he could not enter the room. While in the session he would often ask me the time and say he wanted to go. James' early messy and abstract paintings perhaps indicated his confused understanding of the world. As Francis Tustin has described, 'the psychotic child lives predominantly in a world of black and seething matter pitted with voids which lack any principle of organization' (Tustin, 1972, p.172). Yet early on James was able, to some extent, to picture my absences, for example by means of the vertical mountains with the horizontal linking bridges. Perhaps here one can see the early stages of how the 'building blocks' of an ordered symbolic system come to be formed, by means of a simultaneous vertical and horizontal structuring.

It was only by the end of February that the crisis in the therapy seemed to be over. His being able to stay in the room again coincided with a session in which he spent most of the session making a folder on which he drew some simple musical notes. (His mother had apparently been trying to teach him to play the recorder.) Then he bit off lots of sellotape and stuck it over the notes 'so the marks won't rub away'. I interpreted in terms of sticking things down so they won't rub away, later referring to wanting to stick me down so I wouldn't be rubbed away. Here, I think, was the beginning of attempts at making a 'notation' to make sense of my absences.

The following session, the penultimate before Easter, he drew his family for the first time. The figures were rather primitive – cylindrical and compressed, with a square base for legs and no hands. He talked about going to Wales where he had some relations. 'Us went there before.' He drew some Easter eggs and then a Christmas tree with presents. The presents were what he called 'magic pads', in fact, the toy that Freud described as the 'mystic writing-pad', which he used as a model for the mind. James described carefully how the toy worked – you put something on it and it rubs away. I obviously linked this to his feelings about me and his memories being rubbed away last Christmas, and his concern that this might happen again.

The toy seemed very pertinent to how James' own mind was trying to grasp my absence and to retain memories in consciousness. With him, it was as if there were a faulty connection sheet linking memory with perceptions; or else that a metaphorical 'unseen hand' kept disconnecting the wax slab and the waxed paper, as it were, so rubbing away the writing on the pad of consciousness.

After my interpretation, he angrily wanted to throw away his previous drawings for a while. I would not let him and instead asked him to keep them in some of his folders. He agreed, and then tenderly arranged his drawer, and cut up some of the larger pieces of paper for use the next week. I let him take out one drawing which he wanted to take out, as I felt he needed to take something concrete from the sessions, as he still felt they were rubbed away. In a sense, this was a 'practising remembering' session.

Significantly in the next session, the last before Easter, James began his first attempts at understanding written words. He wanted to make a 'word book'. He would draw, for example, a dog and I would write the letters for him next to the picture. The word game in fact continued as a constant element of the sessions for a few months, as he gradually began to spell words for himself.

One session before a half-term break, he played with toy dolls for the only time. He brought a toy cot and put a baby in it. The mother went shopping and then the baby grew up to become a boy. There was a friendly car who bashed everyone except the boy. Then the boy was playing with a friend, but the mother was dead. I interpreted that he seemed afraid that, if he grew up, his mummy would die. This seemed to hit the target, and later I learned that he had thrown away his potty, slept in his own bedroom and was going around saying he wanted to grow up!

It must have been difficult for James to deal with the lack of correspondence between his mother's fantasy of him as an ideal good child and his being clearly full of primitive terrors. Yet in a sense, James fitted in well with his mother's desire, which she openly expressed – her desire for him not to grow up. His fear in turn was that if he grew up, she would not cope and would die.

James gradually began to bring more elaborate pictures and expressed more structured fantasies. By the end of that year he had begun to read and write simple words. He definitely wanted to be a boy, wanted to go up a class in school, grow up and stick up for himself more. But he also continued to reveal a chaotic and confused side, for which he used the therapy to help him cope.

I think that it was probably significant that his beginning to grow up coincided with his attempt at making a notation and the use of the word game. At last he had a means of making order out of confusion, and he also had a few words for dark feelings, words that seemed to have been denied to him by his mother and rather absent father. As Brecht wrote, 'lamenting by means of sounds, or better still words, is a vast liberation, because it means that the sufferer is beginning to produce something. He's already mixing his sorrow with an account of the blows he has received; he's already making something out of the utterly devastating. Observation has set in' (Brecht, 1963, p.47).

James' slow progress seemed to take place at a number of different levels. He began to make sense of my absences by creating a notation. At first, gaps between sessions were meaningless and the consciousness of sessions was rubbed away. But then the gaps became part of the structure; he was able to order things, however primitively, on the horizontal time axis. At the same time, he became interested in the use of words. It was as if the use of words actually helped him to clear confusions in his understanding and eventually helped him to grow. Maybe the treatment of such children can give us clues as to how consciousness develops. It would seem to involve a complex process in which it is linked to the development of separation, the use of words, the understanding of presence and absence, the creation of a symbolic structure (the horizontal and vertical axes) and a developing sense of time.

Everyday Conscious and Waking Thoughts

Although unconscious wishes and desires are the primary elements involved in the formation of dreams, Freud did describe in detail the role of the other elements such as waking thoughts. He explained this by an analogy:

> A daytime thought may very well play the part of *entrepreneur* for a dream, but the entrepreneur, who, as people say, has the idea and the initiative to carry it out, can do nothing without capital; he needs a *capitalist* who can afford the outlay, and the capitalist who provides the psychical outlay for the dream is invariably a wish from the unconscious. (Freud, 1900, p.561)

In *The Interpretation of Dreams*, Freud emphasized the importance of recent events and the relevance of waking thoughts in the 'entrepreneurial' activity of dream instigation. The significance of recent events and fresh impressions, many of them conscious, has not had time to be lost through repression. The instigating agent of a dream is found among the experiences a person has not yet 'slept on'; that is, these are often undigested experiences. Freud also described how the material that has occupied us during the day dominates the dream and how we can understand dreams as a continuation of waking life, however disguised. He wrote that the 'analysis of dreams will regularly reveal their true, psychically significant source in waking life, though the emphasis has been displaced from the recollection of that source onto that of an indifferent one' (ibid., p.177). In addition, the day's residues, many of which involve conscious thought, have the most numerous and varied meanings and are the psychical material for the dream work to act upon.

The unconscious wish is the essential additional factor in the construction of the dream. Particular unconscious conflicts can, as it were, be 'hooked' on to the recent material, and the latter can provide a point of attachment for such conflicts.

In the psychoanalytic encounter, one may be looking for past conflicts through reconstruction and interpretation, and yet one hopes very much to be working with fresh material from recent events, as this may not yet be bogged down by repression and is often more rich in content. Thus I am emphasizing the psychical significance of waking thoughts, many of them conscious, not only as a point of attachment for unconscious conflicts, but also in their own right.

Particular Functions of Consciousness

So far I have described consciousness as one element of an interacting system. While not wishing to overvalue its place in the system, I have tried to highlight its own contribution. Freud also described several particular functions provided by consciousness.

He described consciousness as a 'sense organ for the perception of psychical qualities' (Freud, 1900, p.615). Excitations flow into consciousness from the external sense organs and are then submitted to a fresh revision before becoming a conscious sensation. At this point, consciousness, by perceiving new sensory qualities, in particular distinguishing and registering *differences* between sensations, directs, distributes and organizes the incoming excitations, eventually forming a conscious sensation. Similarly, Freud wrote that 'consciousness gives us what are called *qualities* – sensations which are *different* in a great multiplicity of ways and whose *difference* is distinguished according to its relations with the external world' (Freud, 1895a, p.308).

Consciousness also receives excitations perceived as different qualities of pleasure and unpleasure from the interior of the apparatus. With the help of its perception of pleasure and unpleasure, consciousness influences the discharge of excitations and can help to discriminate between them. By this means, consciousness plays a part in the regulation of the psychical apparatus. This regulation can also take place by means of the linking of thought processes with verbal memories.

Linked to the process of becoming conscious and to the regulation of the paths taken by trains of thought is the function of 'attention' in the form of mobile psychical energy. Trains of thought may come and go. Those that become conscious can do so if attention is directed toward them by the activity of the preconscious. Consciousness itself may also attract thoughts by a 'hypercathexis', or an additional amount of application of psychical energy. By this means, consciousness can help to provide a 'greater delicacy in functioning' (Freud, 1900, p.602) of the psychical apparatus.

Freud added to the description of attention. Consciousness learned to comprehend psychical sensory qualities when 'a special function was instituted which had periodically to search the external world in order that data might be familiar already if an urgent need should arise – the function of attention. Its activity meets the sense-impressions half-way, instead of waiting for their appearance' (Freud, 1911b, p.220). Bion, one of the few modern psychoanalytic thinkers to have extended our theory of consciousness, uses this quote to fill out his own theory of thinking. He wrote that: 'any experience may be used as a 'model' for some future experience. This aspect of learning by experience is related to, and may be identical with, the function Freud attributes to attention ... the value of a model is that its familiar data are available to meet urgent inner or outer need' (Bion, 1962a, p.74).

Furthermore, Bion used a concept of 'alpha function' as a

> working tool in the analysis of disturbances of thought. It seemed convenient to suppose an alpha function to convert sense data into alpha elements and thus to provide the psyche with the material for dream thoughts, and hence the capacity to wake up or go to sleep, to be conscious or unconscious. According to this theory consciousness depends on alpha function, and it is a logical necessity to suppose that such a function exists if we are to assume that the self is able to be conscious of itself. (Bion, 1962b)

Bion highlighted situations in which the alpha function failed to develop fully and hence when there is a failure to develop adequately differentiation of elements into conscious and unconscious.

To return to Freud, by its contribution to the process of thinking, consciousness can make another contribution to the regulation of the psychical apparatus. It can do so as verbal memories have sufficient residues of quality to draw the attention of consciousness to themselves.

Consciousness also has a role to play in reality testing, the 'function of orienting the individual in the world by discrimination between what is internal and what is external' (Freud, 1915b, p. 232). Perhaps one could say that consciousness has an important role in sorting out sensations and impressions, indicating where they come from and, to some extent, what happens to them.

CONSCIOUSNESS – ONE VOICE OR MANY?

The work of the philosopher Daniel Dennett, in particular his book *Consciousness Explained* (1991), which incorporates research findings from neurophysiology and psychology, provides an interesting new approach to the problem of consciousness and yet also seems to share some of Freud's assumptions while also extending them. Dennett argues that there is no evidence for a special place in the brain where consciousness takes place or where it all comes together for presentation to consciousness. He argues, with the help of experimental data, that there is no single point or boundary line in the brain where all representations are united and where we can read off the results. He calls this model, after Descartes who invented it, the 'Cartesian Theatre'. He believes that there is no evidence of a point in the brain where there is an observer waiting for messages. That is, there is no 'theatre' where representations are projected on to a screen where they are read off by an internal observer, or what Gilbert Ryle (1949) called the 'ghost in the machine'. Yet this is a powerfully attractive model of the mind, one that still dominates psychoanalysis, especially when one thinks of an inner world made up of representations that are somehow read out by the conscious or unconscious subject. The simple logical explanation for this impossibility is that someone would have to observe the observer, and so on, ad infinitum. That is, who observes the observer? Does the unconscious subject observe the conscious subject? If so, who checks on the unconscious subject – the even-more-deeply-unconscious-subject?, etc. There is an infinite regress. Once again one has a version of the issue of the location of the human subject. To some extent, Freud bypassed this problem by emphasizing the interaction between parts of the brain in his *Aphasia* monograph and then the interaction between elements of the psychical system. This bears some resemblance to Dennett's own model of brain functioning, with many parts of the brain working simultaneously and in parallel. I shall continue to examine this important and complex issue on a number of occasions, for example when examining in detail the nature of mental representations and also the relation between subject and object relations.

For Dennett, in place of the 'illusion' of the Cartesian Theatre, he puts forward what he calls a 'multiple drafts' model of consciousness. He thinks of the mind as an intelligent machine, in which all varieties of thought or mental activity are accomplished by parallel, multitrack processes of interpretation and elaboration of sensory input, although he makes no clear distinction between conscious and unconscious arrangements of pathways or functioning. Information entering the nervous system is under continuous 'editorial revision'. These multi-track processes

> occur over hundreds of milliseconds, during which time various additions, incorporations, emendations and overwritings, of content can occur in various orders. These yield, over the course of time, something like a narrative stream or sequence, which can be thought of as subject to continual editing by many processes distributed around the brain. Contents arise, get revised, contribute to the interpretation of other contents and to the modulation of behaviour (verbal or otherwise), and in the process leave their traces in memory, which then eventually decay or get incorporated into or overwritten by later contents, wholly or in part. This skein of contents is only rather like a narrative because of its multiplicity; at any point in time there are multiple drafts of narrative fragments at various stages of editing in various places in the brain. (Dennett, 1991, p. 135)

For him, consciousness is distributed around the brain, and no moment can count as the precise moment at which conscious events occur. He compares the brain to a 'virtual machine', which is like the software programs in a computer. The computer provides the hardware, while the different forms of software program provide different virtual machines. In the brain, the neurones and their architecture provide the organic hardware, while the connections *between* them provide the software programs, made up rather as in Freud's model of the psychical apparatus, of differences in excitations between elements.

An ordinary computer is a 'serial' machine, which essentially per-

forms actions in rapid sequence, one after the other. But the more sophisticated computers can run on parallel pathways, in which various networks of connections can work independently of each other. This
provides a more plastic and intelligent machine that can also deal more
effectively with selective damage – one part of the network can take over
from a damaged area, unlike a sequential machine. Similarly, the architecture of the brain appears to consist of millions of parallel neuronal
networks acting independently and cooperatively to make conscious
experiences in various drafts. Dennett argues that there is

> no single definitive 'stream of consciousness,' because there is no
> Central Headquarters, no Cartesian Theatre where 'it all comes
> together,' for the perusal of a Central Meaner. Instead of such a
> single stream (however wide), there are multiple channels on which
> specialist circuits try, in parallel, ... to do their various things,
> creating multiple drafts as they go. Most of these fragmentary
> drafts of 'narrative' play short-lived roles in the modulation of
> current activity but some get promoted to further functional roles,
> in swift succession, by the activity of a virtual machine in the
> brain. (ibid., p.254)

The notion of multiple, parallel pathways contrasts with the more
traditional view of brain functioning as involving serial, albeit complex, pathways. Freud's early model of psychic functioning, based on
the treatment of hysterical patients, as described in *Studies in Hysteria*
and which formed the basis for his subsequent work, also follows the
serial model with regard to consciousness. Though he describes the
psychical apparatus as having a complicated and multidimensional
organization, he describes consciousness as a narrow 'defile' through
which unconscious thoughts are trying to pass:

> Only a single memory at a time can enter ego-consciousness. A
> patient who is occupied in working through such a memory sees
> nothing of what is pushing after it and forgets what has already
> pushed its way through. If there are difficulties in the way of
> mastering this single pathogenic memory – as, for instance, if the
> patient does not relax his resistance against it, if he tries to repress
> or mutilate it – then the defile is, so to speak, blocked. The work is
> at a standstill, nothing more can appear, and the single memory
> which is in the process of breaking through remains in front of the
> patient until he has taken it up into the breadth of his ego. The
> whole spatially-extended mass of psychogenic material is in this
> way drawn through a narrow cleft and thus arrives in conscious-

ness cut up, as it were, into pieces or strips. It is the psychothera-
pist's business to put these together once more into the organization which he presumes to have existed. (Freud, 1895b, p.291)

In contrast, Dennett describes multiple defiles through which
activity is constantly passing. However, Dennett does not really tackle
the issue of how mental conflicts are produced. Freud's model of a
narrow defile with psychogenic material pushing to be admitted to
consciousness does attempt to account for such conflicts, and would
certainly seem to be particularly relevant in understanding how the
minds of his hysterical patients dealt with conflicts. Thus, although
Dennett's model points to the need to consider that there are many
pathways involved in producing consciousness and not just one
narrow pathway at the end of the process, there is also the need to see
where and how the pathways can be 'blocked', as it were.

For Dennett, rather than a conflict, there is a sort of competition
among many current events in the brain, and a select subset of such
events wins. Discriminations are accomplished in a distributed,
asynchronous, multilevel fashion. There is not a single narrative
thread that comprises consciousness, not a single 'defile', but multiple
fragments of narrative, some of which are more long lasting than
others. There is no Central Meaner or organizer, but consciousness is
just what goes on in the brain. Each act of discrimination is registered
in many places. There is, in Freudian terms, a sort of 'over-
determination' written into the brain.

Dennett's model seems to reflect the experience of the psychoanalytic encounter in that we deal with narrative fragments, with bits of
story, past and present; with elaborations, projections, confusions. We
allow bits of the patient's story to come to light, and we may help to
clear the clutter and allow the unconscious meanings to come through
into consciousness. But, until now, the psychoanalytic theoretical
model of consciousness has not reflected the complexity of what we
do; it has been stuck in the 'serial' rather than the 'parallel' way of
thinking; stuck, that is, with the hysterical model of the mind.

Given the existence of multiple fragments of narrative, Dennett
asks how we still come to experience some sort of continuous stream
of consciousness. He shows, with results from experiments on the
blind spot (Dennett, 1991, pp.323–5) and on jumping eye movements
(ibid., pp. 355–6), that one of the most striking features of consciousness is its discontinuity, and yet we still experience an apparent
continuity. He shows how good the brain is at ignoring gaps in our
experience, in revising the consciousness of perceptions after they
have been perceived, and in creating illusions of continuity when there

is none. For him, there is no self as such except as an abstraction or illusion, an 'as-if' phenomenon, which helps us to feel as if there were a centre of 'narrative gravity', lending some coherence to our personal story. The Cartesian Theatre is a metaphor that the brain has created as shorthand for the functions it uses to organize the fragments of narrative into a story, rather as, one might say, a dream unites the multiple trains of thought into a 'unity,' however precarious, by means of secondary revision. As Dennett writes:

> Our fundamental tactic of self-protection, self-control, and self-definition is not spinning webs or building dams, but telling stories, and more particularly concocting and controlling the story we tell others – and ourselves – about who we are. And just as spiders don't have to think, consciously and deliberately, about how to spin their webs, and just as beavers, unlike professional human engineers, do not consciously and deliberately plan the structures we build, we (unlike *professional* human storytellers) do not consciously and deliberately figure out what narratives to tell and how to tell them. Our tales are spun, but for the most part we don't spin them; they spin us. Our human consciousness, and our narrative selfhood, is their product, not their source. (ibid., p.418)

Of course, it follows from this that one could say that Dennett's own theory of consciousness is just another story about how we think, yet one more attempt by our brains to make coherence where maybe there is none. We then have to ask ourselves how convincing is his story as compared to other stories. Or maybe the point is that we just have to keep creating stories to fill in the gaps, different and alternative ways of talking about ourselves; we are built that way.

One could also speculate that the unconscious might exploit the many gaps and discontinuities provided by the multiple drafts of conscious and preconscious thought processes for its own purposes. The existence of such discontinuities could provide many opportunities for disguise. One could further speculate that this structure might provide for many degrees of freedom in the psychical system. By having many pathways involved in consciousness, the unconscious could be allowed a considerable degree of 'free play', while there may also be a kind of selection process which switches between parallel pathways.

Recent scientific work on 'chaos theory' has also shed light on how systems of neuronal networks may function. For example, studies by Freeman have led to the discovery in the brain of chaos – complex behaviour that seems random but has some hidden order. 'The chaos is evident in the tendency of vast collections of neurones to shift abruptly and simultaneously from one complex activity pattern to another in response to the smallest of inputs' (Freeman, 1991, p.34). He underlines the ability of the brain to respond flexibly to the world and to generate novel activity patterns and ideas. He suspects that chaos in the brain arises when two or more areas 'meet at least two conditions: they excite one another strongly enough to prevent any single part from settling down, and at the same time, they are unable to agree on a common frequency of oscillation. Competition between the parts would increase the sensitivity and instability of the system, contributing to chaos' (ibid., p.41).

Occasionally, the bursts in neuronal activity come together into a Gestalt, an organized pattern. He speculates that consciousness is the subjective experience (or 'dependent concomitant', to use Jackson's and Freud's phrase) of such processes, which helps the brain to plan and prepare actions. Without wishing to push the analogy too far, perhaps one has here the beginnings of a microscopic explanation of how Freud's interactions between neurones take place, how the differences and facilitations between elements of the psychical system are organized.

Whatever happens at the microscopic level, we are still ignorant about how the unconscious itself may be structured. Does the unconscious function through the gaps in the pathways involved in consciousness? Is everything that is not involved directly in consciousness simply unconscious? Is there a basic continuum between consciousness and unconsciousness, or are there parallel networks of consciousness and unconsciousness? Is the unconscious like a dustbin where all the debris of conscious life, the fragments of narrative, are floating, waiting to be put into a narrative sequence by consciousness; or is the unconscious already organized and has to find a way of negotiating through the many pathways of consciousness in order to come into consciousness? Clearly, from psychoanalytic experience, the laws of the unconscious are different from those of consciousness; there is a different logic; and the unconscious has its own structure or language. But this experience has yet to be integrated into the neurophysiological model; and perhaps this is not even possible as we are dealing with different levels of explanation, or different stories.

Dennett has little to say about the unconscious. He does recognize the fact that much nervous activity takes place unconsciously, for example when we act to keep our balance or adjust our posture. He also cites (ibid., pp.305–9) one theory by David Rosenthal that conscious thinking requires the presence of unconscious thoughts, which he terms as 'higher order' thoughts, which constantly back up conscious processes. Again, however, these unconscious processes really refer to the control of ordinary behaviour and not to what the psychoanalyst constantly deals with, eruptions of meaningful impulses that cut across conscious life.

The work of the Russian literary theorist Mikhail Bakhtin on the plurality of consciousnesses can provide some kind of a bridge between Dennett's multiple drafts theory of consciousness with multiple narrative fragments and the day-to-day experience of the psychoanalytic encounter. His work also points towards a subject relations approach to psychoanalysis, by focusing on dialogue and by contrasting the dialogic approach based on interaction between subjects with a monologic approach based on the cognitive subject relating to objects of cognition. In his study on Dostoevsky, Bakhtin took the view that what represents Dostoevsky's unique and revolutionary literary style is that there exists in his narrative a 'plurality of independent and unmerged voices and consciousnesses, a genuine polyphony of fully valid voices' (Bakhtin, 1963, p.6). Bakhtin argued that the novels are 'dialogic'. They are constructed 'not as the whole of a single consciousness, absorbing other consciousnesses as objects into itself; but as a whole formed by the interaction of several consciousnesses, none of which entirely becomes an object for the other' (ibid., p.18). Bakhtin contrasts Dostoevsky's 'dialogic' and pluralistic framework with the traditional 'monologic' form of novel of the single omnipotent consciousness.

The interaction of consciousnesses 'provides no support for the viewer who would objectify an entire event according to some ordinary monologic category ... and this consequently makes the viewer also a participant. Not only does the novel give no firm support outside the rupture-prone world of dialogue for a third, monologically all-encompassing consciousness – but on the contrary, everything in the novel is structured to make dialogic opposition inescapable. Not a single element is structured from the point of view of a nonparticipating "third person"' (ibid., p.18).

That is, with Dostoevsky's novels, there is no fixed position, no Archimideal point, no fixed third position, from which to view his work; rather, the work contains multiple positions.

Dostoevsky's dialogic method contrasts with, for example, Tolstoy's work, which, despite its multiple levels, contains 'neither polyphony nor ... counterpoint. It contains only *one cognitive subject*, all else being merely *objects* of its cognition' (ibid., p.71). What unfolds before Dostoevsky 'is not a world of objects, illuminated and ordered by his monologic thought, but a world of consciousnesses mutually illuminating one another, a world of yoked-together semantic human orientations' (ibid., p.96). Furthermore, the idea in Dostoevsky's novels 'is not a subjective individual-psychological formation with "permanent resident rights" in a person's head; no, the idea is inter-individual and intersubjective – the realm of its existence is not individual consciousness but dialogic communion *between* consciousnesses. The idea is a *live event*, played out at the point of dialogic meeting between two of several consciousnesses. In this sense the idea is similar to the *word*, with which it is dialogically united. Like the word, the idea wants to be heard, understood, and "answered" by other voices from other positions' (ibid., p.88).

Behind the genre of the dialogic novel lies the Socratic notion of the dialogic nature of truth. The dialogic means of seeking truth goes against the notion of monologic thinking, which possesses ready-made truths; dialogic thinking arises out of human dialogue and encounter, which discover truth.

One could assert that Bakhtin's view of communication involves communion between what one could call the '*many voices of consciousness*', both within the individual and between individuals. Consciousness has many streams or voices, or drafts. Through dialogue, in the social field, the themes of these voices may become more or less coherent. In the analytic encounter, one could say that the patient moves from having a single or reduced stream of consciousness, with one or few voices, to the capacity to experience many voices, allowing them to penetrate and overlap, at what Bakhtin called 'various dialogic angles' (ibid., p.266). Clinically, one might distinguish between the capacity to experience the many voices of consciousness, with some sense of coherence or relationship between voices, and various degrees of disintegration of the processes of consciousness, in which a patient may experience the many voices as merely chaotic and fragmented or even as hallucinations. In the clinical setting, there also arises the issue about how much sense and coherence should be fostered by the analyst, how much they should be 'monologic' in the sense of providing a focus on a particular theme, and how much the analyst should foster the 'freedom' of the many and different voices.

A clinical example will illustrate how these kinds of issue might arise in a session. I have chosen material from a patient with a narcissistic personality whose discourse was at times relatively disjointed; but perhaps for this reason illustrates the issues I have raised. By including some of my own thoughts, I hope to convey how I tried to pay attention to a number of different levels or 'angles'.

My patient came into analysis as he was having difficulty sustaining relationships. He showed little empathy for others and was exploitative and sometimes emotionally sadistic. He sought constant admiration and attention to boost his fragile sense of self-worth and also suffered from bouts of feeling empty and deprived of any goodness.

His father was described as stiff and authoritarian, often absent at work; his mother was described as cold, puritanical and anxious. When the patient was young, his mother turned to him for support when his father was absent.

Initially, my patient tested out the analytic boundaries to the limit, with repeated acting out, lateness, and the like. He dealt with separations by denying any dependence on me. In the transference, he wanted me to admire him, to be a servant, to be used and abused as he wished. But he also had a great anxiety, sometimes of psychotic intensity, about being submerged by me/mother and also persecutory anxieties about being exploited by me.

The Monday session I describe here shows a shifting focus of attention with many themes or voices, though there is the central issue about how he dealt with missing me over the weekend. I do not wish to push the analogy of the many voices too far in this material; none the less the notion helped me to make some sense of it. I would also certainly say that he had a fear of ever having a dialogue with me and preferred to keep a kind of monologue going.

The previous Friday, a childhood memory had arisen while he was bringing up concerns about his relationship with his girlfriend, Mary. He recalled that when he was about eleven, he played a game with a girl of his own age that involved tying her up.

The session began with two dreams. In the first dream he was on the phone, but the handset was some way from the receiver, with a long cable between them. Mary was on all fours like a baby or a dog. She had the cable in her mouth and was pulling on it. His associations were that the dream had something to do with a fear about him and Mary thinking about living together and about how they communicated. He made a reference to the phone as suggesting communication; and he was afraid of his own childishness, about which Mary had, in fact, been derogatory.

My thoughts at this time were that the dream image had something to do with the childhood memory of the girl being tied up, with sado-masochistic elements and aggression. I wondered whether the memory had instigated the dream or created anxiety about the analytic relationship. I wondered about his communication with me, particularly what he had done with the memory over the weekend. Did communication with me become perverse? As he made no mention of the memory, I kept it to myself. As he told me the dream, I felt somewhat on the side, fairly attentive but looking on. Was I going to be controlled or involved in some mix-up of projections between baby and adult? I also agreed with Mary's assessment of his childishness and, thinking it might be evidence of his own wish to deny childish dependence on me, and wondered what that meant in the countertransference.

In the second dream, there was an image of a woman called Frankie from a work situation that weekend. She had a haunted, worried look. His associations were that Frankie did not know who she was, that she 'over-blended' with others and was a vulnerable and brittle person. But she had begun to take root at work. He paused and then thought that he and Mary had begun to take root.

At this point, my thoughts began to come together around the two dreams. The haunted figure reminded me of how my patient had looked on occasions. Frankie was a male/female name. She represented a blurring or merging. The first dream may have shown how he projected dependent feelings (the baby) towards Mary and me; the second dream revealed the consequences – there was a haunted subject, an ego deprived of goodness.

Feeling it was time to bring together some of the elements or 'voices' in the session, without hopefully being too 'monologic', I made an exploratory interpretation: that he was perhaps also talking about how he might be taking root with me, and that the dreams had something to do with how he communicated with me over the weekend, without a phone call; and perhaps some thought about needing to talk to me then. He was at first sceptical about needing me, but he paused and, unusually, had second thoughts. He said that in the first dream he was the baby, while I was holding the phone. He felt powerless, humiliated by being beholden to me, having to crawl toward me like a dog.

I interpreted that he was anxious about being in contact with me in his mind that weekend. (I should say that I do not regularly make this kind of interpretation about weekend breaks, but only when I feel that they are particularly relevant.) I think he felt that I was withholding communication, keeping him dangling, and humiliating him. He agreed and admitted to having had some positive thoughts about me during the weekend; but he also expressed fears about being in analysis for ever. I commented that the anxieties in the two dreams seemed to show that, on the one hand, he had a self that wanted to take root; but, on the other hand, there was a frightened, haunted self that hated being dependent on me.

This comment soon led to his making some connections with the childhood memory and he then recalled that the girl begged to be let free. It also led to the issue about how afraid he was that his destructiveness would get out of hand with Mary as it had in the past in other relationships. In fact, it turned out that she had recently told him that she had enacted some sexual bondage with other men, which had disgusted him.

Eventually, thinking again of the Frankie figure, I interpreted that he was afraid that I would keep him in bondage for ever, tied to me; and that he was afraid of being merged with me in some frightening way and would lose his sense of who he was. This provoked some upset, and he held back tears when he suddenly realized that he felt compelled to rescue women whose bodies had been attacked or who abused themselves. He had, in turn, repeatedly abused them as a way of not being intimate. The session ended as he wondered if he could ever look after a woman; he also became concerned not to 'muck up' our relationship. I felt that by this point we had begun to reach a more 'dialogic' level, in which there was some awareness of my existence, and some coherence arising out of a more social interaction.

REPRESENTATION AND CONSCIOUSNESS

The model of the Cartesian Theatre that Dennett (1991) dismissed, and that Ryle (1949) called the 'ghost in the machine', implies that there is an inner private world or space where we inspect our thoughts and feelings and that this is in some way a reflection or copy of the external world. Descartes first put forward the concept of the mind as a single inner space, or what Rorty (1980) called the 'glassy essence,' with an isolated subject only certain of his own thoughts and with a mind and a body somehow separate though interconnected. Since then, the problem of the mind and consciousness has become central to western thought and Descartes' model has become central to much of psychoanalytical thinking.

Yet there are other ways of seeing our minds. Ryle's book *The Concept of Mind* (1949) attempts to destroy what he calls 'Descartes' myth' or the dogma of the ghost in the machine. He first of all describes what he calls the 'official doctrine' about the nature and place of minds, which still exercises such a powerful influence and which, indeed, now seems to be commonplace public knowledge about how the mind works. It is worth summarizing Ryle's description (ibid., pp.13–17) of the official doctrine as the background for the discussion of this issue.

Human beings have both a body and a mind, or are both body and mind. Bodies are in physical space, but minds are not in physical space. The workings of one mind are not witnessable by other observers; its career is private. Only I can take direct cognizance of the states and processes of my own mind. A person is supposed to be able to exercise from time to time a special kind of perception, inner perception or introspection. On the other hand, one person has no direct access of any sort to the events of the inner life of another. Direct access to the workings of a mind is the privilege of that mind itself. When someone is described as knowing, believing or guessing something, etc., these are verbs that are supposed to refer to the occurrence of specific modifications to the occult stream of consciousness. Only the individual's own privileged access to this stream in direct awareness and introspection can provide authentic testimony that these mental-conduct verbs are correctly or incorrectly applied.

Ryle then aims to prove that this theory is completely false as it is based on one major mistake, what he calls a 'category mistake'. This refers to the mistaken application of logical types. For example:

A foreigner visiting Oxford or Cambridge for the first time is shown a number of colleges, libraries, playing fields, museums, scientific departments and administrative offices. He then asks 'But where is the University? I have seen where the members of the College live, where the Registrar works, where the scientists experiment and the rest. But I have not yet seen the University in which reside and work the members of your University.' It has then to be explained to him that the University is not another collateral institution, some ulterior counterpart to the colleges, laboratories and offices which he has seen. The University is just the way in which all that he has already seen is organized. When they are seen and when their coordination is understood, the University has been seen. His mistake lay in his innocent assumption that it was correct to speak of Christ Church, the Bodleian Library, the Ashmolean Museum and the University, to speak, that is, as if 'the University' stood for an extra member of the class of which these other units are members. He was mistakenly allocating the University to the same category as that to which the other institutions belong. (ibid., pp.17–18)

The form of the category mistake is the source for the origin of the 'double life' theory of the mind, that there must exist inside us a ghost person who is actually doing the experiencing, feeling and thinking, not ourselves; that inside our physical bodies there is another category of substance known as mind, as the University would be another category of substance in addition to the colleges. As we mistakenly think of the University as existing as separate from the colleges, so we incorrectly think of the inner ghost as there inside our heads reading off the representations for us.

Ryle then, in the rest of the book, offers an alternative description of how we experience the world. For example, when we 'describe people as exercising qualities of mind, we are not referring to occult episodes of which their overt acts and utterances are effects; we are referring to those overt acts and utterances themselves' (ibid., p.26). We discover other minds in understanding what they say and do, not in wondering what the ghost inside them is saying and doing. 'In making sense of what you say, in appreciating your jokes, in unmasking your chess-stratagems, in following your arguments and in hearing you pick holes in my arguments, I am not referring to the workings of your mind, I am following them' (ibid., p.59). There is no shadow inner world where we are really thinking and feeling, speaking and understanding. 'There is not a real life outside, shadowily mimicked by some bloodless likenesses inside; there are just things and events, people witnessing some of these things and events' (ibid., p.235). The notion of the shadow inner world which follows our words and behaviour is an unnecessary addition, a category mistake like wondering where the University is.

Ryle's arguments do not assert that there is nothing going on in our minds; on the contrary, a lot is going on, there are many processes of thought and feeling, imagination and conjecture, and, I would add, unconscious processes. But their structure is not of the ghostly kind. We have to find other ways of understanding ourselves.

Richard Rorty, very much influenced by Ryle, and also by Dewey and Wittgenstein, develops further the destruction of the shadow inner world, or what he referred to as Descartes' 'invention of the mind'. He argues that the notion of a 'mind' which has an 'essence' and somehow reflects nature was a mere Cartesian invention and has no more status than any other theory (Rorty, 1980). He argues against the notion that knowledge is made possible by what he terms, borrowing from Shakespeare's *Measure for Measure*,* a special 'glassy essence' which enables human beings to mirror nature. And Rorty attacks the notion of the 'single inner space' invented by Descartes,

---

* 'But man, proud man/ dressed in a little brief authority/ Most ignorant of what he's most assured – /His glassy essence – like an angry ape,/ Plays such fantastic tricks before high Heaven/ As makes the angels weep – who, with our spleens,/ Would all laugh themselves mortal' (II.iii. 117–23).

with arguments similar to those I have presented when dealing with the issue of subjectivity and objectivity in Chapter 1.

> We owe the notion of a 'theory of knowledge' based on an understanding of 'mental processes' to the seventeenth century, and especially to Locke. We owe the notion of 'the mind' as a separate entity in which 'processes' occur to the same period, and especially to Descartes. We owe the notion of philosophy as a tribunal of pure reason, upholding or denying the claims of the rest of culture, to the eighteenth century and especially to Kant, but this Kantian notion presupposed general assent to Lockean notions of mental processes and Cartesian notions of mental substance. (ibid., pp.3–4)

Rorty claims that these notions, which are still taken for granted, were merely inventions, metaphors, or, to use Wittgenstein's phrase, 'language games' (see below), with no greater status than any other invention, however useful they have been in enabling us to talk to one another.

Rorty argues that what links contemporary philosophy to the Descartes–Locke tradition is 'the notion that human activity (and inquiry, the search for knowledge, in particular) takes place within a framework which can be isolated prior to the conclusion of inquiry – a set of presuppositions discoverable a priori ... For the notion that there is such a framework only makes sense if we think of this framework as imposed by the nature of the knowing subject, by the nature of his faculties or by the nature of the medium with which he works' (ibid., pp.8–9). Outlining the thinkers who seemed to have most influenced him, he continues to argue against the primacy of the knowing subject who is the source of truth:

> The notion that there could be such a thing as 'foundations of knowledge' ... or a 'theory of representations' ... depends on the assumption that there is some such a priori constraint. If we have a Deweyan conception of knowledge ... then we will not imagine that there are enduring constraints on what we can count as knowledge, since we will see 'justification' as a social phenomenon rather than a transaction between the 'knowing subject' and 'reality.' If we have a Wittgensteinian notion of language as tool rather than a mirror, we will not look for necessary conditions of the possibility of linguistic representation. If we have a Heideggerian conception of philosophy, we will see the attempt to make the nature of the knowing subject a source of necessary truths as one more self-

deceptive attempt to substitute a 'technical' and determinate question for that openness to strangeness which initially tempted us to begin thinking. (ibid., p.9)

Rorty's arguments are dense and complex and cannot easily be summarized, but one of his main points is to show that the notion of an inner mental space was conceived by Descartes and Locke at a particular historical moment, when science was making sense of physical space with mathematical laws. Locke in particular 'made Descartes's newly contrived "mind" into the subject matter of a "science of man" – moral philosophy as opposed to natural philosophy. He did this by confusedly thinking that an analogue of Newton's particle mechanics for "inner space" would somehow be "of great advantage in directing our Thoughts in the search of other Things" and would somehow let us "see what Objects and Understandings were, or were not fitted to deal with"' (ibid., p.137).

This was, for a long time, a useful attempt to create a certain foundation for knowledge of what we are and what we do, in which inner representations are the privileged source of certain knowledge about ourselves; but Rorty argues that the very search for such a foundation is just one, historically based and biased, way of charting a field of inquiry. In contrast, Rorty argues that 'the desire for a theory of knowledge is a desire for restraint – a desire to find "foundations" to which one might cling, frameworks beyond which one must not stray, objects which impose themselves, representations which cannot be gainsaid' (ibid., p.315). Instead he presents a hermeneutic argument, looking at meaning and interpretation.* There is for him no privileged argument which provides the one certain answer about who we are. instead there are many descriptions, many 'voices' in the conversation of mankind. The important thing is to keep the conversation going, to choose new descriptions and new ways of speaking. 'To see keeping a conversation going as a sufficient aim of philosophy, to see wisdom as consisting in the ability to sustain a conversation, to see human beings as generators of new descriptions rather than beings one hopes to be able to describe accurately' (ibid., p.378).

Once the knowing subject as the 'centre' or foundation of knowledge about 'reality' is eliminated, there then follows a particular view about the nature of the human subject as having no privileged central place where 'it all comes together', to use Dennett's phrase. Indeed, in a paper written as a commentary on the work of Donald Davidson and

* I have looked at the relationship between hermeneutics and psychoanalysis in detail in *Freedom to Relate* (Kennedy, 1993), chapter 3.

published at the same time as his book *Philosophy and the Mirror of Nature*, Rorty presents the view that we can even drop the notion of consciousness as it is unnecessary. Ability to report psychological states is not a matter of presenting something to consciousness but of simply using words. Once we drop the notion of consciousness,

> there is no harm in continuing to speak of a distinct entity called the 'self' which consists of mental states of the human being: her beliefs, desires, moods, etc. The important thing is to think of the collection of those things as *being* the self rather than as something which the self *has*. The latter notion is a leftover of the traditional Western temptation to model thinking on vision, and to postulate an 'inner eye' which inspects inner states. (Rorty, 1991, p.123)

Instead, Rorty substitutes, in a way which resembles Dennett's multidraft model of consciousness as eliminating the Central Meaner, 'the picture of a network of beliefs and desires which is continuously in process of being rewoven (with some old items dropped as new ones are added). This network is not one which is rewoven by an agent distinct from the network – a master weaver, so to speak. Rather, it reweaves itself, in response to stimuli such as the new beliefs acquired when, e.g., doors are opened' (ibid.).

Furthermore, Rorty argues that, in a similar way, there is no more a centre to the self than there is to the brain. 'Just as the neural synapses are in continual interaction with one another, constantly weaving a different configuration of electrical charges, so our beliefs and desires are in continual interaction, redistributing truth-values among state-ments. Just as the brain is not something that 'has' such synapses, but is simply the agglomeration of them, so the self is not something which 'has' the beliefs and desires, but is simply the network of such beliefs and desires ... to have a belief or a desire is to have one strand in a large web' (ibid.).

Rorty's argument about the absence of a centre to the self here owes something to Ryle's attack on the concept of mind as a category mistake, as well as to Hume's classical arguments against the existence of any kind of self. The latter argued that he could not distinguish a sense of self from the many perceptions that he experienced, and that we are simply a collection of different percep-tions with no unifying self, a theatre where perceptions come and go, though not a Cartesian Theatre where things then come together:

> For my part, when I enter most intimately into what I call *myself*, I always stumble on some particular perception or other, of heat or

cold, light or shade, love or hatred, pain or pleasure. I never can
catch *myself* at any time without a perception, and never can
observe any thing but the perception ... I venture to affirm that
[mankind is] nothing but a bundle or collection of different
perceptions, which succeed each other with an inconceivable
rapidity, and are in a perpetual flux and movement ... The mind is
a kind of theatre, where several perceptions successively make their
appearance; pass, re-pass, glide away, and mingle in an infinite
variety of postures and situations. (Hume, 1740, pp.252–3)

Marcia Cavell develops the attack on the traditional representational model of the mind and how this relates to psychoanalysis.
Basing herself on Wittgenstein, Rorty and Davidson, she argues
against what she calls the 'assumption of subjective priority', that is,
that 'subjectivity in the form of an inner, private world comes first,
followed by some knowledge of external reality or what we take to be
external reality' (Cavell, 1991, p.142). Instead, while introspection
and self-reflection are important activities, she argues that they
neglect the primary role of social interactions. She argues for the
dependence of mental events, and hence consciousness, on interpersonal interactions in the social field. She also suggests that Freud
himself included such a model when he brought out the importance of
the transference in relationships.

The quandary can be illustrated if we see someone in pain. One
may ask where the pain is located, who feels it and where. Is the pain
felt consciously in the body, in the mind – where? Can one imagine
that a pain is located in the social field, at least at the moment one
begins to express the pain? A pain may not only cause us to suffer, it
may also make us aware of, or may even blunt our awareness of, our
surroundings. For example, those who cut their bodies may feel alive
in the act of cutting or else may use the painful act to merge with their
surroundings. In the analytic setting, whether it be bodily or not, it is
related to what is going on between analyst and patient. Conscious
pain is, then, located not only in the patient's body. Indeed, sometimes only the analyst experiences the pain, or the pain may be located
in a partner outside the session.

Cavell proposes an externalist 'anti-subjectivist' view, which holds
that

while introspection and self-reflection are certainly important
activities, they can yield only a very partial view of the nature of the
mental ... For introspection neglects the relations between mind
and behaviour, the public role that mental states play in the

interpretation of action. And this role suggests that the mental itself has a more public character than the internalist can account for. The mental in general is constituted as such in part by certain relations between creature and environment, also between creature and other creatures. As for particular mental states, any idea, concept, or thought means what it does only in relation to a vast network of other thoughts ... To have a thought is not to have a particular sort of subjective object in or before the mind which is meaningful in and for itself, or which is somehow fitted to receive meaning. Rather, we are creatures who, through our interactions with other creatures in a world we share in common, come to mean something by our utterances. Wittgenstein, for example, will say that to know the meaning of a word or a sentence or a concept requires at least this: knowing how to use it in activities with others. And such activities are also the ground of thought. (ibid.)

As can be seen from the last quotation, Cavell's attack on the primacy of the private inner world follows from the thought of the late Wittgenstein, as does much of Rorty's approach to the issue of mental representations. The early Wittgenstein of the *Tractatus* (1921) had an essentially representational model of the mind, with 'essences' or simple 'objects' lying behind the world, which language reflects in its propositions. As Norman Malcolm put it, 'According to the *Tractatus*, the enduring substance of the world consists of the simple objects. The objects can enter into combinations with one another. The totality of these possible combinations is the form of the world. The totality is fixed, unchangeable. It is prior to the existence of human beings, of experience, of thought, of language' (Malcolm, 1986, p.14).

Furthermore, according to Malcolm's interpretation, the *Tractatus* says that

1. There is a fixed form of all possible worlds.
2. That this fixed form consists of the simple objects, i.e. substance.
3. That in language it must be possible for there to be *names*, which stand for simple objects.
4. That in language it must be possible for there to be elementary sentences, which consist solely of configurations of names. (ibid., pp.56–7).

Malcolm adds that, according to the *Tractatus*, 'anyone understands a sentence who understands its constituent parts (4.024). Nothing else is required. Two sentences with different constituent parts will differ in sense. The sense of a sentence is *fixed* – fixed by its constituent parts. If the sentence is composed of constituents you understand, then you understand the sentence' (ibid., p.13).

But in Wittgenstein's later thinking, he rejects this latter conception. 'To understand a sentence it is not enough that its constituent parts be understood. What must be added is a knowledge of the *circumstances*, previous and present, in which the sentence is employed' (ibid., pp.13–14).

In his later work, he considered that his early thinking was the result of a misunderstanding about how language worked. In his new thinking, the meaning of words is not one fixed thing, not an occurrence or process that 'corresponds' to the word, but is instead the use of the word. In his *Philosophical Investigations* (1953) Wittgenstein called the processes of using words 'language games', of which there are many kinds. For him, meaning arose out of the use of words in context. (One may recall here the clinical example of the disturbed little boy James and how he began to understand meanings through repetition of a word game.) For the later Wittgenstein, the elements of language are not some simple objects that lie behind the world but are like 'tools in a tool-box: there is a hammer, pliers, a saw, a screw-driver ... The functions of words are as diverse as the functions of these objects. (And in both cases there are similarities.)' (Wittgenstein, 1953, p.6).

Language is made up of many different kinds of language game and many different language games. Furthermore, 'Instead of producing something common to all that we call language. I am saying that these phenomena have no one thing in common which makes us use the same word for all, – but that they are *related* to one another in many different ways. And it is because of this relationship, or these relationships, that we call them all "language"' (ibid., p.31). Thus, Wittgenstein emphasized the idea of a language system, made up of elements interacting in a social context, in what he called 'situations', in human customs and institutions.

Using language, which involves mastery of a technique, presupposes that we are already in a human community, in which there is agreement about how words are generally used; that is, it presupposes a community of rule-followers. But for Wittgenstein, following a rule is not about some hidden process going on in the head, but instead it follows a social practice and is openly revealed. As Marcia Cavell has put it in her recent book *The Psychoanalytic Mind*,

> Wittgenstein does not deny the existence of mental images; his point is that they do not have the explanatory force we may have

thought ... Descartes and philosophical tradition held that public discourse follows private; words frame, but in no way help to create, the ideas they communicate. Wittgenstein's revolutionary move was to undermine the notion that we can divorce the private from the public in this way. In his passages about thought as silent speech he warns against the idea that language is a veil cast over thoughts which simultaneously hides and partially reveals them ... He urges that on the contrary silent speech is a derivative from heard speech. As we learn to calculate in the head by calculating on paper, so we learn how to single out something in our minds, how to think of it as a face, a farce, a seduction, from telling things and being told ... First there is private thought – including wish and desire – Augustine supposes; then a fitting of that thought to public speech. This is a picture, we notice, that only a creature who can both think and talk might have. In the picture Wittgenstein draws the direction goes the other way: first there is the child's induction into a form of life, which at the same time is its learning of language, and with this induction an entry into thought ... As for reference, it is socially fixed, not determined by private entities in individual minds/brains. (Cavell, 1993, pp. 24–5)

As for what takes place when we speak, Wittgenstein considered that 'Knowledge is not *translated* into words when it is expressed. The words are not a translation of something else that was there before they were' (Wittgenstein, 1967, p.33). He denied that the picture of an inner process, and hence of a private inner space, was an accurate one. There were not 'meanings' going through the mind in addition to words. The words simply expressed the thought. Instead of there being internal objects that become translated into meanings, meanings arise out of the use of words in a social context, the language games. Intentions are embedded in human institutions, or, as he vividly put it, in 'forms of life'. Knowledge is no longer a matter of presenting thoughts to consciousness but of understanding the use of words in context, in social situations where we find ourselves as 'living human beings' (Wittgenstein, 1953, p.97).

Wittgenstein also does away with any notion of some correlation between mental events and brain processes. As he wrote in the collection of thoughts called *Zettel*:

No supposition seems to me more natural than that there is no process in the brain correlated with associating or with thinking; so that it would be impossible to read off thought-processes from brain-processes. I mean this: if I talk or write there is, I assume, a system of impulses going out from my brain and correlated with my spoken or written thoughts. But why should the *system* continue further in the direction of the centre? Why should this order not proceed, so to speak, out of chaos? ... It is ... perfectly possible that certain psychological phenomena *cannot* be investigated physiologically, because nothing physiological corresponds to them ... I saw this man years ago: now I have seen him, I recognize him, I remember his name. And why does there have to be a cause of this remembering in my nervous system? Why must something or other, whatever it may be, be stored up there *in any form*? Why *must* a trace have been left behind? Why should there not be a psychological regularity to which *no* physiological regularity corresponds? If this upsets our concept of causality then it is high time it was upset. (Wittgenstein, 1967, p.106e)

If we are to agree with Wittgenstein and those like Rorty who have extended his scepticism about inner representations, then much of what passes for psychoanalytical theory needs revision. It follows that subjective experience is not so much an issue about individual minds or about merely an inner process, but has to include the social field. We certainly need to look more closely at the nature of the social context of subjective experience, a theme I will develop subsequently. But what is also put in question is particularly the notion of the subject/object distinctions and the privileged nature of the inner world. On the other hand, perhaps the actual 'raw' analytic experience is at least in tune with this scepticism. After all, the analytic encounter is a special kind of conversation or language game. Analytic conversation, like neurophysiology, does, however, appear to suggest that there may be some stable mental structures, however chaotic they may become. Perhaps having such structures is like having the rules of a game laid down in a guidebook. The actual game will depend on the moves made between players in the social field, but they keep shifting and changing and may or may not remain fixed.

Perhaps an essential function of consciousness is constantly to create, eliminate and re-create pictures of the world. By this I do not mean that there inner representations reflecting outer experiences as in a mirror. What we see is the picture we are constantly creating. There is no other observer or ghost observing us observing. We are the ones who make the picture. That is, we do not see things in our head but in the world. This is not to deny that we have various kinds of images in our mind; but, as silent speech is derived from heard speech, so most of these images are derived from things seen. If there is, in addition, a separate and organized internal world, it is perhaps a kind of unconscious storehouse of rules, memories, and differential excitations, out of which we make the pictures we see. Furthermore, perhaps we can say that while introspection does give us a certain amount of information about what we think and say when we turn our attention to some of the streams of thought, it is only one aspect of the human situation. It is only in an encounter with another person that matters become interesting and that true dialogic understanding can happen.

Perhaps it would be more accurate then, or at least more useful, to talk about our 'subjective world', rather than our inner world, as I suggested in Chapter 1. That way, we leave in suspense the philosophical problem of inner and outer, and whether or not there are mental representations and what they are. We have instead to consider what we have to deal with every day, what it is like to be a person, and how subjective experience is made up of many elements, some coming from ourselves and some from others, in a complex network, a unique subjective world.

CONCLUDING THOUGHTS

One may ask, what are the implications of what I have presented in this chapter both theoretically and clinically? Overall, I think that one can say that, far from having a simple or auxiliary role in the mind, consciousness has a complex part to play in mental functioning and is not merely some sort of elaborate sense organ. Freud himself outlined a number of other functions for consciousness. Presumably he was cautious about over-emphasizing the role of consciousness as he was intent on doing away with its former over-valuation. Any new model of consciousness would have to take account of recent scientific findings that emphasize that consciousness involves multilayered and multitrack processes. Presumably the unconscious is also structured in similar ways but with different rules. The scientific findings are compatible with, and influenced by, some kinds of recent philosophical thought, which tends to undermine the traditional ideas about mental representation. Other kinds of thought emphasize the importance of dialogue, social interaction, forms of conversation and a plurality of voices in human discourse. Such ideas may help us to think about our clinical work in new ways. They may even influence the way we listen to patients, as I have indicated in the second clinical example of this chapter. They may guide us to pay closer attention to the patient's various streams of thought and yet not necessarily provide monologic closure. I can also think of another patient whose mother had many helpers during his childhood. By closely listening to his discourse, I could detect a central mother figure and also subsidiary caretakers having their say. Similarly with the patient I presented, it seemed important to attend to a number of levels rather than stick to one level that might have missed the nature of his conflicts.

I have approached the difficult issue of whether or not the many voices of consciousness, the many streams or tracks, ever become unified, and have presented arguments for considering that there is no place in the mind or brain where this can be seen to be localized. However, from the thought of the late Wittgenstein, one can suggest that if anything comes together it is in the social field, and I shall develop this theme in subsequent chapters. As I shall discuss, the social psychology of George Mead develops in detail the consequences of this assumption and provides backing for my own notion of a subjective organization which encompasses the individual and the social fields. Briefly, for Mead the field of the mind is not confined to what goes on in the head, but is coextensive with, and includes

> all the components of the field of the social process of experience and behaviour, i.e. the matrix of social relations and interactions among individuals, which is presupposed by it, and out of which it arises and comes into being. If mind is socially constituted, then the field or locus of any given individual mind must extend as far as the social activity or apparatus of social relations which constitutes it extends; and hence that field cannot be bounded by the skin of the individual organism to which it belongs. (Mead, 1934, p.223, fn.)

Even if nothing really comes together in the brain, this does not imply that there is no possibility of achieving some kind of integration of different viewpoints and different activities somewhere. We do need our 'auxiliary' spaces where we can play with different positions. Perhaps our fascination with art and literature comes from the powerful way that we can achieve new combinations of thoughts on the canvas or on the page.

Freud himself was not that clear about the degree to which there was a self that draws everything together in some way, except in the analytic dialogue. For example, in *The Interpretation of Dreams*, he does ask the question about 'to whom does a wish-fulfilment bring pleasure?' His answer is that it is

> to the person who has the wish of course. But, as we know, a dreamer's relation to his wishes is a quite peculiar one. He repudiates them and censors them – he has no liking for them, in short. So that their fulfilment will give him no pleasure, but just

the opposite ... Thus a dreamer in his relation to his dream-wishes can only be compared to an amalgamation of the two separate people who are linked by some common element. (Freud, 1900, pp.580–1)

Perhaps we are, then, merely an amalgamation of two or more people; or, rather, an amalgamation of many fragments, narrative threads and voices, as a dream is an amalgamation of many different themes. One could compare the mind, as does Hume, to a play. There are a number of different parts, characters that come and go; but there is no unity separate from what the players say and do.

If one eliminates the need for a unified self and for the primacy of a private inner world, then one could argue, with Wittgenstein, that much of the clutter of our mental grammar is cleared. For example, to have a so-called conscious intention could at times be seen as having a disease. Thus when a postman delivers a letter through the door, you go and pick up the letter. You may say to yourself, 'There is the letter I have been expecting.' But on the non-representational model, you do not have an intention to go, brought on by something called a self, and then go. There is no intermediary state of mind because, if there were, you would have to postulate an intermediary behind the intermediary, and so on, ad infinitum. That is, there would be an infinite regress of ideas. If you do have something like an intermediary idea that signifies the need to pick up the letter and that then makes you pick it up, you are likely to be suffering from an obsessional or schizoid condition, or a dissociated state. In the normal state, our contact with the world is a direct one and not through some mental intermediary.

It is uncomfortable to think of the absence of a unifying self or private inner world of representations which underlie our actions. On the other hand, if we abandon this notion, at least for the most part, psychoanalysis can no longer be seen to be limited and esoteric in its scope, for it has to confront legitimately social, and even perhaps political, questions.

3 TRANSFORMATIONS OF THE SUBJECT, OR THE COMEDY OF ERRORS

SUBJECTIVE ORGANIZATIONS – SUBJECT 'OF' AND SUBJECT 'TO'

The term 'subject' that I have been using captures a basic dual aspect of the human situation, that we are both subject 'of' and subject 'to' various phenomena. That is, the term refers both to our sense of 'I-ness', who we are, that we can be authors of our actions and our history, while at the same time it also indicates that we are subject to various forces outside the orbit of the 'I' who speaks, forces which arise both from the individual and from the environment. Although Freud rarely used the term 'subject' as such, his use of the language of ordinary experience – the I, the It, the Over-I – to describe the agencies of the psychical apparatus would seem to imply that the issue of subjective experience was at the heart of his formal description of his discoveries. I would suggest that, because of its dual implications, the term 'subject' is well qualified to describe the organization of Freud's psychical agencies. It encompasses both the sense of positive identity and the sense of a threat to identity, some force opposing subjectivity. In addition, of course, in the traditional Cartesian model of the mind, where there is a subject there is also an object. I have presented arguments against the too ready use of the Cartesian model, particularly in the sense of a private inner world reflecting the outer world as in a mirror, and I shall return in detail to the issue of the subject–object relation; but in the meantime, I aim to focus more on the subject side of this equation. For even if one were to retain some aspects of the model of subject–object relationship, some kind of interrelationship, however modified, I think that the subject aspect of the relationship has been rather neglected in favour of the object aspect.

As I have discussed, Freud conceived of the psychical apparatus as a whole system, with various interacting parts and functions; there is a dynamic play of forces between the various elements of the whole system. The apparatus is made up of a system of relations between elements, the functions of the psyche take place as a result of interactions between parts or subsystems. No one place is the privileged seat of the soul or psyche. But there still remains a fundamental issue for psychoanalytic theories – how much the elements of the whole system, or the subject, are brought together and how much they are kept separate, even when interacting; that is, how the elements are *organized*.

Ogden also highlights this key issue particularly in the thought of Freud, Klein and Winnicott. His answer to it is to use the term 'dialectical' when describing the interplay of systems, basing himself on the thought of Hegel and Marcuse, and the commentary on Hegel by the French thinker Kojève, who incidentally profoundly influenced Lacan, as I shall take up later. For Ogden,

> Dialectic is a process in which opposing elements each create, preserve, and negate the other; each stands in a dynamic, ever-changing relationship to the other. Dialectical movement tends towards integrations that are never achieved. Each potential integration creates a new form of opposition characterized by its own distinct form of dialectical tension ... In addition, dialectical thinking involves a conception of the interdependence of subject and object ... One cannot begin to comprehend either subject or object in isolation from one another. (Ogden, 1994, p.14)

Applying this dialectical thinking, Ogden proposes that the 'experiencing subject can be conceptualized as the outcome of an ongoing process in which the subject is simultaneously constituted and decentred from itself by means of the negating and preserving dialectical interplay of consciousness and unconsciousness' (ibid., p.15). As Freud proposed a model of the mind in which there is no privileged position in which to locate the subject, so the subject is constituted for Ogden in the relations between consciousness and unconsciousness (ibid., p.18).

Ogden repeatedly uses the term 'dialectical' in his thinking, for example there is the dialectic of presence and absence, of Klein's paranoid-schizoid and depressive positions, of I-Me mirror interactions in Winnicott, of splitting and integration, and of his own autistic-contiguous position. Though I do not disagree with the notion of a dialectical interplay of elements, I am not sure what this tells us specifically about the interactions, beyond the fact that there is a dynamic interplay between the elements. Describing interactions as dialectical certainly sounds as if it means something, but my problem is that it seems at the same time to stop any further thinking. I think that he uses the term too widely and to explain too much. I would suggest that one needs to be more specific about the way that elements are organized and how they interact. However, I agree with Ogden that one can view Klein's theory of 'positions' not only as a basis for an object relations theory, but also as a prototype of a theory of subjectivity, and that Winnicott's descriptions of primitive subjective states of mind – for example, that of the subject coming to feel alive – are of fundamental importance in having a fuller understanding of human subjectivity. I have found Ogden's clear discussions in this area very useful as a starting point for my own speculations.

In the clinical setting, through emphasizing the dialectical interrelationship of subject and object, Ogden proposes a model in which analyst and patient are also interdependent, and, in terms rather reminiscent of Sartre's relations between self and Other as described above, are seen 'as subjects creating and created, destroying and destroyed by the other' (ibid., p. 4). Ogden introduces a 'third term' to take account of the analytic experience, which refers to what analyst and patient create jointly, and what is separate from each other, rather along the lines of Winnicott's 'transitional space' between mother and infant. 'In the same moment that analyst and analysand are created, a third subject is generated that I shall refer to ... as the *analytic third*, since it is a middle term sustaining and sustained by the analyst and analysand as two separate subjects. More accurately, analyst and analysand come into being in the process of the creation of the analytic subject' (ibid., p.5). The analytic third is not experienced in the same way by each of its creators, while at the same time each of them is no longer the same as a result of its creation.

It would seem here that Ogden is describing an important element of the analytic relationship, where analyst and patient are in a mutual and creative relationship, even when negating one another. It highlights the fact that there are two subjectivities in play in analysis. My unease, which is increased when examining Ogden's clinical material, is that this approach can become an opportunity for the analyst's constant and rather unlicensed use of his own free associations and personal reverie, supposedly in the service of the analysis. Indeed, in his clinical chapter on the analytic third, Ogden shows how 'the intersubjective experience created by the analytic pair becomes accessible to the analyst in part through the analyst's experience of his own reveries, forms of mental activity that appear to be nothing more than narcissistic self-absorption, distractedness, compulsive rumination, daydreaming, and the like' (ibid., pp.94–5).

While I would not wish to rule out in principle the use in the analytic session of any kind of thought process, if it is induced by the

interaction between patient and analyst, I think that Ogden's consistent use of his own reveries is rather different from the disciplined use
of the analyst's countertransference, although I may have misunder-
stood him. I have tried in the previous chapter to give an example of
such a use when illustrating how the patient may move from
monologue to dialogue. I have the impression from a number of
intersubjective analysts that there is not enough distinction between
the subjective positions of analyst and patient. The analytic relationship, though an intimate one, is also a distorted one, where the
subjectivities of analyst and patient are not the same or are not at the
same level; the patient's world is to be examined in the open, while the
analyst's is essentially private, or masked, except at a few contact
points with the patient. How the mask may be lifted, or not, may have
important bearings on what is going on in the session.

Perhaps my difficulty with Ogden's approach and a number of
intersubjective thinkers who do seem to advocate a similar approach
has more to do with, first, an over-emphasis on the 'positive' aspects
of the analyst–patient interaction, and not enough attention to how
the subjectivities of patient and analyst do not overlap and constantly
fail to connect; and second, with the basic model of the human subject
that is presented, that perhaps could do with more elaboration.

I would suggest that we need to see how some aspects of the
personality may become organized in pathological ways, to use John
Steiner's useful model of 'pathological organizations' (Steiner, 1987).
Incidentally, I think that this can be seen in part at least as a
proto-theory of subject relations, and it has clearly influenced my own
use of the term 'subjective organization'. For Steiner, a pathological
organization can be considered to be in an equilibrium with the
paranoid-schizoid and depressive positions. This is a highly organized
defensive structure, held together by narcissistic intrapsychic relationships in which perverse gratification plays an important role as the
glue holding it together in some way. The organization of defences
seems to be designed to produce a real or illusory safety from the
anxieties experienced in the other two positions. The strength of this
model is that it does seem to illuminate the way that borderline
personalities deal with anxiety. But perhaps it is questionable how far
it can be applied in general to other kinds of personality. My own
model is not that of a defensive organization, or an organization held
together by perverse forces, though I could imagine that a subjective
organization could become a defensive or pathological organization
under abnormal conditions.

To address the issue of the complexity of the human subject, I have
found the thought of Jacques Lacan to be seminal. His understanding

of the human subject is complex and very much influenced by philosophical thought. The subject for him is essentially 'alienated', 'lacking' and 'fading'. There is no place for a unified sense of who we are; and for this reason his theory has appealed to the current postmodern fashion for thought which emphasizes cultural fragmentation. Incidentally, Ogden does not find Lacan relevant for his own project, as being too much of a 'deconstructionist'. Ogden views Freud, Klein and Winnicott as working 'entirely within a dialectical, hermeneutic framework wherein the analytic dialogue (as well as the intrapersonal dialogue) is based on a mutually interpretive discourse in which meanings are clarified and elaborated and in which enhanced understandings of the experience of oneself and the other are enhanced' (Ogden, 1994, p.28). I would suggest that this over-emphasizes again the 'positive' aspects of communication and ignores the way that communication may break down, be inadequate, come up against lack and loss, conflict and absence, all very much part of the Lacanian and, I would suggest, Freudian discourse. Lacan, for Ogden, over-emphasizes the alienation of the subject and the discordance between subject and Other, signifier* and signified. 'The Lacanian subject is not simply decentred, but is radically disconnected from itself leaving a central "lack" or void resulting from the fact that the speaking subject and the subject of the unconscious are irrevocably divided by the unbridgeable gap separating signifier and signified' (ibid., p.30). I would agree with Ogden that Lacan may have pushed his notion of the alienated and lacking subject too far, that his model of the subject is virtually always being subject 'to' rather than subject 'of', but I would not completely dismiss the usefulness of much of Lacan's elaborate thought about the ambiguities and complexities of human subjectivity.

For Lacan, the subject and the Other are inextricably linked; and when the subject appears in one place, he disappears in another. There is a constant tension between subject and Other, reminiscent of Sartre's dialectic of self and Other. Though it is difficult to summarize Lacan's notion of the subject, I shall take a few relevant lines from my study of him as a pointer:

> [The] subject comes into being through confronting the question of his lack, and the anguish that arises when the subject is faced by the failure of the Other to live up to his or her supposed perfection.

---

* According to Saussure (1915), the linguistic sign is a double entity, made up of a concept, the signified, with the sound image, the signifier. Thus the Latin word *arbor* is formed from the signifier 'arbor' and the concept 'tree'. Signifier and signified are intimately united, like two sides of a coin, and the bond between them is arbitrary.

The Lacanian psychoanalytic discourse revolves around the problem of lack and of the lacking object. The subject is seen as marked by castration and lack from birth. Language represents the subject, but in so far as it represents what is prohibited. The subject is confronted by the unconscious, which is striving to express what is really forbidden to the speaking subject ... This inevitably creates tensions and splits in the subject, who continues to be de-centred, lacking, fading. On the one hand, he tries to speak, and on the other he is faced by the impossibility of doing so. It is out of these tensions, which the subject relives in the psychoanalytic situation, that the subject comes into being. (Benvenuto and Kennedy, 1986, pp.181–2)

For Lacan, it is at moments of failure, disruption, discontinuity that the unconscious appears, described by Freud in, for example, slips of the tongue, jokes and dreams, where linguistic mechanisms can be seen clearly to operate. The unconscious appears, is made manifest, through a split in the subject, so that the subject is always surprised by what then appears (see Lacan, 1973, p.28).

The thought of Lacan is illuminating with regard to the way that social structure *transforms* the subject. Lacan was influenced by the anthropologist Lévi-Strauss, who argued that the unconscious imposes structural laws on the emotions, memories and impulses of subjects (Lévi-Strauss, 1958, p.203). Lacan described how the subject is formed and transformed by networks of 'chains of meaning', or chains of signifiers, which cross his path. He vividly illustrated this notion, which he used as a way of interpreting Freud's repetition compulsion as the repetition of a chain of meaning in a symbolic circuit, by commenting on Edgar Allan Poe's detective story *The Purloined Letter* (see Benvenuto and Kennedy, 1986, pp.91–102).

The subject of the story is a love letter stolen from the Queen of France by an unscrupulous minister. Though we never know the letter's precise contents or from whom it comes, we infer that it concerns the Queen's unfaithfulness to the King. The minister's power comes from his keeping hold of the letter and threatening to use it, without actually doing so. Poe's detective, Dupin, manages to discover the letter by looking where no one else had looked, in front of everyone's eyes, disguised on the top of the minister's desk. Secretly, and undetected by the minister, Dupin substitutes another letter, thus shifting the balance of power between the characters in the story. The minister, once powerful because he possessed the letter, becomes weak in relation to the Queen, who, unknown to him, now has the upper hand. The minister takes the place of the Queen as the one in the

Other's power. The King, the figure of paternal authority, remains, like the police, blind to the situation. Dupin, rather like an analyst, intervenes to shift the dynamic between the characters.

Lacan traces the effect on the characters as the letter changes hands and follows a complicated path, its routes and displacements determining the action and destiny of the characters. The letter, which he compares to a signifier, travels in a definite path, forming a symbolic circuit which cuts across the subjects of the story, transforming each of them in turn as it moves along the circuit. 'One can say that, when the characters get a hold of this letter, something gets hold of them and carries them along and this something clearly has dominion over their individual idiosyncracies ... [A]t each point in the symbolic circuit, each of them becomes someone else' (Lacan, 1978, pp.196–7). Each subject is caught up in a network of other subjects; there is an intersubjective field, made up of criss-crossing chains of meaning, a network of unconscious social structures.

This model seems to correspond to the analytic experience, where one may be listening for the way that chains of meaning, narrative structures or 'voices', criss-cross, intermix, fade, dissolve or occasionally cohere. The analyst may, as it were, have to receive many letters from the patient. This is perhaps most vividly portrayed by those severely traumatized patients who present with a horrifying history which they tell with little feeling. They may describe the most awful story of massive trauma, fostering as a child, early loss of a parent, etc., which may make the analyst feel incredibly sad, while the patient seems unmoved. If such patients start treatment, there is the likelihood of an early major enactment, a sudden opting out, or a major crisis, as if they are gripped by the chains of meaning which dominate their lives. They seem to be subject 'to' the past, not subject 'of' their history. In this context, it is perhaps of some interest that the man with the 'chairman' dream, in Chapter 1, developed a particular attitude to history. As a boy, he became fascinated by old buildings, particularly old churches, mediaeval castles and Gothic cathedrals. He was not at all interested at that time in the people who used and lived in the buildings. He retreated into history as a way of escaping from the realities of his lonely family life, which resulted in his not finding a place for himself in his own history.

Lacan emphasized how the path of the purloined letter, like a signifier, determined the acts and destiny of the subjects. As he put it:

If what Freud discovered and rediscovers with a perpetually increasing sense of shock has a meaning, it is that the displacement of the signifier determines the subjects in their acts, in their destiny, in their refusals, their blind spots, their end and fate, their innate gifts and social acquisitions ... without regard for character or sex, and that, willingly or not, everything that might be considered the stuff of psychology, kit and caboodle, will follow the path of the signifier. (Lacan, 1956, p.60).

When we look for the subject, we have, for Lacan, to look within the structure of the signifying chain, for he is indeed this very chain. The Lacanian subject 'keeps running along the chain of which he is part, as the signifiers (of which he is made) slide away from the signified, from the "something". The result is that the subject's lack of being, or void, his truth, is expressed in the very process. On the one hand, he can be represented by the signifier, but only to be reduced to being no more than a signifier; so that the same moment as he is called to speak, the subject is petrified. It is this process which is summarized in Lacan's definition, "The subject is what is represented by the signifier, and the signifier can only represent something for another signifier. The signifier represents the subject for another signifier"' (Benvenuto and Kennedy, 1986, p.118).

Thus Lacan's model is of a subject slipping through the signifying chain, where you are only left with signifiers; the signified is always out of reach, but what is available is the chain of signifiers. It is the analyst's task to uncover the many and varied relationships between signifiers. The danger with this conception of psychoanalysis is that one may become carried away by the fascination with language, with the power of the signifier. However, I think that it does highlight an important area with which psychoanalysis deals, in particular how the subject cannot be conceived of without reference to social structure, as I shall explore in more detail later.

Lacan was against any notion of 'unity' to the way that the subject is organized; for him there is always alienation and fragmentation, the subject is always fading, losing meaning, appearing and disappearing. Whatever one may think about this view of subjectivity, his thought does highlight the issue of how the subject may or may not cohere. Each analytic theory has a different stance on this issue. For example, in self psychology there is a particular emphasis on the cohesion of the self. There are useful clinical accounts of states of fragmentation and of disruptions to the analytic session (Wolf, 1988, pp.109–18); but there is a basic position that cohesiveness and integration are both possible and desirable, while conflict and the negative aspects of communication tend to be underplayed.

The issue of unity versus diversity or plurality, or unity versus fragmentation, was what in ancient philosophy was called the problem of the 'One and the Many' and which still seems relevant today. The philosopher Habermas has recently highlighted how this ancient problem still gets played out in modern thought, thinkers coming down on one side or other of the 'one and many' dynamic:

> 'The One and the Many,' unity and plurality, designates the theme that has governed metaphysics from its inception. Metaphysics believes it can trace everything back to one. Since Plato, it has presented itself in its definitive forms as the doctrine of universal unity; theory is directed toward the one as the ground of everything. Prior to Plotinus, this one was called the idea of the good or of the first mover; after him, it was called *summum ens*, the unconditioned, or absolute spirit. During the last decade this theme has taken on renewed relevance. One side bemoans the loss of unitary thinking ... the other side attributes responsibility for the crises of the present to the metaphysical legacy left by unitary thinking within the philosophy of the subject and the philosophy of history. This side invokes plural histories and forms of life in opposition to a singular world history and lifeworld, the alterity of language games and discourses in opposition to the identity of language and dialogue, and scintillating contexts in opposition to univocally fixed meanings. (Habermas, 1992, p.115)

In contrast to what he sees as a polarization of viewpoints, Habermas proposes that we need to look at both aspects of the one and the many, that plurality and unity are in a constant relationship, that 'the unity of reason only remains perceptible in the plurality of its voices' (ibid., p.117).

The issue of one and many, of the interplay between unity and fragmentation, or the issue of the self as continuous and discontinuous, is at the heart of Klein's analytic theory. The movement between the paranoid-schizoid and depressive positions represents the interplay between the unity, the oneness, of the depressive position, in which there is recognition of the One whole object, and the fragmentation of the paranoid-schizoid position, where only Many part-objects are recognized. Rather than focus on the object side of this dynamic, I would like to emphasize how Klein's theory can be seen as a prototype for a subject relations theory. What is novel in her thinking is not only the way that objects are experienced as a unity or diversity, but how the subject who does the experiencing goes in and out of different structural positions, throughout his life. She has subtly sidestepped the issue of the subject's unity by offering a model where unity is a factor, but part of a dynamic process. However, I think there is a danger in this model of holding to a moralistic, or even religious, attitude, by too readily equating, in a Platonic fashion, the perception of the whole object, the one, with the good. That is, being a good or 'healthy' person in this way of thinking can mean the capacity to experience the whole object, and being a not-so-good person means being fragmented, rather than accepting, to follow Habermas, that being a person involves the duality of the one and the many. I suspect that this theoretical trap accounts for some of the religious fervour that accompanies the political organization of the followers of Klein, and to some extent to those of Lacan, who tend to act as if they have the best way of doing analysis and are the possessors of the truth, the absolute 'good', the only 'one' way of doing analysis, as laid down by their prophet.

ORGANIZATION AND DISSEMINATION

Returning to theoretical issues, while in Lacan the subject never has a sense of integration, I have suggested that with Klein integration is part of a duality. I feel that this movement away from and towards the possibility of some kind of integrating organization corresponds more faithfully to what we see in the session and what we observe in baby's experiences, both areas of which are, after all, not always totally chaotic!

I have repeatedly and purposively used the term 'organization' as it is rather a general one, and can be understood in a variety of overlapping ways. It has been used in the sciences in a number of different contexts. For example, it can be used as a general term for the distinctive feature of organic life. '[W]e use the term "organism" synonymously with "living entity". In the higher members this organization becomes more and more distinct. This greater complexity of organization runs parallel with increasing range and power of adaptation, attained by the setting apart of special structures (organs) for the performance of definite functions' (Starling and Lovatt Evans, 1962, p.3). There is an increasing amount of organization as animals show increasing differentiation of structure in their parts; in particular, the organization of the nervous system becomes increasingly more complex in the course of evolution.

The organization of visual perception has been of particular concern to scientists as a way of understanding brain function, as the visual apparatus is fairly easily accessible to experimentation. It seems that while there is a certain amount of innate organization in the way that the visual apparatus is organized through its neuronal connections, there is also a need for interaction with the environment for the apparatus to develop fully in complexity and organization. For example, kittens, monkeys (and probably human babies), are born with at least 25 per cent of the cells of the primary visual cortex specified to detect contours; development proceeds rapidly, provided the animals are exposed to light during a critical period of four to six weeks (Young, 1987, pp.169–70; Zeki, 1992). This points to what one could call a basic principle of the nervous system – that *use* leads to increasing organization. There is thus a basic innate organization built into the visual cortex, but the presence of the social field is required for the organization to develop in complexity, the visual system has to be used to become fully organized. This finding is perhaps compatible with the suggestion that the subject is in possession of various functions and structures that need to be used in social interaction for their full realization. It is in this sense that I would conceive of a subjective organization comprising the individual within a social field, 'hungry' for interaction, for social input.

As for the organization of the higher brain functions, I have already discussed Freud's view of language functions as involving the whole language system, as well as the complexities of how consciousness can be conceived as involving multiple parallel pathways. The Russian neurologist Luria, however, reminds us that what distinguishes human mental activity from reflex animal activity is the former's socio-historical origin, including the role of culture and language, and its structural organization.

[T]he higher mental functions which, at a first approximation, may appear direct, simple, and indivisible properties of mental life or direct functions of circumscribed areas of brain tissue, in fact, are the result of historical development and are social in origin and complex in psychological structure. This was well expressed by L.S. Vygotsky (1960), who stated that: 'a function which initially was shared by two people and bore the character of communication between them gradually crystallized and became a means of organization of the mental life of man himself.' This historical genesis and complex structure are essential features of the higher mental functions of man. (Luria, 1966, cited in Pribram, 1969, p.49).

Thus the very structural organization of human mental life involves interaction between people, social interaction. The term 'organization' is of course used in sociology to define various kinds of social relationship. For example, Weber (1968, p.48) defines an organization as a social relationship which is either closed or limits the admission of outsiders, when its regulations are enforced by specific individuals, such as a chief or administrative staff. Lévi-Strauss (1962, pp.75-6) shows how the sociological field in primitive societies and indeed to some extent our own can be organized by the use of any system of differentiating features, such as the use of opposing terms. These terms can be used like a code to convey messages, which can be transposed into other codes.

As for the relationship between self and others in the social field, I have already described how in Sartre the Other consists of a group of phenomena outside of me, yet which have a fundamental role in organizing my experience, like a skeletal framework. Mead (1934, p.175) also highlights the role in the structure of the mind of the organized attitudes of others.

One could also use the term 'organization' in quite general terms, as Locke did in his Essay Concerning Human Understanding (1689, p.331), where he describes the structure of a plant or animal as an organization of parts of matter in one coherent body. Similarly for Dewey (1929, p.209), the term refers to an empirical trait of some events involving an organism, where whole and parts are in interaction; each part of the organism is itself organized and so are the parts of the part; but for him, psychic organization does not refer merely to the individual but also to the individual's place in the social field.

Lichtenstein (1977) points out that several analytic thinkers have taken up the issue of organization in early mental development in order to account for the development of the personality. Sandler (1960) writes about an 'organizing activity' which begins to occur early in life, which he relates to the synthesizing function of the ego. Spitz related the concept of an 'organizer' in embryology, which triggers successive changes in the embryo, to a similar process in the psyche. He conceived of a variety of elements in the psyche becoming integrated through a process of organization. Hartmann borrowed from biology the concept of organization of the organism as the lawful correlation of the organism's individual parts, and used this to describe a process of 'fitting together' of elements of the psyche. These notions are essentially about the development of a whole self having a sense of unity; they emphasize the synthetic action of the ego, and underplay the movement away from organization towards disorganization.

Lichtenstein attempts a formulation of how the psychic structures are related to one another by avoiding conceiving them as related to the whole person. Instead, he defines the self as 'as the sum total of all transformations which are possible functions of an early-formed invariant correlation of the various basic elements of the mental apparatus. This definition seems to be compatible with the observation that the self-experience includes all the past selves of one's life and the not-yet-lived future. It also seems consistent with the fact that in the self-experience the potential selves that we could have been are merged with the actualized selves that we were and are' (Lichtenstein, 1977, pp.241–2).

He conceives the invariant element involved in human identity as the primary relationship to the mother. It is a 'thematic configuration, arising in the earliest, most primitive contact of the infant with the mothering adult. Borrowing from ethology, I thought of this earliest identity theme as an imprinted configuration which from then on constitutes the invariant in the development of the individual' (ibid., p.251). He suggests that 'it is likely that every individual is endowed with multiple developmental alternatives, and not just one self, which by definition excludes all other potential selves' (ibid., p.257). I shall return to Lichtenstein's thought later, when considering more fully the nature of the term 'identity'.

One suspects that developmentally early psychic organizations are very much based on sensations and body zones, and that they require the continuous care of the mother for their establishment. One could imagine that there are particularly intense early experiences, such as moments of engagement between mother and baby, which can form the basis of a fully subjective life, and could be seen as the template for an early subjective organization. One could describe the baby as already a proto-subject, one that is beginning to form meaning as it elicits care from its caretaker. I would presume that the early mother–baby relationship forms the matrix for the subsequent more sophisticated subjective organization, which is my main focus. In the analytic situation the relationship between the early and later organization may be fairly obvious at first or may take time to clarify.

To show what I mean, I have in mind a brief clinical example, from the beginning of the analysis of a young woman. She had come for help because of a great worry about her capacity to sustain relationships. She was worried about getting into unsatisfactory relationships with men, following the recent breakdown of a long-term one. She had also become rather socially isolated, and had a poor image of herself. Her mother, a powerful influence in her life, had gone through two divorces. The last one, relatively recently, had particularly affected the patient, as it had seemed to her to represent the loss of hope that relationships could last, and was clearly very relevant to her presenting problems.

At the beginning of analysis, she talked with considerable pressure, and it was difficult to make a contribution. She talked in considerable detail about family rows, clearly concerned about what would happen in the analysis. She later talked about all the many things she had to do in her life, of which analysis was just one, which was interpreted as related to the issue of whether or not there was going to be time and space for analysis in her life. She was also afraid that there would be no room for her in the analyst's life, that she could easily be displaced. Very rapidly there developed an atmosphere in the session, which could be described as the patient doing everything on her own. This seemed to be the theme of her life. For example, she got little real support from her mother after mid-adolescence. She very much had to grow up on her own, be self-reliant and make her own way in life. As a result she had become involved too early in a long-term relationship that had eventually broken up. All her thoughts, memories and her way of relating seemed to have become organized around the theme of being self-reliant, as if she had developed a cocoon of protection. The problem was that she constantly re-created this cocoon, so that the analyst felt left out, on the sidelines, a presence but one that had difficulty making live contact with the patient. It was then possible to link this kind of organization to the early relationship with her mother, who had been busy and preoccupied when the patient was an infant. It was also then possible to look at different ways she could relate. I would consider that the kind of organization she revealed could not be fitted into the Kleinian paradigm, whether it be the paranoid-schizoid axis or Steiner's pathological organization. The kind of organization I am describing is not necessarily pathological but a habitual way of organizing subjective experiences.

When there have been more major environmental impingements, such as chronic deprivation or various kinds of abuse, then early organizations become precarious. In later life, the subject may turn to all sorts of unsatisfactory solutions, such as perverse behaviours, self-harm or secret, almost delusional, fantasy worlds to maintain some sort of equilibrium.

Atwood and Stolorow describe similar possibilities through their intersubjective perspective. First of all, they propose that a central motive in the patterning of human action is 'the need to maintain the organization of experience' (Atwood and Stolorow, 1984, p.35). The organizing principles of a person's subjective world, which are unconscious, can operate positively, giving rise to certain configurations in awareness, or negatively, preventing certain configurations from arising. Atwood and Stolorow emphasize how patterns of conduct serve to maintain the organization of experience in two ways:

On the one hand, a pattern of conduct may serve to maintain a *particular* organization of experience, in which specific configurations of self and object, deriving from multiple origins and serving multiple purposes, are materialized. Such configurations when actualized may in varying degrees fulfill cherished wishes and urgent desires, provide moral restraint and self-punishment, aid adaptation to difficult realities, and repair or restore damaged or lost self and object images. They may also serve a defensive function in preventing other, subjectively dangerous configurations from emerging in conscious experience. (ibid., p.91)

They also make the valuable point that, 'On the other hand, a pattern of conduct may serve not so much to materialize a particular configuration of experience, but rather to maintain psychological organization per se, as when behavioural enactments are required to sustain the structural cohesion and continuity of a fragmenting sense of self and other' (ibid., p.92).

Stolorow and Atwood (1992, p.44) describe how sensual experiences and fantasies can become psychic organizers for the self. For example, sexual fantasies can be used as a defence to maintain cohesion and prevent fragmentation. Brandschaft and Stolorow describe how 'developmental traumata can derive lasting significance from the establishment of invariant and relentless principles of organization that remain beyond ... the influence of reflective self-awareness or of subsequent experience' (Brandschaft and Stolorow, 1990, p.108).

Bollas points to the pivotal existence in mental life, brought out in psychoanalysis by the use of free association, of a fundamental and creative process of fragmentation or disorganization, or rather what he calls 'dissemination' or 'cracking up'.

Unconscious mental life operates according to an oscillation that ensures its continuous – indeed ceaseless – function, as on the one hand unconscious work brings together through condensation otherwise disparate ideas, and on the other hand the process of free association then deconstructs these condensations. When Freud asked the analysand to free-associate to the dream, he frequently stressed that in so doing the patient dispersed the manifest content of the dream. What was created as an act of condensation – the dream event – is destroyed by the work of free association. Both processes, however, – bringing together and cracking up – are important features of the unconscious ... Free association is creative destruction. (Bollas, 1995, p.54).

Bollas suggests that Freud minimized the radical act of free association in order to emphasize the fact that dreams could be interpreted and had meaning. But for Bollas, free association 'not only divests the manifest content of the dream of its textual integrity but indicates its seminal power, since each dream image drives thousands of further associations that disseminate along a multitude of pathways' (ibid., p.54). Bollas suggests that there is in mental life a 'continuous simultaneous oscillation between psychic intensities (cohesions) and their disseminations (fragmentations)' (ibid., p.60).

I would suggest that Bollas is describing the use of a radical process of dissemination in the way that the subject discovers his own truth and, in Bollas' terms, elaborates his personal 'idiom'. This contrasts with the Kleinian notion of the fragmenting paranoid-schizoid position as essentially pathological and as avoiding the more 'healthy' unitary depressive position.

Bollas highlights what one could describe again as the issue of whether or not there is a central organizing psychic structure. He points towards a notion of multiple processes of cohesion and dissemination, with no actual centre as such, at least not in the usual sense. He does use the idea of a self, but for him this self can, at times, name 'an essential elusiveness, an organization in being that is inexplicable, that cannot be represented or located' (ibid., p.157).

I think that there is a further important and specific element in trying to account for the way that the psyche is organized, and this concerns how much unity and organization are used at very early levels to ward off pain, and how much they are used to recognize pain. Ferenczi suggested that, by means of a kind of empathy into the infantile mind, one could hypothesize that 'To a child kept immune from any pain the whole of existence must appear to be a unity – "monistic", so to speak. Discrimination between "good" and "bad" things, ego and environment, inner and outer world, would only come later; at this stage alien and hostile would therefore be identical' (Ferenczi, 1926, p.366). Klein (1946, p.4), quoting Winnicott, emphasized the infant's early lack of integration, followed by the gradual build-up of cohesion of the 'self' (or what I would call the 'subject') which coincides with introjection of the good breast. For her, unity at the depressive position is a way of recognizing pain in a more realistic way. I should add that, though Winnicott emphasized the early lack of integration, I would agree with him when he considered that the paranoid-schizoid position was a pathological development.

Of course, we are here at the margins of what is knowable and have to use our empathy with the infant as well as our experience from analysing early anxieties in adults. Perhaps there are different kinds of early organization. There could be a kind of defensive unity, aimed at warding off threats from the environment; and there could be other kinds of organization where there is a reaching out for new experience, a taking in of something new, but then a reorganization. At these moments of reorganization, the infant is vulnerable to states of disruption and fragmentation. Whatever the details, I think it is worthwhile to focus on the nature of the organization, how its elements are organized, how the subject is built up, how the organization is experienced in the analytic situation, as I have indicated in the brief clinical example above, as well as the way that object relations theory points to the way that objects are built up. That is, I want to look more at what does the building up. In classical theory, this would be equivalent to how defences are organized in order to deal with specific anxieties. I would add that one would need to look in addition at how the various defensive levels interact.

I would suggest that, regardless of whether or not one actually uses Klein's model, any theory of subject relations would need to take account of how the subject shifts and moves between positions, or between different kinds of organization. These movements will in turn affect the way that the subject relates to other subjects, the way that others impact on the subject and the orientation of the subject towards objects. I suspect that one has only just begun to understand something about different kinds of subjective organization. One could think of 'closed' or 'open' organizations, 'embodied' or 'disembodied' subjects, 'precarious' and 'relentless' organizations, 'rigid' structures, as well as states in which the subject feels empty or dead.

The following clinical example is a further example of how the issue of the subject's organization may be taken up in analysis. Mr A, a middle-aged man, came into analysis because of depression, doubts about himself and work problems. He had been feeling increasingly desperate about himself, and had found it increasingly difficult tolerating times when he was on his own, when his feelings of depression became most acute. He also had a problem with his thoughts, finding it difficult to have a sense of their belonging to him; or, to put it another way, he had difficulty in the area of subjectivity, of owning his own subjective processes.

He had never felt particularly close to his parents. They had had high expectations for him to succeed, which to some extent he had fulfilled, though he could never believe in his success. His mother came across as rather harsh and ungiving; his father, a housemaster in a boarding school, as more kindly but uninvolved, more interested in other children than himself.

At first in analysis he was often preoccupied by what he was to do, how to get it right, both with me and in the world outside. Although he was keen to come to the sessions, he found silences persecuting; he quickly felt abandoned and alone with chaotic thoughts. He was also a somewhat obsessional and controlling person. I noted how he liked to check up on the time as the session was under way, which was not only about a fear of abandonment. He had an automatic response to when I called time at the end of the session, which was to look at his watch and nod in agreement. He found it very uncomfortable in one session when, for some reason, he had forgotten his watch and could not keep checking the time. At the same time, he was concerned that he could not get his thoughts into a proper order, as they were often taken over by feelings of chaos, where he would then lose his sense of who he was.

One Monday session, I was expecting him to ring the consulting room bell, when I heard the sound of clearing up outside the door. In fact, it turned out that a severe gust of wind had blown over one of the large flower pots outside the room, breaking the pot into pieces, and he was tidying it up for me. When he came into the room, he made some friendly remark about what had happened. Not quite knowing what to do, I just vaguely smiled. I was struck by his wanting to be helpful, possibly reparative, but also wondered about what he may not want to face in the session, what mess there might be for me to clear up, and how much he might want to control me. I mention this interaction, as it does convey something of the flavour of the analysis.

He began by saying, in a rather strangled voice, that it felt today like coming to see a harsh authority who could see into all his crimes and misdemeanours. He said that last night he had felt bad, he could not get to sleep. He had become increasingly desperate and had felt more and more chaotic. There was something about his alarm clock which preoccupied him; you could never be sure that it would work, but he had done nothing about it. He finally went to sleep after curling up into a foetal position.

I made a comment that perhaps his desperate feelings last night, which were resolved by curling into a foetal position, becoming a baby, had something to do with feeling dependent on me over the weekend. But then those feelings were avoided by seeing me as a harsh authority. That was what I had become by the time he came to see me. (I was then thinking that perhaps the clearing up of the broken pot was an attempt to divert or appease me.) He commented that maybe the two sorts of feelings were actually linked together. He then talked a little about what he had been doing over the weekend. There was a lot of mess in the garden, bits of branches on the lawn, etc. He hired a

chain saw from a hire shop. The man there was very doubtful about
whether or not he would be safe with it. But he managed to use it; he
cut up bits of wood, branches of trees, and made neat piles from the
mess. (Rather like his action at the beginning of the session, I was
again thinking.) He added that he had different feelings on a Monday
from the other days here. It was easier coming on other days.

The image of the chain saw was obviously rather powerful, an image
of aggression, and of cutting to pieces. I commented about this and how it
seemed to me to indicate a cutting off of emotions, of dependent feelings.
This linked to seeing me as an authoritarian figure.

He responded by a comment about his chaos. 'What about that?', he
said, choking with desperation. This led to an exploration of his situation. The authority image, with all the aggression and cutting up with
which this was associated, seemed to *organize* the chaos associated with
dependency over the weekend. In addition, one of his constant concerns,
as it was that day, was about his own thought processes, and what he felt
was a difficulty in being creative, or of getting his thoughts together. The
chaos was always interfering. One could see how this chaos could be
organized by the aggressive cutting up.

He agreed with this formulation. He recalled that on Friday his wife
had rejected his sexual advances, which had left him feeling less of a
man, and lacking in male authority (one of his other central
preoccupations). The he recalled seeing the film *An Officer and a
Gentleman*, starring Richard Gere. He described how Gere was
organized, however reluctantly, by the authoritarian sergeant-major.
Finally, the Gere character learned to become an officer by putting
someone else first, by offering help to a fellow cadet. But, he
commented, Gere had had no alternative but to go through with the
training, as he had nothing else to go back to. (No doubt a link to the
analysis.) This led to memories of childhood, when his father was a
housemaster at the boarding school, where Mr A was also a pupil. He
did not know where he fitted into his family; there were always so
many other children taking up his parents' attention. He recalled
going to see his mother and feeling he did not get what he wanted from
her. She was a rather harsh, or anyway ungiving, maternal authority.

The session ended with some thoughts about how he might allow
something different to evolve, where he might be able to tolerate
dependency, the maternal aspects of coming to see me, which often
left him feeling chaotic; rather than organize these feelings by an
aggressive authoritarian, 'paternal' organization. I think, too, that one
could see here how he had difficulty with what Bollas describes as the
radical process of dissemination, allowing the subject's unconscious to
disrupt discourse. Mr A felt such a process as persecuting and had to

organize his experience to avoid or deal with the threat of such a process. As in the beginning of the session, the pieces had to be cleared up and put in a neat pile. However, I did feel that there was something of a shift in the session. This was possibly confirmed by the fact that the next session was concerned with how he could be more responsive to members of his family and less isolated.

As well as looking specifically at how the subject may organize elements of their life and how this may relate to the transference, as with Mr A, I suspect that one may also reach an understanding of the nature of subjective organizations by looking at what one could call the 'quality' of the transference. This refers to the form the transference takes rather than its content or its sensory and material qualities; in short, what it feels like. I gave an example of this with the young woman whose subjective organizaton felt in the transference like she was going around in a cocoon. The quality of the transference will include the quality of the language used by the patient, its physicality, its expressiveness or lack of it, and the shape of the flow of speech. This may have been what I was getting at when I compared a 'rigid' transference to a more 'fluid' transference incorporating its 'dual aspect' (Kennedy, 1984). The latter refers to the way that the analyst can become simultaneously the receiver of the patient's projections, the analyst as a fantasy object, and as different from these projections; oscillating between these two aspects. John Padel develops the theme of the oscillation between positions in a number of areas; for example, between two- and three-person modes of being, and between self and other. He describes 'how the capacity to do both things at once – to perceive the real while also distorting it or mending it in phantasy – is something on which the success of an analysis may depend, but to entertain both the real perception and also the version altered in phantasy, sometimes alternately and sometimes together ... is perhaps one of the most fundamental characteristics of the human animal. It seems to me to be the source of creativeness. Binary thought consists of finding or creating pairs of polar opposites ... and creating pairs of opposed ideas is the natural preliminary which leads to searching for a new way to reconcile them' (Padel, 1994, p.6). Padel points out that Grotstein (1978) has also put forward the existence of the capacity to do two things at once, or what he calls a 'dual track' hypothesis. It is a feature not only of the transference but also of early experiences of the human being and which continues throughout life.

One could propose, then, that being a subject involves some capacity to take up different positions, without their becoming fixed in a kind of frozen state of being. For example, with Mr A, one could suggest that he was stuck in one way of organizing his subjective life;

for example, around particular notions of maternal and paternal authority. Perhaps this was what Ogden was referring to when he described a 'dialectical' movement between various psychic positions. I think that one could describe the position which the analyst takes up in a session in similar terms. The analyst may have to bear being in a number of different subjective positions, or 'vertices', to borrow from Bion (1970), with the patient, rather than allow himself to become fixed in one place; though, at any moment, he may find himself 'moored' in one place more favoured than another. This can be seen vividly in the analysis of adults who have been sexually abused as children. Though of course it may be important to recognize when abuse has occurred (see Kennedy, 1996), the analyst may be forced into a position of, say, either denying the abuse or of agreeing that it took place; there may be a strong pull towards taking sides rather than seeing different sides. The analyst may find himself taking up a position between the neglectful parents on the one hand and the victimized child on the other, rather than seeing the different sides of the situation and bearing the uncertainty of being in and out of different positions.

I would suggest that the analyst's free-floating attention consists of a subjective oscillation between different positions or 'moorings', or 'placements'. This may mean having to tolerate a considerable amount of ambiguity, uncertainty and paradox. In this sense, the analyst is poised at the point at which the paradox of human subjectivity arises; and, as Winnicott emphasized (1971, p.14), paradox accepted can have positive, therapeutic value.

However, the patient may find ambiguity quite intolerable; he may become caught up within a vicious and maddening circle, in which toleration of ambiguity and paradox, so vital to subjective life and so inevitable given the uncertainty of where the subject is located, becomes unbearable. I will try to illustrate this issue with a brief clinical example.

Ms X was severely sexually abused as a child by her stepfather. He would deliberately accuse her of being naughty so that he could take her up to her room as a punishment. Then he would sexually abuse her. Her mother turned a blind eye to what was going on. Ms X grew up with major psychiatric problems, which came to a head after the birth of her daughter. She often felt suicidal, drawn to cut her body, and was occasionally violent, when she would throw chairs or break windows. Though she managed to look after her daughter, she needed periods of respite care, as there were times when she felt violent towards her. Luckily, she recognized that something was wrong and she sought help. In therapy, she revealed that she went in and out of dissociated or disorganized states, particularly when she had to face her child's vulnerability and need for her, such as at bath- and bed-times. In these states she experienced an almost delusional sexually exciting fantasy world, where she re-experienced being abused as she was so special. At the same time, the excitement about being special in this way made her feel unbearably guilty. It was only the thought of cutting her body, or of becoming violent towards physical objects that could eliminate the guilt.

Most of her subjective life had become organized around this constellation of excitement, guilt and cutting, all of which was focused on her abused body. This is a common and at times intractable problem in many severely abused women. They often have great difficulty in taking responsibility for their actions. They remain subject to an abused body and an abusive view of the world. Subjectivity is experienced as dangerous because of the volatile mixture of excitement and aggression, which produces a precarious subjective organization. Though originally set up to defend against unbearable psychic pain, the organization then becomes the central organizer of experience.

Ms X would often hide from people, afraid that they would see how destructive she was; while she remained addicted to her unstable fantasy world. Coming to feel in touch with her child was at times almost impossible, as it produced an almost unbearable situation or subjective position. Whenever she had to experience vulnerable and maternal feelings towards her daughter, she tended to blank them off. To be a mother meant having to identify with her own neglectful mother, the one who had allowed the abuse to occur without protest. As so often in these situations, Ms X was put then into an 'impossible' conflict about being simultaneously a mother and a sexual woman. She felt she was in a vicious circle of excitement and abuse; it felt maddening to be in the circle and also to feel that there was no way out of it. But she was also fairly resistant at first to face moving into a more benign sort of circle, which one could say is really the aim of therapy with such people. This is a difficult process because of the almost impossible subjective position which they occupy, as a result of which they tend to blank out dependent feelings to themselves and their children; but of course this leaves them vulnerable to allowing abuse of their own children and to ignoring it, blanking out the reality of their children's suffering. There is thus the real danger of a repetition of their own history, when a child's subjective reality was cruelly displaced or disorganized by the intrusion of adult subjective reality.

One may ask what this way of looking at clinical material may add to the understanding of the abused patient. I would argue that the issue of subjectivity is at the heart of the abused patient, who often feels robbed of a subjective life, and not responsible for themselves. Moving from a victim role to a more active view of themselves means moving from being subject 'to' to being subject 'of' their destiny.

I think that one could say that there may be something specific to what one might call 'body immersed' organizations, such as those with Ms X. I am thinking of her and other patients who have persistent somatic symptoms and preoccupations. They may have a preoccupation with physical sensations and body parts, as if the body itself has become a central organizer of their psychical lives, while insight into ordinary psychical life is noticeably lacking, as if they do not have a 'map' of subjective life. One suspects that such patients have been traumatized in an early bodily way; that there has been major interruption in the continuity of bodily care. They may have then resorted to self-care, and turned to sensations around body parts as a way of organizing experience, and this then becomes held on to very tenaciously. This contrasts with normal development, when the subject comes to feel *embodied*, with a sense of their body feeling alive and owned, which I take to be a fundamental aspect of being a human subject.

THE SUBJECT AND THE DRIVES

This last point leads on to the relationship between the subject and the drives, which originate from the body. For Freud, as I mentioned in Chapter 1, a drive is on the border, or frontier, between the physical and the mental; we can only know the drive from the mental representation of it, and yet it is also a biological process. It could also be said that in this difficult area of analytic theory, we are at the frontier of theory itself, of what is knowable. In the opening paragraphs of his paper 'Drives* and their vicissitudes', Freud suggests that any new theory needs certain basic hypotheses, or conventions (*Konventionen*), to make it work, and that these lack a certain precision at first. The notion of a drive is one such 'conventional basic concept ... which at the moment is still somewhat obscure, but which is indispensable to us in psychology' (Freud, 1915a, p.118).

The drive concept is still obscure, so much so that a number of modern analytic thinkers leave it our entirely. Yet I think that this would be a mistake, and would seem to leave out of account clinical

* I use the more accurate term 'drive' to translate the German *Trieb*, rather than 'instinct', which is used for the German *Instinkt*.

evidence from, for example, the perversions, adolescent disturbances and psychosomatic disorders. In Freud's view, what underlies the drive is a constant source of stimulation coming from within the body, which contrasts with momentary stimuli arising from the external world (Freud, 1905a, p.168; 1915a, p.118). However, observation of young babies, in my view, yields simple evidence that at certain moments they are taken over by physiological processes but at discrete moments. For example, up to about four months of age, one can see a baby responding in his social world, looking around, responding, smiling at the mother from time to time, etc., but then something else suddenly takes over. His eyes seem to be elsewhere, they are no longer in contact with the social world, and he fills his nappy; or at another time, his attention may be taken over when he suddenly experiences wind. The clear division between these periods of being taken over by physiological processes, or what I would see as drive activity, and returning to the realm of the social-psychological, seems to be lost at around five months. There is then a much smoother transition between the states. In my view, this kind of observation points to the dual nature of the drive, that it is attached both to a physiological organization and yet also touches on the developing subject's organization. For example, I would suggest that one can see how the baby goes in and out of drive-dominated states. When the drive takes over, it is as if the baby loses his primitive subjective awareness, his relatedness to others.

Perhaps relevant to this process is what Darwin, in his book *The Expression of the Emotions in Man and Animals* (1872), describes as the third principle of expression. This is that, 'certain actions which we recognize as expressive of certain states of the mind, are the direct result of the constitution of the nervous system, and have been from the first independent of the will, and to a large extent, of habit' (Darwin, 1872, p.66). So that one could see how at those moments when the baby seems to be elsewhere, there is a direct action of the nervous system, through the mediation of the drive and excluding the baby as subject, or taking the baby out of the realm of being a subject.

The physiological and psychological organizations may act in accord to some extent or in conflict. Thus the drives may disorganize the subject. This is perhaps particularly true of the sexual drives, which, as Freud emphasized (1911b, p.222), may become detached from the other drives, and being not so susceptible to influence and modification, they may take over the subject to some extent.

I wonder whether psychosomatic conditions reveal that the physiological organization, as represented by the drives, and the psychological organization can become too linked or fused together. There needs to be some continuing separation or distinction between these realms for normal development to take place. But if there has been, for example, some kind of disruption to the early care system, one could see how subjective experience could be constantly 'contaminated' by the intrusion of somatic experiences, leading ultimately to a psychosomatic, or body immersed, organization.

This would contrast with how the subject can gradually, through development, organize the drives. In Freud, this is a gradual process that is only complete after puberty. In *Three Essays on Sexuality* (1905a, pp.167–8), Freud describes how the drives in childhood are not unified in any way, but consist of a number of different components, or partial drives* (*Partialtriebe*), each with a special connection to an erotogenic zone, a part of the body giving rise to a form of sexual excitation. Using evidence from, for example, the perversions where the partial drives fall apart, Freud describes how normally the sexual drive is put together from the various partial drives into what he calls a firm 'organization'. This only happens at puberty, when the primacy of the genitals is finally beginning to be established.

> The final outcome of sexual development lies in what is known as the normal sexual life of the adult, in which the pursuit of pleasure comes under the sway of the reproductive function and in which the partial drives, under the sway of a single erotogenic zone, form a firm organization directed towards a sexual aim attached to some extraneous object. (ibid., p.197)

The erotogenic zones then fit themselves into this new arrangement, with the genital zone as the leading one. The new organization is a result of a combination of the partial drives into a unity.

> [T]he sexual drive [is] something put together from various factors ... in the perversions it falls apart, as it were, into its components [*Komponenten*]. The perversions were thus seen to be on the one hand inhibitions, and on the other hand dissociations, of normal development. Both these aspects were brought together in the supposition that the sexual drive of adults arises from a combination of a number of impulses of childhood into a unity [*Einheit*], an impulsion with a single aim. (ibid., p.232)

---

* In the Freud *Standard Edition*, *Partialtriebe* is translated as 'component instincts'; but I have followed the German in using the term 'partial drives', as it seems to me a more accurate translation.

The partial drives are thus synthesized into some kind of unity by the adolescent subject, though there is the constant possibility that the sexual drive may be fragmented into its components. Laufer and Laufer (1984) offer their own interpretation of this process by emphasizing how the unity of the mature body image at adolescence plays a crucial role in creating the final sexual organization. The task of adolescence is essentially to establish the final sexual organization. What usually takes place is the integration of the old and the new, coming to terms with the loss of the old immature body and accepting the reality of the new maturing body, with the integration of the new body image. For Laufer and Laufer, breakdown of functioning at adolescence occurs as a result of a 'developmental breakdown'. There is an unconscious rejection of the sexual body, with an accompanying feeling of being passive in the face of demands coming from the body. This results in the genitals being ignored or disowned. What occurs is a breakdown in integrating the physically mature body image into the representation of oneself. The specific interference in the developmental process is contained in the adolescent's distorted view of and relationship to his body.

While agreeing in essentials with this formulation of a developmental breakdown, I would add that one also needs to consider the infantile and childhood precursors of the breakdown which lay the ground for future disorder. Also, I would add that once breakdown occurs in the adolescent, then all the levels of the mind may be affected, so that there may be a fragmentation of infantile, childhood and adolescent elements.

One can also see in some adolescents how they may wish to hold on to the immature body image quite tenaciously as a way of dealing with the reality of the maturing body (see Kennedy, 1989). The infant's body takes a long time to develop. Lacking coordination of functions, the baby is dependent on others for a lengthy period. The baby only gradually becomes aware of a whole body; for example, the legs are a rather mysterious part of the body with which they just vaguely thrash around for the first few months. Later, the child acquires an imaginary mastery of his body, linked perhaps to the ego ideal, where he sees himself as having a totally functioning body. This image of himself as being able to coordinate himself could be seen as the first organized form in which the individual identifies himself. At adolescence, the wish to hold on to the early immature body image, one without the functioning genitals, conflicts with the growing mature body image. An attack on the new adolescent body and body image, as in self-harm and suicide attempts, may be seen as, in part, a wish to cling to the old immature body image and the old helplessness, as well as an attack on the new, sexual body. One can often see in these adolescents the use of a particular kind of whole body image underlying their masturbation fantasies. This image may be either an idealized image of what the body should be or is felt to be, or an alienated and psychotic ideal unity which cannot be reached and hence makes the subject feel incomplete.

Freud's drive theory thus points towards ways that the subject may become organized or disorganized, through the way that the partial drives are unified or fragmented at adolescence around the primacy of the genitals. Laufer and Laufer point towards the specific role of the body image in providing for the process of organization. This seems to contrast with Freud's various theories of psychical agencies, where, as far as I can tell, there is no detailed description of how the mind comes together. It is as if drive theory and the rest of Freud's theory are proceeding along different paths. Laufer and Laufer believe that the developmental tasks of adolescence should be subsumed under the main task of integrating the body image, and that this process dominates all others; one might add that it makes for the synthesis by the subject of all the partial drives. I would agree that this process is important, but I think that there are other important processes going on, as described by Freud in his paper 'Drives and their vicissitudes', particularly those involving how the subject relates to others and how the subject is transformed in various ways by the drive.

It is perhaps significant that in this paper Freud, I think uniquely in his writings, uses the term 'Subjekt' on a number of occasions. He seems to be describing an elaborate relationship between the subject and drives, where the subject appears and disappears at various points in the complicated 'circuit' or 'route' of the drive. He uses four terms, 'pressure', 'aim', 'object' and 'source', in reference to the concept of a drive. The pressure of each drive is its active element, the demand for work. The aim is of the drive is its satisfaction. He makes the point that, though the ultimate aim of each drive is the same, there may be different paths leading to the same aim, and that intermediate aims may be combined or interchanged with one another. I think that here is evidence that Freud used the drive concept to bring in a rather flexible and undetermined element into his thinking. There may be an ultimate aim for the drive, but on the way the drive can be diverted along many different kinds of path. The object of a drive, which can be a part of the body or something external, through which a drive can achieve its aim, is not originally connected to the drive, but becomes assigned to it. The object is what is most variable about the drive. A close attachment of the object to the drive only occurs in 'fixation'. Again, there is a looseness and flexibility about the drive pathway, this time with regard to the object. The somatic source of the drive remains somewhat unknowable and obscure, the part of the drive which leads from and to the purely physiological processes.

Much of the rest of the paper concerns the sexual drives, which use many pathways to achieve satisfaction. 'They are numerous, emanate from a great variety of organic sources, act in the first instance independently of one another and only achieve a more or less complete synthesis at a late stage ... They are distinguished by possessing the capacity to act vicariously for one another to a wide extent and by being able to change their objects readily' (Freud, 1915a, pp.125–6).

Drives may undergo a number of different vicissitudes, or take a number of different pathways, such as reversal into the opposite, turning round upon the subject's own self (die eigene Person), as well as repression and sublimation. To attempt to tie down some of the routes which the sexual drives take, Freud examines in some detail two pairs of opposites – sadism/masochism and scopophilia/exhibitionism. Masochism can be seen as sadism turned around on to the subject, and exhibitionism includes the subject looking at his own body. Both these perversions involve a double enjoyment, that of the passive subject who is suffering or being looked at, and the active subject who causes the suffering or is exhibiting himself. 'Analytic observation, indeed, leaves us in no doubt that the masochist shares in the enjoyment of the assault upon himself, and that the exhibitionist shares in the enjoyment of [the sight of] his exposure' (ibid., p.126). That is, there are two subjects here, first of all the one who is subject 'to', that is the 'passive' subject of masochistic or exhibitionistic pleasure; and second, the other subject, (der fremde Subjekt), the extraneous subject (ibid., p.128), the one who is subject 'of' and who takes over the 'active' role in the perverse relationship, who tortures or looks at the other. Freud traces how the drive, experienced as sexual enjoyment, weaves its way through the relations between these two subjects, transforming them as it goes.

The object of the drive in these two perversions also comes into the picture. Freud in fact, confusingly, uses the term 'object' in two senses in the text. He first uses it to mean the passive partner of the perversion, the object of the other subject. That is the partner is treated like an object, with no subjectivity of their own; they are there merely to fulful the other's sexual pleasure. In fact, the active partner is also treated in this sense like an object with no subjectivity of their own, as they need to be hurt or looked at by the other in order to obtain satisfaction. The term 'object' is also used more specifically as whatever will fulfil the aim of the drive. This may be a part of the subject's body – for example, if they exhibit a part of their body to the other – or it may be a piece of clothing, or a part of the body, that incites the other to cause pain, etc.

Thus I would suggest that fundamental to the vicissitudes of the drive, or how it is transformed, is the position taken by the subject in relation to the other subject. It is in this sense that I would picture the drive as a process, a complicated pathway, capable of transforming the subject, while the drive itself can be transformed by the different positions taken up by the subject. Involved along the way in the perverse pathway is the loss of subjectivity, usually by each subject desiring to control the other, using them as an object in the sense of someone whose only function is to elicit sexual pleasure for the other; so that one could say that in this process one subject is replaced by another subject.

THE SUBJECT AND DESIRE

At this point I think it is necessary to add into the picture of the relationship between drives and the subject, the role of desire as the essential psychical element involved both in the drive pathway and in the structure of the subject. Before, however, tackling the role of desire in the specifically psychoanalytic field, it is necessary to turn to some philosophy for clarification of the nature of desire.

The issue of desire in the subject can be summarized as the difference between the 'cognitive' or 'knowing' subject and the 'desiring subject'. The German philosopher Dilthey highlighted the limitations of considering a merely knowing subject when he wrote that most philosophers, including Kant, 'had explained experience and cognition in terms of facts that are merely representational. No real blood flows in the veins of the knowing subject constructed by Locke, Hume and Kant, but rather the diluted extract of reason as a mere activity of thought' (Dilthey, 1883, p.50).

Dilthey went on to consider the other aspects of the subject, including willing and feeling, and to maintain the importance of what he called the 'lived experience' of the subject, which other thinkers later took up with modifications. For example, I have already mentioned how Husserl wrote of the importance of considering the 'life-world' in the structure of the subject, the world that is actually experienced by human subjects as opposed to the theoretically constructed objective world. More recently, Habermas (1985) has put the structure of the life-world into his theory of intersubjective communication. He considers that what is unique to psychoanalysis is its discovery of a particular kind of self-reflection through which human subjects can free themselves from states in which they may have become a mere object for themselves (such as in the perversions), a thing or a commodity. He uses his reading of psychoanalysis to put forward an emancipatory theory of communication between subjects in the life-world, or community of subjects in interaction. As I have commented in detail elsewhere (Kennedy, 1993, pp.125–8), much of his theory remains valuable for psychoanalysis, but, in my view, it holds to a rather utopian view where it is possible to have an ideal form of communication; whereas psychoanalytic experience points to the many ways in which communication breaks down and can never be ideal. He also leaves out of full consideration the place of the unconscious and that of desire.

The essence of desire is well described by Plato in *The Symposium*, where the nature of love (eros) and desire (epithumia), which in Greek are interlinked, is debated over a long banquet. Socrates says that:

> whoever feels a want is wanting something which is not yet at hand, and the object of his love and of his desire is whatever he isn't, or whatever he does not have – that is to say, whatever he is lacking in ... Love is always the love of something ... and ... that something is what he lacks. (Plato, 1951, 200e)

Desire is thus always desire for what is lacking; hence the feeling of emptiness that may occur when one has fulfilled a desire. What gets desire going is the absence of fulfilment. Lack is the motor force driving desire. But in addition, there is the place of the other in desire. It is in Hegel as interpreted by the French thinker Kojève that the issue of the desiring subject in relationship to the other arose and which, as Lacan drew attention to, is in a form that is particularly relevant for psychoanalysis. Kojève (1947, p.3) emphasized that the person who contemplates and is absorbed by what he contemplates, that is the 'knowing subject', only finds a particular kind of knowledge, knowledge of the object. To find the subject, desire is needed; the desiring subject is the human subject.

As Kojève explores, what distinguishes the human from the animal is the fact that human desire is not just directed towards other objects but towards other desires. There is a basic sort of desire in man, akin to animal desire – for example, the desire for food experienced through hunger – so that man begins to become conscious of himself through such a basic experience of lack. This would correspond to the physiological element of the Freudian drive. Human reality can be formed and maintained only within a basic biological reality, an animal life. But what is essentially human about desire is at another level, that of self-consciousness, when it is faced by another self-consciousness, and where both are struggling for acknowledgement or recognition. As Hegel wrote:

> Self-consciousness exists in and for itself when, and by the fact that, it so exists for another; that is, it exists only in being acknowledged ... Self-consciousness is faced by another self-consciousness; it has come *out of itself*. This has a twofold significance: first, it has lost itself, for it finds itself as an *other* being; secondly, in so doing it has superseded the other, for it does not see the other as an essential being, but in the other sees its own self ... It must supersede this otherness of self. (Hegel, 1807, p.111)

This would correspond to what is essentially psychological in the relations between subjects in the drive pathway. Desire is only human, according to Kojève, if one desires, not the body as such, but the desire of the other, if he wants to possess or assimilate the other's desire:

> that is to say, if he wants to be 'desired' or 'loved', or, rather, 'recognized' in his human value, in his reality as a human individual. Likewise, Desire directed towards a natural object is human only to the extent that it is 'mediated' by the Desire of another directed toward the same object ... Thus, an object perfectly useless from the biological point of view (such as a medal or the enemy's flag) can be desired because it is the object of other desires. (Kojève, 1947, p.6)

Similarly, in the case of the drive, one can see how the physical object is merely there to achieve the aim of the drive, and can be anything at hand to achieve this purpose; but it is desire, which is linked up with various fantasies, that makes the drive human as opposed to the merely animal. Thus, for example, in exhibitionism, one subject desires to be looked at; it is the gaze of the other that is desired. In masochism the subject desires to be dominated, which fits in with the sadist's desire for control of the other's desire. In perverse situations like these, however, there is little desire for recognition by the other; on the contrary, such a desire is constantly being extinguished; there is a domination of what Freud called the primitive 'narcissistic subject' (Freud, 1915a, p.132), which has little sense of otherness.

But in ordinary life, the mutual desire for recognition plays a fundamental role in structuring human relationships. The 'doubling of self-consciousness' (Kojève, 1947, p.9) is the essential dynamic

structure of relations between subjects, in which there is simultaneously activity by the individual and activity of the other, a dynamic
which one would now call 'intersubjective'. Incidentally, I would add
here that the essence of the intersubjective relationship is that it takes
place *at the level of desire* and not at the level of, say, the real. In my
view, this is where intersubjective psychoanalytic thinkers can make a
mistake in confusing levels. This is why I suggested that they are
essentially describing an interpersonal relationship and not an intersubjective one.

The movement between the subject and the other in a constant
search for recognition of their desires constitutes human reality, what
is truly intersubjective. Desires are directed towards other desires.
Desire is a fundamental element of the human subject. Desire is
always involved with the other, not only because it is driven by lack
and the need to find the other to fulfil this lack, but also because
within its structure there is always the other's desire.

Desire is the element of otherness essential to the subject. This
description seems to capture an important element of the psychoanalytic relationship, in which the subject's desires, or wishes, dreams
and fantasies, are the material on which analyst and patient work.

In Lacan's view, the object of human desire is the desire of the
Other in at least two senses: one can translate the French *le désire de
l'Autre* as both the Other's desire (not mine, but the Other's), and as
desire *for* the Other. Thus, as the subject's desire is at first unknown
to him, he looks for it in the Other, and his desire becomes the Other's
desire. I would add that in the perversions one can see this dynamic in
an extreme version, where is a merging of desires, with no actual
recognition of the other, and hence a loss of subjectivity. There is an
attempt to displace the other's desire by making it one's own.

The infant early on tries to identify himself with the mother's
object of desire in order to be that object of desire, while in addition
he has desires *for* her. For Lacan, the basic structure of desire
follows from the law of the signifier, in that it signifies something
only in relation to another signifier, so desire is always desire for
another thing.

But there is the additional point that while there may be different
desires in play, the subject at some point usually has to take up one
position or another with respect to desire in order to resolve the
Oedipus Complex and assume their sexual organization. And this is a
very complex matter indeed, one which perhaps includes the recognition of desires. People may have great difficulty in taking up a main
position on one side or the other of of the Oedipal constellation, so
that they may hover between positions, or be confused about their

desires. In the usual resolution of the Oedipus Complex, there must take place, for example, the fantasized death of the rival in order for the subject to assume his own desire. That is, the other's desire has to be confronted in some way, rather as in Hegel's master–slave dialectic, where master and slave fight to the death for recognition (Hegel, 1807, pp.111–19).

I would also add that recognition of desires is quite a complex activity, involving sophisticated discriminations; and that before this is possible presumably there has to be some basic registering of desires. Emotionally deprived patients with traumatic early histories, such as Ms X above, often seem to illustrate this latter point. They may be greedy for reassurance, desperate for recognition and basic care; yet they so often never find what they want, or else denigrate potential caregivers. They may feel constantly empty of feeling, and try to fill up the emptiness by eating food, or by attacking their bodies through cutting and other forms of self-harm. There is a desperate search for the fulfilment of a basic desire for recognition; but as their early desires were never given adequate attention, they themselves are never fulfilled, never satisfied. They confuse desire with need. The problem is one of an empty or unfulfilled desire which they experience as a need or a physical emptiness. The move from experiencing such physical emptiness to a more symbolic form of functioning where desires can be registered and experienced is, to put it simply, the task of therapy, though it is far from easy with these patients.

IDENTITY AND OTHERNESS; THE PLAY OF SUBJECTS

The notion that desire is that element of otherness essential to the subject leads on to consider the elusive nature of human identity, of who and what we are, how we may appear or disappear as subjects, where subject and other come together or fail to connect, in what one might call a 'play' of subjects. In *The Comedy of Errors*, Shakespeare illustrates what I mean. He vividly portrays a number of aspects of the dilemmas of human identity, involving issues of separation, loss, failed encounters and restoration of what was once lost. Briefly, the plot involves two sets of twins – two masters, who are twins and both called Antipholus, and two servants, who are also twins and both called Dromio. After a storm at sea when they were young, the children were separated, leaving one Antipholus and Dromio, from Syracuse, who remained with their father, and the Antipholus and Dromio who remained with their mother, though they were soon stolen and ended up in Ephesus.

At the beginning of the play, the father has not seen his pair of twins for some years, as they went in search of their lost brothers. The master and servant from Syracuse arrive at Ephesus, not realizing that both their twin brothers live there, nor that their father has been arrested there and is threatened with death, nor that their mother is now living in a convent there. *The Comedy* turns round a series of misunderstandings and misrecognitions when, for example, the Antipholus from Syracuse meets the Dromio from Ephesus or the Dromio from Syracuse meets the Antipholus from Ephesus, each thinking the other is attached to them when they are not. There is of course on the one hand simply a comedy at work; the various failed encounters are funny. At the same time, there is a tragic theme; for example, there is an underlying sense of loss. As Antipholus from Syracuse says at the beginning, thinking of his lost family:

> He that commends me to mine own content
> Commends me to the thing I cannot get.
> I to the world am like a drop of water
> That in the ocean seeks another drop,
> Who, falling there to find his fellow forth,
> Unseen, inquisitive, confounds himself.
> So I, to find a mother and a brother,
> In quest of them, unhappy, lose myself.
> (I. ii. 33–40)

The wife of Antipholus of Ephesus, Adriana, becomes distraught when the person she takes for her husband, who is really Antipholus of Syracuse, falls in love with her sister. Echoing in some ways the speech I have just quoted, she says, with despair and heart-rending yearning, to the 'wrong' Antipholus:

> Ay, ay, Antipholus, look strange and frown;
> Some other mistress hath thy sweet aspects.
> I am not Adriana, nor thy wife.
> The time was once when thou unurged wouldst vow
> That never words were music to thine ear,
> That never object pleasing in thine eye,
> That never touch well welcome to thy hand,
> That never meat sweet-savoured in thy taste,
> Unless I spake or looked or touched or carved to thee.
> How comes it now, my husband, O how comes it,
> That thou art then estrangèd from thyself?
> Thyself I call it, being strange to me,

That, undivided, incorporate,
Am better than thy dear self's better part.
Ah, do not tear away thyself from me;
For know, my love, as easy mayst thou fall
A drop of water in the breaking gulf,
And take unmingled thence that drop again
Without addition or diminishing,
As take from me thyself, and not me too.
(II. ii. 111–30).

All is eventually resolved, true identities are revealed, and even the twins' parents are reunited. Along the way, one could say that something fundamental about human identity is also revealed; for example, that it is an elusive and precarious entity, nothing about it can be taken for granted, and that perhaps we rely too much on things being the same for reassurance about who we are. Furthermore, the play seems to emphasize how having an identity and being identical are not the same thing. In a sense this play 'plays' on the ambiguity of these two elements. Despite the appearance of being the same person, one Antipholus or one Dromio is not the other. We may rely on things being the same, but identities can be easily transformed. It does not take much for despair to set in, and with it a sense that one has lost the ground for being certain about one's subjectivity. One subject can easily turn into another subject, while appearing to remain the same. There is often in life a play of subjects; it can make us feel dizzy.

There is also perhaps the issue of how we are all incomplete to some extent, and that we need the other to feel more ourselves. Or, as Ricoeur put it, 'Oneself as Another suggests from the outset that the selfhood of oneself implies otherness to such an intimate degree that one cannot be thought of without the other, that instead one passes into the other' (Ricoeur, 1990, p.3). This is illustrated in an extreme way by the yearning of the Antipholus from Syracuse for his double in order to feel complete; and in a more ordinary way by Adriana who yearns for the return of her husband, and who pleads with the wrong man, 'Ah, do not tear away thyself from me.'

Some productions of The Comedy of Errors have highlighted the ambiguity of identity by having one actor taking the role of one lot of twins, although that makes the final unmasking scene somewhat difficult to bring off. That kind of technique does underline the issue of identity; not only is there the comedy of errors as Shakespeare wrote it, with all the failed encounters, but there is the additional comedy that the person you think is different is actually the same, as he is played by the same actor. That is, there is a further doubling of the fact that where there is sameness there is in fact difference, and vice versa. Furthermore, attention is drawn to yet another duality which is embodied in the actual performance, that of actor as both himself and as taking a role.

One could say that different dramatists, actors and directors have different views about how much the actor should be himself and how much he should be totally identified with the role. If one actor plays one set of twins, then it might be very difficult to be too identified with one role; it might be better technically for the actor to show the audience that he is aware of being two people at once, in order for both audience and actor not to feel confused, and it also highlights the comic confusion. This would be the method recommended by Brecht (1948, p.194) for all theatre, as he thought that, in order to release the actor and audience from their usual expectations, the actor should be aware the whole time that he is a man who is acting a role, and that he should convey this dual aspect clearly to the audience in an open way.

Brecht considered that there should be no illusions that the player is identical with the character and the performance with the actual event. But I would suggest that this proposition is itself an illusion, for there are always two aspects, only there are variations in the degree to which the two aspects are merged. In the theatre of Grotowski, for example, the actor becomes the man, living in a small permanent community devoted to perfecting the art of theatre. Stanislavski came somewhere between Brecht and Grotowski, recommending that the actor pay particular attention to his state of mind and the fusion between the actor's inner life and that of the character.

In all theatre there is often some kind of process of masking and unmasking, which has parallels with the psychoanalytic process. The analytic subject, like a character in a play, starts from a position where various kinds of truths or information are concealed and then, in the course of the analytic process, are revealed.

The mask itself has a long history in the theatre. Originally in the Greek theatre it had to cover the actor's face and yet allow the voice to sound through. The Latin word for mask became 'persona', referring to the process of sounding through. In Greek, the mask or prosopeion refers to the actor turning his face or prosopa to the audience. In addition, as Arendt has shown (1963, pp.107–8), the Greek word for actor was *hupocrites*, the actor himself and not the mask he wore. Persona became a metaphor for the individual's public face. To become a person meant having to put on a mask; but paradoxically it also meant becoming part of the social network, becoming a human subject with legal rights. Stripped of a persona, one is left with the 'natural man' without rights, a person but not a subject. While the hypocrite is one who, by always being an actor, never has a mask or persona, he never really enters society and is thus scorned.

Peter Brook has shown how the mask is a powerful means of revealing human emotion. A mask is not a dead object; on the contrary, really good masks enable the actor to reveal fundamental truths. By liberating the actor from his own conscious self he is enabled to reach hidden depths. The mask frees the actor, as it

> gives you something to hide behind [and] makes it unnecessary for you to hide. This is the fundamental paradox that exists in all acting: that because you are in safety, you can go into danger. It is very strange, but all theatre is based on that. Because there is greater security, you can take greater risks, and because here it is not you, and therefore everything about you is hidden, you can let yourself appear. And that is what the mask is doing: the thing you are most afraid of losing, you lose right away – your ordinary defences, your ordinary expressions, your ordinary face that you hide behind. (Brook, 1988, p.231)

Similarly, the psychoanalyst has a kind of mask-like function. He is out of sight and is not fully known by the patient. The patient's ordinary defences are then lost and there is potentially greater access to the unconscious. The analyst wears a mask in order to help reveal the patient's truth. This is not to say that the analyst only wears a mask, for there are times when his human aspects are and need to be revealed, as I shall discuss in detail in the next chapter. But this takes place in a context in which he appears and disappears from behind the mask. Without the mask, psychoanalysis cannot take place. Thus, however much the analyst uses his countertransference, however much he may need to examine his own subjective responses to the patient or reveal some of his human aspects, his unmasking to the patient is necessarily only limited.

The dilemmas of personal identity were first put forward in a philosophical way by Locke, who remains the seminal influence both for modern philosophical treatment of the issue and also, as Heinz Lichtenstein (1977) has shown, for the psychoanalytic contribution. In his *Essay Concerning Human Understanding*, Locke places his consideration of the problem of personal identity in the context of a general consideration of the nature of identity. The identity of a simple physical object depends on the identity of its constituent parts; if one part is removed, the object is changed. But with a living thing, whether it be a tree or a horse, the parts may change, such as when there is growth, but it remains the same. Here identity consists in the organization of the parts; they are 'united in that continued Organization, which is fit to convey that Common life to all the Parts so united' (Locke, 1689, p.331).

Similarly for man, 'the Identity of the same *Man* consists ... in nothing but a participation of the same continued Life, by constantly fleeting Particles of Matter, in succession vitally united to the same organized Body' (ibid., pp.331–2). This definition of man has certain parallels with what Wittgenstein considered was essential in understanding the nature of human experience, that it was 'Only of a living human being and what resembles (behaves like) a living human being, can one say: it has sensations; it sees; is blind; hears; is deaf; is conscious or unconscious' (Wittgenstein, 1953, p.281). Norman Malcolm considered that this was one of Wittgenstein's most profound, if largely ignored, insights, clarifying the nature of mental operations, for 'The thing which perceives, thinks, imagines is neither a non-corporeal entity that "inhabits" the body, nor a brain – but a living human being' (Malcolm, 1986, p.186).

To return to Locke, having defined man in terms of one 'fitly organized body', he comes to the issue of personal identity, and to do this he defines what we mean by a person. This is a

thinking, intelligent Being, that has reason and reflection, and can consider it self as self, the same thinking thing in different times and places; which it does only by that consciousness, which is inseparable from thinking, and as it seems to me essential to it ... For since consciousness always accompanies thinking, and 'tis that, that makes every one to be, what he calls *self*; and thereby distinguishes himself from all other thinking things, in this alone consists *personal Identity*, i.e. the sameness of a rational Being: And as far as this consciousness can be extended backwards to any past Action or Thought, so far reaches the Identity of that *Person*; it is the same *self* now that it was then; and 'tis by the same *self* with this present one that now reflects on it, that that Action was done. (Locke, 1689, p.335)

Thus personal identity is defined as consciousness of the self's present and past thoughts, in a unity of life. However, Locke also uses psychological observation to point out certain difficulties in this assumption. For example, there are times when consciousness is interrupted by forgetfulness, or by drunkenness or by sleep. At these times, when consciousness is interrupted, we lose 'the sight of our past *selves*, [and] doubts are raised whether we are the same thinking thing ... i.e. the same substance or not' (ibid., p.336). Locke argues, again rather on the lines later put forward by Wittgenstein, that it is not substance as such that provides for the definition of personal identity, but rather the 'unity of the continued Life'. 'For it being the same consciousness that makes a Man be himself to himself, *personal Identity* depends on that only, whether it be annexed only to one individual Substance, or can be continued in a succession of several Substances' (ibid.).

For Locke, then, it is not substance but consciousness that makes for personal identity. (Similarly in *The Comedy of Errors*, what becomes clear is that it is not being the same substance or being identical in body that makes for identity, but something else.) For example, if a man claims he is Socrates, or an incarnation of the philosopher, he is not Socrates unless he shares the same consciousness with the historical figure. Whatever 'has the consciousness of present and past Actions, is the same Person to whom they both belong' (ibid., p.340).

Lichtenstein (1977, p.133) interprets the assertion that different substances are united into one person by consciousness as similar to Freud's description of the psychical apparatus being like a compound instrument made up of different agencies. However, he also pointed out that, as was described in detail in chapter 1, Freud never took up as a central issue how a person became united as a person. By grounding personal identity in consciousness and memory, as well as pointing out the issue of gaps in memory, Locke's thinking certainly anticipated psychoanalytic findings. Furthermore, Locke also showed how personal identity as the capacity to remain the same in the midst of constant change, had its limits. For example, he pointed towards the possibility of the existence of multiple selves united in one body. He raised the uncomfortable possibility that one body could house more than one consciousness and that one consciousness could be housed in more than one body. In fact, it does not require a great leap of thought to imagine how this could now be done, with the aid of modern technology. Thus, one could imagine how a memory chip containing a person's essential memories could be implanted in more than one person's brain, or else how one or more memory chips could be implanted in the same person's brain.

The phenomenon of the 'split brain', involving severely epileptic patients, monkeys and cats, who have had the connections cut along the corpus callosum, which unites the right and left cerebral hemisphere, provides further evidence for the complexity of how we view personal identity. Although the interpretation of experiments with these patients is open to some doubt, Nagel's paper (1971) on the phenomenon remains seminal in questioning what we understand as the unity of a person.

By performing carefully controlled experiments on how both hemispheres process sensory information from different parts of the visual field, it has been shown how each hemisphere has the capacity to process information separately from the other hemisphere, and indeed there may even arise conflict between each hemisphere. The question then arises about how many minds there are in the brain, or at least how integration is achieved, or not, between different and potentially independent systems. As Nagel puts it:

> The experimental situation reveals a variety of dissociation or conflict that is unusual not only because of the simplicity of its anatomical basis, but because such a wide *range* of functions is split into two noncommunicating branches. It is not as though two conflicting volitional centres shared a common perceptual and reasoning apparatus. The split is much deeper than that. The one-mind hypothesis must therefore assert that the contents of the individual's single consciousness are produced by two independent control systems in the two hemispheres, each having a fairly complete mental structure. If this dual control were accomplished during experimental situations by temporal alternation, it would be intelligible, though mysterious. But that is not the hypothesis, and the hypothesis as it stands does not supply us with understanding. For in these patients there appear to be things happening *simultaneously* which cannot fit into a single mind: simultaneous attention to two incompatible tasks, for example, without interaction between the purposes of the left and right hands. (Nagel 1979, pp.159–60).

Nagel argues that there is no whole single mind that these patients can be said to have, and that the 'attribution of conscious, significant mental activity does not require the existence of a single mental subject ... [C]onsideration of these very unusual cases should cause us to be skeptical about the concept of a single subject of consciousness as it applies to ourselves ... The natural conception of a single person controlled by a mind possessing a single visual field, individual faculties for each of the other senses, unitary systems of memory, desire, belief, and so forth, may come into conflict with the physiological facts when it is applied to ourselves' (ibid., pp.163–4).

Such a view is compatible with some of the neurophysiological data I have already discussed in Chapter 2 concerning the multiple drafts of consciousness, as well as the notion of the existence of the many 'voices' of consciousness. It certainly alerts us to the complexity and uncertainties of what we mean by personal identity. Parfit even goes as far as to consider that personal identity is not what really matters in understanding who we are. Instead, he proposes that:

> we cannot explain the unity of a person's life by claiming that the experiences in this life are all had by this person. We can explain this unity only by describing the various relations that hold between different experiences, and their relations to a particular brain. (Parfit, 1986, p.445)

The psychoanalyst Heinz Lichtenstein takes account of some of the ambiguities based on Locke's account of personal identity, and, as I briefly mentioned above, then goes on to develop a concept of human identity as a 'theme with variations'; there is a basic invariant theme and later variations on this theme. Thus:

> The mother imprints upon the infant not an identity, but an *'identity theme.'* This *theme* is irreversible, but is capable of variations, variations that spell the difference between human creativity and 'a destiny neurosis.' What in the adult is referred to as his social identity (Erikson's ego identity) – being a worker, a farmer, a hunter, etc, – is, at its best, a successful variation of the identity theme imprinted upon the infant. At its worst, it is an artificially imposed part, the playing of which is experienced as alienation by the individual, because it is incompatible with his identity theme. (Lichtenstein, 1977, p.78)

Lichtenstein proposes that the

> decisive factor in making for either success or failure of integration is the patient's ability to find the appropriate terms to implement the invariant identity configuration. In patients confronting an 'impossible' identity theme, the finding of the appropriate terms may be a never-ending search throughout the patient's life. A great variety of implementations are tried and rejected, and new levels of symbolic implementation are discovered, which may lead to a surprising new integration, without, however, a guarantee of lifelong stability. (ibid., pp.255–6)

This is certainly a useful way of looking at how the personality may be organized around certain essential configurations. It allows for the possibility of multiple themes, or narratives, or 'voices', becoming organized around one or two basic patterns. In addition, one can see how in some patients there is little sense of a basic and secure 'invariant' identity theme. Without this basic element, they may become too easily merged with the other, and hence either retreat into a citadel of unrelatedness or else constantly find themselves becoming confused with the other. Thus, there may be a variation around a theme, but if the basic theme is not grounded, the variations may become fragmented, rigid or confusing.

Thus in any consideration of human identity, one needs to examine the relations between subject and other including what Ricoeur describes as the 'need, hence lack, that drives the self toward the other' (Ricoeur, 1990, p.185). Ricoeur's account of the dilemmas of selfhood is ultimately concerned with ethical issues, of how our notion of the self may determine the kind of life we may wish to live. He makes a basic distinction between two forms of the meaning of identity, which overlaps what I have already described with regard to Locke's and Lichtensteins' views. There is identity as *sameness* – Latin *idem*, and identity as *selfhood* – Latin *ipse*. Selfhood is not sameness. This is of course well illustrated by the confusion of identities based on apparent sameness in *The Comedy of Errors*. Ricoeur provides a rich discussion of how identity is constituted by an interweaving 'between the pole of character where *idem* and *ipse* tend to coincide and the pole of self-maintenance, where selfhood frees itself from sameness' (ibid., p. 119).

Ricoeur emphasizes how it is in narratives that one can find some constancy and consistency in one's life. Being affected by narrated events becomes the organizing principle of subjective life, where one may gather together one's life. He also points out how literary narratives and personal narratives interlink and are complementary and are not necessarily mutually exclusive (ibid., p.163). In fiction the connection between action and its agent is often easier to perceive than in life and so can provide for an illustration of, or a kind of imaginary experiment about, issues such as the nature of the self. Networks of narratives united in plots, involving characters in interaction, are ways of organizing the actions of agents.

I would also add that for an author to write about characters in interaction, there is a fundamental need to *transform* himself so that he can see himself through the eyes of the other; only then can he imagine these interactions in a live way. This may require some stepping back from himself while also immersing himself in the life of the other. In this sense, the literary activity is very relevant to one's understanding of subjectivity. The author makes a character, a subject, who appears to be outside himself in some way; and yet the character arises from the author himself, often unconsciously, from some 'other' place. The created literary world appears to be separate from the writer, and separate from the real, mundane, world in an imaginary space. And yet, maybe the subject of the story, the subject that is created by the author, is true to life in more than the literal way. Usually, the subject of the story is seen as just fiction. But maybe this subject is a true subject. We are all subjects of a story, which is perhaps why we like reading and can feel that a novel or a play makes us feel more alive. When we enter a story, we come into contact with something alive in us, we enter into a deep relationship with our own subjectivity, where subject and other are in an alive and a 'playful' interaction. After seeing a good production of a play, we feel more in touch with ourselves. Fiction in this sense is not escape but discovery; we find ourselves, our sense of being a subject, through a play of subjects, through the playful transformation of subjects.

For Ricoeur, there are also ethical implications concerning the subject's narrative which arise from how one takes account of one's life and how one is also accountable to others. Thus he writes that:

> we admitted that selfhood-identity covered a spectrum of meanings, from the pole where it overlapped with identity as sameness to the opposite pole, where it is entirely distinct from the latter. The first pole appeared to us to be symbolized by the phenomenon of character, by which the person can be identified and reidentified. As for the second pole, it appeared to us to be represented by the essentially ethical notion of self-constancy. Self-constancy is for each person that manner of conducting himself or herself so that others can *count on* that person. Because someone is counting on me, I am *accountable* for my actions before another. The term 'responsibility' unites both meanings: 'counting on' and 'being accountable for.' It unites them, adding to them the idea of a *response* to the question 'Where are you' asked by another who needs me. This response is the following: 'Here I am!' a response that is a statement of self-constancy. (Ricoeur, 1990, p.165)

Such ethical considerations lead naturally on to the thought of Charles Taylor whose book *Sources of the Self* (1989) makes a detailed examination of the history of modern identity as a starting point for a renewed understanding of modernity. Rather than see identity in the terms first described by Locke as involving self-consciousness, he sees identity in terms of a 'space of moral issues' (Taylor, 1989, p.49). The self for Taylor is not neutral or disengaged; it is inevitably engaged with others in moral or ethical activity. He deals with issues of relevance to psychoanalysis, particularly if one accepts the view, which I have argued elsewhere in detail (Kennedy, 1993), that one can see psychoanalysis as essentially an ethical activity, concerned with the quality and pattern of a person's life, how they may reach the point, if they have not already been able to, of choosing how to lead their life. Furthermore, his inquiry brings to light aspects of the history of identity that psychoanalysts may too easily ignore, though at the same time they are often using concepts without being aware of their history.

For Taylor, the term 'identity' designates 'the ensemble of (largely unarticulated) understandings of what it is like to be a human agent: the sense of inwardness, freedom, individuality, and being embedded in nature which are at home in the modern West' (Taylor, 1989, p.ix). He believes that in order to grasp the richness and complexity of the modern identity it is necessary to see how our modern sense of the self has developed in time. He focuses on three main areas: first, what has led to our notion of 'inwardness', our sense of ourselves as beings with inner depths; second, the affirmation of 'ordinary life', concerned with production and reproduction (that is, labour involving the making of things needed for life) and with our sexual life, including marriage and the family; and third, the notion of nature as an inner moral source, which then leads to the notion of an inner voice or impulse through which we can find the truth within, particularly in our feelings and our sense of solidarity with other people.

Taylor organizes his history of identity around the notion of the 'good'; that is, he is concerned with what he calls 'moral sources', with the nature of the good life, with 'our sense of what underlies our own dignity, or questions about what makes our lives meaningful or fulfilling ... the respect for life, integrity and well-being, even flourishing of others' (ibid., p.4) Surely, very much what psychoanalysis is centrally concerned with.

The term 'identity' for Taylor is also 'defined by the commitments and identifications which provide the framework or horizon within which I can try to determine from case to case what is good, or valuable, or what ought to be done, or what I endorse or oppose. In other words, it is the horizon within which I am capable of taking a stand' (ibid., p.27).

Taylor's task is to show the connections between the modern moral outlook and its multiple sources. Although the notion of identity as such is a relatively modern one, there are many aspects from the past which go to make up the elements of identity, But, as he points out, we are in a particularly confusing time, in that 'frameworks' today are problematic. No framework is shared by everyone, or can be taken as the main framework for any system of thought. In addition, there is a general 'loss of horizon', a sense of loss of self, of emptiness, a lack of purpose or meaning. One way of coping with this situation is to make a system of thought around the loss of self, to 'deconstruct' rather than reconstruct, or to take as a central feature of thinking the notion of lack, as Lacan did, with his 'fading' subject, the subject possessed of an empty centre. Taylor's project is to reconstruct a history of modern identity around the themes I outlined, which may help us to provide an alternative and more 'empowering' (ibid., p.520) view of the subject, one which takes account of multiple sources and different characteristics.

The multiplicity of moral sources arose after the gradual abandonment of religious belief. As a moral source originating from within and which excluded God, creative imagination and artistic enterprise represented one important solution to this confused situation. Art enables us to transform our view of the world, enabling us to overcome despair and dread. In addition, turning towards ourselves can help us make choices about what kind of life we wish to live. Echoing Winnicott, Taylor writes that 'We choose our real selves; we become for the first time true selves. And this lifts us out of despair' (ibid., p.450).

In the twentieth century, we have turned inward, exploring and even celebrating subjectivity; and yet at the same time – particularly, one could add, since the discoveries of Freud – we have become disorientated. 'There would seem to be a slide to subjectivism and an anti-subjectivist thrust at the same time' (ibid., p.456). This could be explained by the discoveries made by the act of turning inward, which has taken us, 'beyond the self as usually understood, to a fragmentation of experience which calls our ordinary notions of identity into question' (ibid., p.462). The modern identity has to take account of this dilemma, the existence of multiple sources, the fragmentation of experience, and what I have described as the elusiveness of the subject.

– – –

In this chapter, I have covered a number of different aspects of subjectivity. I have suggested that the term 'subject' captures a basic aspect of the human situation – that we are both subject 'of' and subject 'to' various phenomena. I have tried to build up a picture of the psychoanalytic subject, using ideas from a number of thinkers. I have suggested that psychoanalytic subjectivity implies being in several, perhaps overlapping, positions or viewpoints, in relation to others. The subject moves between positions, or between different kinds of subjective organization. One can think of various kinds of closed or more open subjective organizations, as well as body-immersed organizations. I have also indicated some of the kinds of basic issues concerning the way that organizations both arise and are sustained, how organization is both maintained and undermined, issues first tackled psychoanalytically by Klein. I think that my interpretation of Klein offers a view of her theory that is less deterministic than her followers have believed. In addition, as emphasized by Winnicott, ambiguity, elusiveness and paradox are the almost the hallmark of being a subject. He also showed how the beginning of subjective life is facilitated by the mother allowing the infant to have an ongoing sense of being, and also by providing living experiences, the basis for subsequent live contact with others, where subject truly encounters subject.

Subjects are marked and transformed by chains of meaning that traverse the social field. There are perhaps many different kinds of subjective organization, in which the elements of the individual subject interact and are organized and disseminated in the social field. A subject relations theory needs to take account of the analytic subject as more a desiring subject than a knowing subject; and, in my view, needs to take account of how drives both transform the subject and are transformed by the subject. Such a theory also needs to look carefully at the way that subjects interact in the social field, including how identities can merge and shift in various symbolic circuits, in a constant 'play' of subjects.

It also follows naturally, from a model in which psychoanalysis is fundamentally concerned with subject relations, that the subjectivity of the analyst, the theme of the next chapter, plays an inevitable part in the analytic relationship.

4 THE ANALYST'S SUBJECTIVITY, OR THE HUMAN ASPECTS OF THE PSYCHOANALYTIC RELATIONSHIP

THE HUMAN MASK

As I mentioned in the previous chapter, the analytic relationship, though an intimate one, is also a distorted one, where the subjectivities of analyst and patient are not at the same level; the patient's world is to be examined in the open, while the analyst's is essentially private, or masked, except at a few contact points with the patient. However, how the mask may be lifted, or not, may have important bearings on the conduct of an analysis. Yet it is also difficult to disentangle what belongs to the analyst and what belongs to the patient, when both are so intensely involved in the analytic relationship. I agree with thinkers like Ogden and Aron that the subjectivities of both analyst and patient are in play in the analysis, and that the analytic experience is created by both partners. But this does not necessarily imply that the analytic relationship is truly interpersonal or that the analyst's own subjectivity should be open to the patient, though I would consider that the analyst's subjectivity should certainly be open to himself.

Perhaps one could argue that my approach is illogical, given the fact that I have argued that there is a need to develop a subject relations theory of psychoanalysis, and that it is in interaction between subjects that the subject finds coherence. However, what I have asserted does not imply that subjects start from similar positions, or have similar subjective organizations, or that the analytic relationship is a mutual one, though there may certainly be mutual influences. Nor does fostering the patient's exploration of his own subjectivity, which I would consider essential in analysis, imply that the analyst shift in his position as basically a point of reference, however mobile this may become.

Yet, at the same time, I am not advocating a classical neutral stance for the analyst, nor that one should ignore the subjective states of analyst and patient. On the contrary, I think it vitally important to try and tackle what can be loosely called the 'human' aspects of the psychoanalytic relationship, which make it a risky, worthwhile, spontaneous, complex and very personal endeavour. But I think that one avoids tackling the complexities of the analytic relationship if one ignores the fact that the analyst does, as it were, wear a mask, however human it may be.

There has been in recent years increasing emphasis in the psychoanalytic world on clarifying and exploring the subjective states of analyst and patient. For example, Bollas (1987, 1989) explores the analyst's use of his subjective experience in order to clarify important aspects of the patient's early experiences. He recommends that 'the clinician should find a way to make his subjective states of mind available to the patient and to himself as objects of the analysis even when he does not yet know what these states mean' (Bollas, 1987, p.201). Aron emphasizes the need to analyse the patient's experience of the analyst's subjectivity in order to 'open the door to ... explorations of the patient's childhood experiences of the parents' inner world and character structure' (Aron, 1991, p.37). The intersubjective approach to psychoanalysis, for example as explained by Stolorow et al. (1987) pays particular attention to the way that the subjectivity of patient and analyst interact. Self psychology emphasizes the need for the analyst to have a particular subjective approach – for example, the capacity to be empathic with the patient by offering 'optimal responsiveness' (Bacal, 1985, p.202), in contrast to the classical technique of offering optimal frustration. Wolf also describes how 'discrepancies in subjective experience between analyst and analysand are bound to become the foci of the working through process' (Wolf, 1988, p.153). Finally, many contemporary clinical presentations from a wide variety of analytic schools show how enactments between patient and analyst are an inevitable and necessary part of the analytic work, reflecting how subjectivities of patient and analyst are in constant interaction.

As important as these developments are in making sense of what takes place between analyst and patient, and I shall refer to some of them where relevant, in my view they frequently omit something important – the individual, personal or human element as such and as distinct from the subjective state of mind induced in the analyst by the patient, or the patient's view of the analyst's subjectivity, or what one might call the general methodology of analysis. It seems to me that this human element, or the shape and pattern of the mask, as well as what the analyst is like when he takes off the mask, or tries to, or tries not to, is what often gets in the way of fostering the patient's subjectivity; at the same time, attention to the human element as such may help foster the analytic process.

Few analysts have tackled the specific role of the personality of the analyst in analysis, as distinct from the methodology; John Klauber being the notable exception. He emphasized how too much concentration on the method of psychoanalysis ignores the personal factor, 'though in fact the personal factor is central to the method. It determines what the analyst selects for interpretation, in what way he views what he selects, and even perhaps what the patient brings' (Klauber, 1981, p.xxiii). He suggested that 'all analysts are aware of the importance of the personal factor, but ... its systematic study remains a lacuna in psychoanalytic theory' (Klauber, 1987, p.43).

Despite recent attention to the issue of subjectivity in analysis, I would suggest that this lacuna still remains, for there has been little attention to the subject as an individual. Much of what Klauber put forward for consideration about this difficult area still seems to me to be relevant to our current work and much could be developed further. To cite a few of his main ideas as a backdrop to what I am putting forward: he considered that there was a neglect in the theory of technique of the significance of choice of individual paths determined by the analyst's personality (Klauber, 1981, p.126); that every analyst, particularly when his identity as an analyst is established, has his individual atmosphere (ibid., p.30). He emphasized the way that the value systems of patient and analyst inevitably interacted and that the direction of the analysis was affected by the analyst's values (ibid., p.134). He considered that what was sometimes classed as resistance could be provoked by the analyst, by his unexpressed personal feelings towards the patient (ibid., p.xxiii); and that the analyst is dependent on the patient as much as the patient is dependent on the analyst, though in different ways (ibid., p.xxx) – for example, the analyst needs the patient to fulfil his own creativity. The analyst 'needs the patient in order to crystallize and communicate his own thoughts, including some of his most inmost thoughts on intimate human problems which can only grow organically in the context of this relationship' (ibid., p.46).

For Klauber, the first requirement of psychoanalytic technique was to 'facilitate the patient's capacity to communicate his feelings and thoughts as fully as possible' (ibid., p.59). He was particularly concerned with the nature of how interpretations could facilitate this process, and where occasionally the analyst needed to be spontaneous in order to do this effectively (ibid., p.115), and to minimize the otherwise traumatic quality of the transference, its flight from reality and stirring up of powerful feelings that usually could not be gratified. Finally, I would point out the underlying belief that seemed to permeate his work, that analysis has a basic long-term aim to foster the development of the patient as an autonomous subject by means of the analytic process, which will help him in the much longer period of his life after the analysis has ended (ibid., p.110) – 'perhaps the criterion of successful personal interaction between analyst and patient may lie partly in the degree to which the patient shows an ability to make his own synthesis – that is, in part to conduct his own analysis and translate its results into life' (ibid., p.138).

Of recent thinkers, Nina Coltart is one of the few who, like Klauber, tackles the difficult issue of what we actually do in the day-to-day work of analysis, in the secrecy of the consulting room, rather than what we say we do. She compares this work with that of a tightrope walker. 'The tightrope itself is the years-long stretch of sessions, in which we try to do, in partnership with our patients, something which has been called impossible and is by any standards unusual' (Coltart, 1992, p.95). Certainly, to tackle the thorny issue of how the psychoanalyst's personal attitudes come into the analysis as distinct from his general psychoanalytic attitude does feel like being on a tightrope. One has to proceed very cautiously with an awareness of impending danger, but practice does help.

Scattered around the literature there are occasionally papers that address one particular human issue. For example, I shall refer to papers on humour by Baker (1993) and Christie (1994); one on irony by Stein (1985); that of Viederman (1991) which tackles the real person of the analyst, concentrating mainly on the analyst's emotional availability; and a paper by Coen (1994) tackling the delicate issue of love between patient and analyst. However, it seems to me that it is only Klauber who has comprehensively brought into focus the degree to which the analyst's humanity needs to be coordinated with his analytic function (Klauber, 1987, p.8), and it is rare to find descriptions of what actually takes place in analysis which are as convincing as those of Coltart.

Paula Heimann, who influenced Klauber, wrote about the need for the analyst to be natural with his patients, such as not attempting to know everything, recognizing mistakes, using ordinary courtesy, being honest and straightforward about what they feel. She deplored the notion of the analyst being neutral. As she put it vividly, 'In my opinion, there is only a short distance from the neutral analyst to the neuter' (Heimann, 1989, p.313). But she also described how such naturalness does not necessarily come about easily; she recommended the constant use of critical self-observation, continued self-analysis and self-supervision; that is, 'tamed naturalness' in the analyst's personal attitude. 'As so often, both in analysis and in the human condition, there is a paradox; only tamed naturalness is creative. With growing experience we acquire the criteria for distinguishing both a patient's authentic understanding and our correct intuitive interpretations from impulsiveness, naive or wild' (ibid., p.317).

But does the personality of the analyst make a difference to the outcome of the analysis? No doubt a full answer to this question would require a systematic follow-up study of analytic patients and a detailed examination of many analysts' working methods, neither of which seem likely, if only because of issues of confidentiality, not to mention the reluctance of many analysts to have their work examined in such an intensive and possibly intrusive way. In the meantime, we may have to be content with the results of accumulated experience, anecdotal information and general argument. A similar question could be put with regard to the outcome of a child's development. Does the personality of the parent make a difference to the child's development? It would seem obvious, except in rare circumstances, that it makes a profound difference, and that psychoanalysis is based on exploring this difference. There is a distinction between the parental function and the person of the parent; but obviously parents who function only without any feeling or who do not put the stamp of their personality into their parenting are damaging to their children. Although analysts are not parents, we do have to deal with the fact that our patients become very dependent on us, that we foster and have to work with sometimes profound regression.

I mentioned earlier that Bettelheim (1983) reminded us that Freud considered that psychoanalysis was ultimately the treatment of man's 'soul', and that Freud meant by this what was most valuable in man while he alive, what makes us human. Yet there still remains a profound fear about acknowledging the consequences of what we are doing with our patients' 'souls' and what we believe about child development. Indeed, it would seem that a number of fears abound in the practice of psychoanalysis. Some of them arise from the institutional frameworks in which analysts work and a number arise directly out of the psychoanalytic encounter itself, both out of fear of the analytic relationship and fear of the effects of the unconscious on us. I think that these fears, a number of which I shall examine in detail, all go to make up the analyst's subjectivity; they give shape to the human mask.

FEAR OF SEDUCTION

One powerful fear, which seems to motivate the attitudes of analysts both in their individual work and in their institutional behaviour is that of being 'seduced' by the patient. As is well known, the threat of the patient's seduction arose at the birth of psychoanalysis, when

Breuer was frightened off by Anna O's sexual feelings towards him. Freud himself later moved from considering that many of his hysterical patients had been seduced by their fathers to the notion that most of the time his patients were telling him about fantasies of seduction, and that he had thus over-valued reality and under-valued the role of fantasy in their lives (Freud, 1896). Today, with our increased awareness of the reality of child abuse, we would emphasize both the need for caution in making assertions about the status of memories of seduction and also the need to take seriously the possibility of abuse in the patient's history. I would also add that we may also undervalue the analyst's fear of being seduced by the patient sexually or in other ways. There is fear of 'negative' seduction – such as being taken for a ride, made to turn a blind eye to difficulties and of being sucked into the patient's pathology. And there is fear of 'positive' seduction – such as being seen to be too supportive, too helpful, too much ourselves and even too creative.

Perhaps in order to cope with these kinds of fears, Freud's technical papers seem to oscillate between encouraging strictness with respect to basic technique in order to prevent 'wild' analysis, and the need to be aware of the power of the unconscious and how the analyst has to follow unconscious processes. Thus he recommends that the analyst be guided by the unconscious. For instance, dream interpretation should 'not be pursued in analytic treatment as an art for its own sake, but that its handling should be subject to those technical rules that govern the conduct of the treatment as a whole' (Freud, 1911a, p.94). But, he adds, 'Occasionally, of course, can one act otherwise and allow a little free play to one's theoretical interests, but one should always be aware of what one is doing' (ibid.). A certain amount of free play but not too much would thus seem to be in order, and I myself would agree with this view.

In addition, for Freud, the analyst should 'simply wait and not bother about whether he is keeping anything in mind' (Freud, 1912, p.112). Also, 'he must turn his own unconscious like a receptive organ towards the transmitting unconscious of the patient' (ibid., p.115). He emphasized how the various rules he had developed were like rules of the game and that there should be no mechanization of the technique (Freud, 1913, p.123).

Thus there is a constant interplay, or a duality, between the need for the analyst to keep to certain rules and boundaries and the need to be receptive to the primary process laws of the unconscious. I would suggest that for the analyst to come down too much on one side of this duality would be a great technical error. Excessive rigidity of technique or, on the contrary, excessive intrusion into the patient's unconscious may be damaging to patient and analyst. To put the technical issue in another way, a fear of being seduced by the patient in a negative way may make us idealize technique as a defence. My impression from listening to scientific presentations and conducting clinical seminars is that this defence is a common one. It produces an ascetic attitude, where the analyst is aloof, self-satisfied and hence ungiving; the analyst may be obsessed with having perfect technique and may idealize the power of psychoanalysis. They may believe that there is only one way of doing psychoanalysis and anything else is 'not analysis'. That is, they may be seduced by their own technique as a defence against being seduced by the patient. Furthermore, idealization of our technique and over-concern about deviations from some imagined ideal may interfere with our ability to be appropriately responsive to our patients.

The other temptation, the fear of being positively seduced by the patient, includes concern that the analyst will be taken over by a fascination with the unconscious, or may indulge in mutual free association and in excessive disclosure. I should add that when the issue of the analyst's human presence is discussed, there often seems to be a powerful fear that what may be recommended is that the analyst should actively disclose aspects of himself to the patient. This is certainly not what I am putting forward. This fear may blind us to the need to examine more fully what we are actually and unknowingly disclosing, and also how we need to examine how our personality affects what we say and do in analysis.

There may also simply be times when one has to obey one's intuition. Heimann was against an analyst communicating his feelings to the patient and giving insight into his own private life, because this burdens the patient and distracts him from his own problems; but she was not against occasionally communicating feelings to the patient in so-called violation of the rules (Heimann, 1989, pp.317–18). She gave the example of saying to a patient that what the patient told her, about a clever adolescent with a mind of an old person, made her shiver. Though this intervention produced indignation, when Heimann thought of alternative ways of getting through to the patient, they all seemed relatively cramped and inhibited. It was only a direct approach that got the message across.

Fear of seduction can become an alive issue when the patient brings the analyst a gift of some kind. Should the analyst always refuse gifts and remain 'untouched' by ordinary social processes? Obviously it would be quite wrong for the analyst to actually encourage gift giving; that really would be a real seduction by the analyst of the patient. But there may be the odd occasion when gifts can be given in good faith. For example, most of the patients who have ended a proper period of treatment with me have given me a present of some kind, such as a plant, a bottle of drink, a small sculpture or a book. I have never, knowingly at least, asked for these gifts. They just brought them to me at the last session, usually giving it to me at the end of the session, not at the beginning, as if to mark a distinction between the work of analysis and the fact that we are both human. It would seem to me churlish to refuse such gifts. I would suggest that this would be tantamount to saying to the patients that I could not bear their generosity, which they have demonstrated despite all the hard and painful work of the analysis.

Though the analyst should not directly communicate about his private life, I believe there is a paradox here – for I think that our patients at times, and perhaps often, are only too aware of our problems. It is naive of us to think that our patients do not notice us and are not constantly translating us for ourselves. After all, one of our main tasks is to help foster the patients' awareness of their relating, and we spend so much time focusing on ourselves in order to facilitate this awareness. For this reason, we need to listen to the patients' assessment of us in the session.

I would even go so far as to suggest that, at least with very disturbed patients, they are constantly acting out our own character problems in various minor and even, on occasions, major ways. Although I cannot give clinical evidence for this suggestion for reasons of confidentiality, I have noticed it when doing supervisions and when I was in a support group with analytic colleagues for the treatment of psychotic patients.

One can also notice this in various ways with analytic colleagues who may be over-identified with their training analyst. For example, they may act out their analyst's conflicts about political issues within their society, or reveal apparently similar character traits.

With the fear of being seduced by the patient, analysts are often tempted to put the patient down, at least when they present their work in public. To caricature this attitude somewhat, the patient is described, literally or implicitly, as some kind of dreadful monster whose only aim is to destroy the good endeavours of the almost saintly analyst. In this scheme of things, only the analyst who can constantly deal with the negative transference is considered worthy of the name; any other attitude is considered 'soft' or simply not that of an analyst. Though I would agree, particularly from my experience of working with highly disturbed in-patients at the Cassel Hospital (Kennedy et al., 1987) that there is a fundamental need to deal firmly with the negative transference in these situations, one can too easily forget the need to provide a holding environment for the patient, and to provide and promote ego support, particularly at moments of crisis. One may become so seduced by the patient's severe pathology that the analyst can think that only, for example, attention to primitive object relations should take place, as if the patient had no adult ego nor any sexual life. In addition, as Harold Searles (1963) described, the concept of transference can be used in these situations as a defence for the analyst to protect himself from the full emotional impact of the patient. Referring to the treatment of psychotic patients, Searles writes that, with deeply ill patients:

> it is essential for the therapist to be able not only to endure, but also to enjoy, a wide variety of transference-positions in relation to the patient, before the patient can become able, acknowledgedly and explicitly, to accept him as a *therapist* to such a degree as to be able to attend to verbalized transference-interpretations from him. To try to do this prematurely, before the therapeutic-symbiosis phase has been allowed to develop and has come towards the end of its usefulness to the patient, is tantamount to the therapist's using the concept of transference as a kind of shield to protect himself from the necessary degree of intimacy with the patient, in a way quite analogous to the patient's own unconscious use of his delusional transference as a kind of shield to protect himself from experiencing the full reality of the therapist as a person in the present. (Searles, 1963, in Buckley, 1988, p.215)

This came home to me when I had to take over the analysis of a disturbed man who had broken off his previous analysis following a severe psychotic episode. It certainly seemed that the previous analyst had done much good work around the patient's destructiveness and aggression, which had helped him a lot. But from what I could piece together, she had neglected to take up the patient's secret loving feelings towards her, and had tried to explain away the patient's sexual feelings towards her as irrational. It was perhaps then no surprise when in his psychotic episode he became obsessed with wanting love from a particular woman who was a tease, who showed interest in him but did not respond to his advances. He did experience considerable relief when I took up how his unacknowledged love for his previous analyst had played a major role in the psychotic episode.

The issue of the analyst actually having sexual feelings for the patient can be a difficult one, particularly when there may be a mutual attraction, separate from any transference, if this is possible. In this context, I recall something my analyst, Klauber, said to me after I had just begun with my first training patient, who was worryingly showing signs of an erotic transference. I had rather proudly, I suppose, announced that I had no sexual feelings towards her. Klauber commented that this was worrying, as it was natural to have such feelings. I was certainly somewhat stunned by his comment, but it got me to think more clearly what was going on with my patient, not to mention my analysis.

Obviously there needs to be a clear boundary with regard to displaying sexual attraction to the patient, though unfortunately, we all know of occasions when this boundary has broken down. But there may be more subtle situations, when there is a certain amount of sexual charge between analyst and patient, which may or may not be acknowledged. The problem is that if this is ignored by analysts, then it may be acted out by either party in one form or another, or patients may find themselves keeping secrets from their analysts as they can pick up some increased defensiveness on their analyst's part. There may be no rigid rule for what to do with these feelings. In my own limited experience, I would look both at the nature of the transference and into myself for guidance. For example, if there is a history of sexual abuse in the patient, then the sexual charge may have something to do with an unconscious incitement to be abused, or to test out the safety of the analytic setting.

Perhaps again out of fear of being seduced by the patient, analysts may emphasize that it is dangerous to want their patients to get better, for, rightly, they may pick this up and react in such a way as to make the analysis ineffectual. This is perhaps different from thinking that the best way for patients actually to get better and not merely have an interesting but irrelevant and ultimately frustrating experience in analysis is to attend to the duality of free play and the technical rules. It may even be important to let in the occasional notion of constructive hope, as has been argued persuasively by Stephen Mitchell. Indeed, Mitchell suggests that some of the most popular clinical concepts become popular, not because of their accuracy as such, but because:

they provide a compelling, more hopeful way for the analyst and analysand to think about and live through difficult, uncomfortable clinical situations. Kohut's empathic stance makes it possible for the analyst to respond to noisy, otherwise insufferable demands not as pathological self-absorption but as a striving for narcissistic equilibrium. Winnicott's distinction between developmental needs and instinctual wishes makes it possible for the analyst to respond to entitlement not as an incessant claim for infantile fulfilment but a self-healing return to points of parental failure. The contemporary Kleinian notion of projective identification makes it possible for the analyst to regard the often intolerable anxiety, boredom, and terror that accompanies work with very disturbed patients not as a cause for alarm and escape but as evidence of the patient's unconscious efforts to communicate features of dissociated experiences of early life. I am not suggesting that any of these widely applied clinical concepts is necessarily wrong or inaccurate, but rather that one of their greatest values lies in the imaginative yield they open up for the analyst to find new possibilities in old conditions. (Mitchell, 1993, p.222)

Coen argues that 'the analyst needs to feel a certain degree of caring, concern and optimism for the patient to be able to help the latter change and grow ... this seems especially necessary in order to analyze negative, hateful, rejecting, exploitative aspects of the patient. Otherwise the patient will tend to experience (*correctly*) the analyst as judging and condemning rather than assisting with change' (Coen, 1994, p.1132). This view, however, contrasts with that of many other analysts, particularly in the British Society who, like Enid Balint (1968), point out that friendliness can make the patient feel lonelier, as the ill part of the patient will feel neglected. However, I suspect that she was not implying a rigid or cold technique; rather, a careful and respectful one.

Perhaps the point is that the analyst will find himself reflecting back to the patient in a variety of ways, sometimes with rather cool irony, and at other times with a warm, empathic attitude, and more often somewhere between these points, on a continuum. I would thus agree with Viederman (1991) who argues in detail against the rigid application of the stance of strict abstinence and anonymity, which can only distort the analytic relationship and generate unnecessary hostility.

The 'right' attitude for the analyst to take is thus a complex affair, with analysts taking different positions. I shall return to this problem later when I address the issue of interpretation. But I would like to add at this point that it may be inadvisable for an analyst to hope too much that his patients get better, but if none of them do then I personally find it difficult to imagine why on earth he would be working as an analyst.

In addition, I would suggest that there are times when it is important and appropriate to respond truthfully and feelingly as one human being to another, and also to be honest about one's feelings with the patient, including admitting genuine mistakes. Furthermore, if the analyst always maintains a rigid stance, for example never answering questions, but always putting them back to the patient, then there is the danger of facilitating a false self in the patient. Equally well, if the analyst allows too much constant intrusion into the patient, then the patient can feel traumatized. As Klauber pointed out, it is inevitable that the patient will struggle against and/or identify with the analyst's values, however much the analyst tries to remain neutral. Indeed, neutrality itself represents a particular and questionable value system. It is perhaps better to recognize this dilemma rather than pretend it does not exist, otherwise the patient will harbour secrets from the analyst, or will develop a split-off enclave of fantasy life. There is a danger of producing such enclaves by being too friendly, but also by being too unempathic.

STRAIN OF RESTRAINT

Of course, it is not just fear of seduction which influences analysts' attitudes to their patients, but also the traumatic experience of listening to and bearing with the patients' very painful experiences day in and day out. As Klauber (1981, pp.52–3) described, there are considerable personal strains for the analyst in doing this work, particularly at the beginning of one's career, before one finds a more secure analytic identity. It is difficult bearing the loneliness of the consulting room and the frustrations of having to be constantly restrained emotionally with patients. As Tarachow aptly described, 'The psychoanalyst must be capable of withstanding all degrees of ... necessary deprivation, tension and task, especially tolerance for loneliness' (Tarachow, 1962, p.380).

Perhaps somewhere the analyst has to bear the cost of having to hold on to hate and love for the patient. Time and again the analyst has to sit back and prevent himself from expressing an opinion about some aspect of what he hears, in order to maintain the analytic stance, though there are of course slightly questionable ways of cheating, when the analyst can make his opinions known with an interpretation, such as making an intervention which begins with 'I wonder what stops you from ...' or 'You seem to have difficulty in ...'.

The political opinions of the patient may have an impact on the analyst, particularly when they clash with those of the analyst. Of course these opinions may fit in with the psychotic aspects of the patient, such as with a delusional structure. In a sense, that is easy to deal with because it fits in with pathology. But when the opinions fit with the whole character of the patient, it can be quite a strain to have to sit back, if one's own opinions are very different from those of the patient. In this context, I recall a difficult patient I saw for therapy some years ago. A homosexual, he presented with a life-threatening illness (not AIDS), and difficulty in forming relationships. He broke off treatment after presenting me with a long dream, which took nearly a whole session to relate, in which he clearly moved from homosexuality to heterosexuality. He did then give me a term's notice but refused the offer of full analysis, no doubt afraid of change. He did recover from his illness, but otherwise I am not sure what I did for him. However, at least he himself was pleased to report that as a result of therapy he no longer voted for Margaret Thatcher! He himself linked this change to a different way of seeing his mother, no longer as a harsh and rigid authority.

Analysts in countries plagued by political turmoil obviously have to take account of the clash of political interests in a more active and even suspicious way. Very difficult ethical issues may arise; for example, if a patient is involved in torture or political suppression. It is difficult to see how the analyst can remain neutral in these situations. I think that in this area I am really referring again to what Klauber pointed out concerning the inevitable interaction between the values of patient and analyst, and the need for the analyst to be aware of this interaction. It is inevitable that analysts have ethical views about many aspects of life, but an obsession with normative behaviour seems to me inappropriate, although there is a tendency among some analysts to preach about what is or what is not appropriate and normal behaviour.

However, we cannot be unaffected by what we hear. For example, a narcissistic patient described how he had decided not to give his ex-wife and children any child maintenance, as she had remarried. Legally he was obliged to continue his anyway minimal payments, but the Child Support Agency was reluctant to pursue self-employed fathers, as it was too much bother and often ineffectual. He then described how he went round to his ex-wife's house and offered her some money for a few summer activities for the children. He was outraged when she declined his offer, accusing him, rightly, of not fulfilling his ordinary duty as a father by re-establishing his regular payments, while he wanted to give the false appearance of generosity. The effect of this man's narcissistic character – for example, the way that he constantly distorted the truth, of which this was only a small example – outraged me. Working with that feeling was important for his treatment, but none the less was a great strain.

One could say that during an analysis the analyst is not infrequently making some sort of judgement of the patient's character: how much, for example, they can relate to others; how just and 'decent' they are as people, etc. When analysing analytic candidates, this may be very important indeed, particularly in the British Society, where analysts report back to the training committees and have a say in the candidate's progress, though it is very difficult to be precise in making judgements in this area.

One may wonder whether the general need for restraint accounts for the way that analysts at times can be so unrestrained in their institutional behaviour, when they come together in group settings. For example, there is the bitchiness about colleagues that can arise, usually centred around whether or not they are really analysts, whether or not they really work with the transference, or whether or not they are 'just crazy'. Also, analysts are notoriously prone to particular sorts of character problems which limit their capacity to be ordinarily human and sociable, at least in the analytic institutional setting, perhaps again out of the strain caused by the restraint required of them in their work, as well as the collective awareness that analysts work with powerful forces that they can barely understand, however much they are supposed to. The temptation is to over-use the frozen, polite smile, the guarded look, the ever-so-civilized stab in the back. Such attitudes may be in part a result of living too much in the incestuous world of psychoanalysis and psychotherapy, with few social contacts with other kinds of world.

Behind the fear of standing out too much or of not being a real analyst there may also be economic worries, the need to get referrals to make a living. Here the personal factor about trusting an analyst with someone's 'soul' is crucial, though not talked about much. As one colleague put it, there are two kinds of analysts – those to whom you would refer a relative and those to whom you would not.

In addition, perhaps we are not clear enough about the possibility of and the need for a personal fit between patient and analyst, or of its role when it is lacking and an analysis breaks down. Such a possibility can be seen more clearly in dealing with the training of analysts. From my own experience on the Student Progress Committee of the British Society there have been a few times when candidates have changed analysts, apparently for such reasons. Equally, there have been times when candidates have gone on and on with an unsatisfactory analytic experience out of a misguided sense of duty, and have needed help to extricate themselves.

The institutional behaviour of analysts is a complex phenomenon, one which no doubt would benefit from a detailed sociological analysis. The element of history has to be taken into account; both the early history of psychoanalysis, with Freud's fears that psychoanalysis would become adulterated or tainted by heresy, by the personal views of a heretic; and, in London, the 'controversial discussions' centred around whether or not Melanie Klein was a heretic or an innovative genius but essentially faithful to Freud. As Viederman describes, perhaps with history in mind, there is still a fear that 'To give theoretical status to the personal attributes and responses of the analyst ... generates concern that the definition of the analytic process will be clouded and its scientific status compromised' (Viederman, 1991, p.459).

The issue of what is orthodox in analysis and what is heresy still plagues us today; there are analysts who consider themselves 'strictly orthodox' and those who are 'liberal' or 'reform', to use a metaphor from the structure of contemporary Judaism. Whatever the origins of this sort of attitude, I am focusing more on the inevitable tensions that arise from the analytic work itself, and how the personal element may become detached, or split off, from the analytic function and then may be acted out in institutional settings. Perhaps the way that the controversial discussions became focused around personalities was indicative of just such a split; although of course there were also real personal differences involved. Alongside the detachment of the personal element, there may be in fact a fear of integration of the personal and the more rule-based aspects of psychoanalysis.

THE NEED TO INTERPRET

Why do analysts interpret? Although the answer to this question would seem to be obvious because interpretation is what we are meant to be doing, there remain a number of difficult issues to face about our need to interpret. Bion, in his characteristically ironic fashion, made the point that interpretations can be made by the analyst in order to deny the anxiety aroused in him by what is unknown and hence dangerous to him (Bion, 1963, p.18). Winnicott, also characteristically, said that he interpreted mainly in order to let the patient know the limits of his understanding (Winnicott, 1971, pp.86–7). He also expressed the thought that, looking back over his career as an analyst, he had made too many interpretations, and had been too keen on wanting to appear to be clever. I think that there is a recognition by Bion and Winnicott that interpretations can be reductive and not facilitating, particularly when they respond more to the needs of the analyst than to those of the patient. Klauber suggested that the skill of the analyst could be measured by the analyst's success in balancing the reductive aspects of psychoanalysis with those which made it liberating. 'He does this in a number of ways: by the moral qualities at his disposal for interest in the patient and identification with him; by showing the positive value of primitive mechanisms, as for example, when envy and oral incorporation are used for the ego's acquisition of new ideals; by the education in accepting the realities of the id which implicitly accompanies interpretation; by the analysis of current anxieties in everyday terms; and by the innumerable exchanges between patient and analyst which make the analytic experience a humane one' (Klauber, 1981, p.27).

Thus along with the actual process of making an interpretation there is a complex atmosphere surrounding the interpretation, whose aim from the analyst's point of view is to provide a suitable environment in which it can be effective. Each analyst has their own personal atmosphere, as of course does each analysis. There are also considerable differences in how analysts view both the giving of interpretations and the role of the personal atmosphere. To caricature the differences as two opposite attitudes – there is the 'wait and see' approach and the 'keep the interpretations going' approach. The former approach involves the analyst waiting for the patient to speak and then gradually making sense of what he says, eventually formulating an interpretation – possibly a transference interpretation, but just as likely an interpretation that may lead up to a transference interpretation. The ultimate aim is to facilitate the patient's capacity to think for himself, to find his own subjective way of being and hopefully to make deep emotional contact with the patient. In this method, it is important to allow time for the patient's fantasies – for example, about the analyst – to develop. This tends to be my main personal style, though at times I may take a more active or interventionist approach, depending on the patient and what I am hearing; for example, I may be more active with ill patients and those in a crisis. Also I am more active in this way when doing psychotherapy, when a more focused approach may be required. With the wait and see approach, I think one needs to be on one's guard against being too passive and letting the patient go on too much before intervening.

The more active, 'keep interpreting' approach involves making frequent interpretations, in a lively and constant toing and froing with the patient, quite often being guided by the countertransference. This method can be a powerful way of making contact with the more psychotic aspects of the patient, but I think one has to be on one's guard against both infantilizing the patient and also over-exciting him. Constant and ongoing interpretations can give the appearance of rigour, but can also be a way for the analyst to defend himself against being with the patient, bearing the unknown and facing his full emotional impact. There are obviously many finer distinctions between these two basic technical positions. Each has its uses and abuses. By waiting and seeing, the analyst can be facilitative and encourage the more liberating aspects of analysis, but there is the danger of not doing enough. With the other approach, the analyst is actively engaged in an alive way with the patient, but this can become too reductive.

The kinds of interpretations we give have some relation to our past, our analysis, training, idealizations, identifications and transferences to other analysts, as well as to the authority of prevailing fashions. At some point we are hopefully ourselves. But it may take many years, if ever, before we give interpretations that do not remind us directly of our own analysis.

Whatever the particular style or idiom of the analyst, interpretations continue to be made. I would suggest that there are at least three reasons why analysts need to make interpretations. The first need is intellectual, the need to make sense of what is happening in the analysis, to give or discover meaning. This need is driven by the analyst's curiosity. I would add that there are also two different ways that interpretations can discover meaning. Meaning can be given by the analyst to the patient, which seems to be more common in the 'keep interpreting' mode of making interpretations, or the meaning can be discovered, arising out of the encounter of analyst and patient, through interaction between the horizons of analyst and patient. Of course there are various mixtures of giving and of discovering interpretations. Sometimes the most effective interpretations arise just as you are making another interpretation; one may be surprised by what appears as one speaks.

The second need is an emotional one, that of wishing to make contact with the patient. It can feel unbearable to have to be out of touch with a patient for long periods of time. Interpretations are one powerful and acceptable way we have of trying to keep some contact going, however difficult this may be with some patients. For example, I recall a long analysis with a vulnerable woman, early on in my analytic career, who originally came for help because of severe colitis. She soon revealed a severe suicidal disposition and also went through a long period of experiencing a negative transference, which at times was difficult for both of us to tolerate. She had had an emotionally deprived upbringing, her mother never gave her affection and she was also subjected to beatings by her father. She eventually revealed that when she lay on the couch she thought I would beat her up, and she constantly had to fight the temptation to run out of the room. I was a frightening figure for her for many years. Though in the outside world she was reasonably successful both personally and professionally, with me she revealed a terrifying world in which she felt trapped. It also turned out that, during the period of intense negative transference, which lasted about four years, she was afraid of the words I used and how I used them; in particular, my interpretations about any unconscious emotion made her fear that I was going to drive her mad. These fears seemed related to the fact that her strange mother never accepted her; she treated her like an object, even speaking to her in the third person. There was thus a fundamental difficulty about giving interpretations, as they were experienced as attacks on her sanity. However, there was no alternative, as things felt worse if I kept silent, leaving her to imagine that I was in reality a hateful and potentially violent figure.

I have to say what eventually helped her to get out this difficult situation was a perhaps rather despairing intervention on my part. One day, when she was again bitterly complaining about the awfulness of what she was experiencing, I said that perhaps we really did need to consider whether or not it was in her interest to continue the analysis for much longer, if indeed it were making her worse. She did not experience this intervention as a threat but as a relief. A little later she said that because I had indicated that I would not let her continue to suffer as she had been, then she finally realised that I could not be such an evil figure after all. Perhaps now, some years later, I would be able to deal better with this whole situation, but I suspect I had to experience the despair of interpretations apparently not getting anywhere in order to reach the point of making an effective intervention. Also, I suspect that I often needed interpretations in order to keep myself sane, during the long period of having to deal with what was basically a psychotic transference.

As I mentioned before, the analyst also has a deep emotional need for the patient in order to crystallize his thoughts, to fulfil his own creativity. In addition, I think that one needs the patient in other more private ways. I think that the use of what I would call one's private area of suffering is a vital and therapeutic element of the analytic relationship. It is what is missing in accounts of an analysis. It was, Freud said, left out of *The Interpretation of Dreams* for reasons of tact. But, as Paula Heimann wrote, 'Driven by suffering, the patient turns to the analyst in the hope of finding help. The analyst can provide help if he himself originally came to analysis as someone who was ill – and in some regards still is ill – but had the courage to do without falsehoods and tricks, in this way making something creative out of his illness' (Heimann, 1989, p.311).

I feel that we need to tap into the private area of suffering, a particular area of subjective experience, not explain it away with jargon as countertransference. Sometimes, perhaps often, patients are in touch with this area and use it for their own purposes, to avoid conflict, to get the analyst to collude with them, or simply share their own suffering. Thus the analyst's private sufferings are not only a nuisance, something one hoped that one's own analysis would have dealt with, but also an inevitable part of the analytic work. If used wisely, they can also be the source of much creativity. I think that analysts need to listen to the patients' conscious and unconscious assessment of their private areas of pain and suffering. They may not know what they are reacting to, nor does the analyst have to tell them exactly; but the analyst will, hopefully, know – provided he does not retain his God-like stance. Patients will reflect back to the analyst their own suffering; they may even wish to protect the analyst from themselves, which is perhaps particularly seductive and dangerous for the analysis. Doing analysis certainly can test the analyst's capacity to withstand considerable amounts of distress and survive with the interpretative capacity still intact. That was certainly a major issue with the treatment of the last patient I mentioned.

The third need that the analyst has of interpretation is as a defence against the impact of the patient on himself. To some extent I have touched on this throughout the paper. But more specifically I am referring to what Klauber has described about the threat to the analyst which arises from being in contact with primitive processes in the patient. There is the constant possibility of identifying with the patient's primitive impulses. 'The analyst's underlying anxiety must ... be concerned with the danger of introjecting the patient and, having introjected him, of responding to him at the level of the warded-off sexuality which underlies his character and values. Interpretation must therefore serve to reduce the danger of excessive sexual stimulation for the analyst as well as for the patient' (Klauber, 1981, p.38).

However, he also points out that interpretations not only limit and frustrate sexual desire, but can also arouse excitement by offering the possibility of cure. Inherent in psychoanalysis is a struggle between the exciting and frustrating elements, which can be experienced as a constant tease.

HUMOUR AND IRONY

Freud distinguished between humour, the comic and jokes. In the case of the comic, two people are in general concerned: besides myself, the person in whom I find something comic. With jokes, 'the psychical process is accomplished between the first person (the self) and the third (the outside person) and not, as in the case of the comic, between the self and the person who is the object' (Freud, 1905b, p.144). With humour, 'It completes its course within a single person; another person's participation adds nothing new to it. I can keep to myself the enjoyment of the humorous pleasure that has arisen in me, without feeling obliged to communicate it' (ibid., p.229). Furthermore,

> There are two ways in which the humorous process can take place. It may take place in regard to a single person, who himself adopt the humorous attitude, while a second person plays the part of the spectator who derives enjoyment from it; or it may take place between two persons, of whom one takes no part at all in the humorous process, but is made the object of humorous contempla- tion by the other ... When [for example] ... a criminal who was being led out to the gallows on a Monday remarked: 'Well, the week's beginning nicely,' he was producing the humour himself; the humour is completed in his own person and obviously affords him a sense of satisfaction. I, the non-participating listener, am affected as it were at long-range ... I feel, like him, perhaps, the yield of humorous pleasure. (Freud, 1927, p.161)

The essence of humour is that one spares oneself the affects to which a situation would usually give rise, such as the painful one of being about to be hanged in the above example, and dismisses the possibility of the expression of the emotion with a humorous remark. Freud suggested that it was through humour that the super-ego consoled the ego in order to protect it from suffering. There is thus something noble and elevating about it, lacking in the telling of jokes. There is a triumph over the traumas of the real world by the production of pleasure.

I have begun this section with a long preamble about Freud's description of humour as it seems to me to describe what is an essential human accompaniment of the psychoanalytic relationship. I have never told a joke to a patient, as it has never seemed appropriate; it would be like doing analysis in the street or at a party, in the presence of the 'third person', where joke telling would be appropriate, whereas a touch of humour on occasions may make all the difference to the analytic process. Baker writes that 'to deny humour access in an analysis may be to deprive the analysis of a useful corner of creative and growth-promoting exploration' (Baker, 1993, p.955), but he also cautions us to be wary of its use, particularly with certain patients who are not healthy enough to cope with a humorous intervention, and to be careful of using humour to distract us from analytic work.

Christie (1994) and Baker both suggest that the spontaneous use of humour can at times be facilitating to the analytic process, as can a good interpretation. It can provide both for relief and for insight during a long and difficult struggle with painful issues. It can help the patient to take some distance from their suffering as well as lightening the load a little. I will give one small example from the end of an analysis with a somewhat schizoid man. He originally had a great fear of becoming intimate with people, and was quite inhibited emotionally. He would often fill up his time with courses and study rather than stay still for one moment and just live a little. But he made good progress, including establishing a good long-term relationship. He had to deal with an early abandonment by his mother, which made the ending particularly difficult. During one session, he described all the courses he was thinking of doing in the future – the further education, the extra weekends away, etc. At one point, I simply wondered with him when he was going to relax. He laughed at this remark and realized that he was going back to his old way of filling up time in order not to live. What I had said was not 'funny'; I was certainly aware of his need to experience the pain of loss. I suppose I was worried that he might actually mar his relationship by not staying at home long enough. What came out of my mouth seemed to make contact with his harsh super-ego, and help him to look at himself. But I should add that this man had a sense of humour, and thus I knew he could deal with my intervention.

This use of humour in analysis is one way that the analyst can use spontaneity for analytic purposes. This matches Klauber's belief that, under certain circumstances, the analyst's spontaneity can be liberating for the patient, bringing together patient and analyst and enlarging the area of communication between them. In general, he thought that the 'spontaneous processes are responsible for the artistic and most creative aspects of the analysis ... It is the spontaneous communication of a new idea which evokes a spontaneous reaction in the patient and gives both a feeling of a constructive session which will lead to further development' (Klauber, 1987, p.33).

Klauber distinguishes this kind of spontaneity from impulsiveness, and emphasizes that it is wiser to use it only after mastery of basic analytic technique. I would agree that sometimes this kind of response is the only or most effective way of bringing to light deeply unconscious conflicts, especially as the analysis continues and the patient becomes familiar with the analytic process, and may even become too adept at being a patient. The analyst in turn may become too familiar with the patient, and can find himself accepting too readily what he might not have accepted in the beginning of the analysis. Both sides become used to one another. I myself often find that I can have my most useful ideas about an analysis in the first week after a holiday break, when I can have a fresh look at what has been going on.

I would suggest that the spontaneous response of the analyst also refers to a particular way of being an analyst, of using one's subjective awareness, one in which the analyst is alive and open to many aspects of a situation, while listening to many voices and narrative themes, and having a continuous sort of unconscious dialogue both with oneself and with the patient. As I have discussed in Chapter 2, there arises in the clinical setting the issue about how much sense and coherence should be fostered by the analyst, how much they should be 'monologic', in the sense of providing a focus on a particular theme, and how much the analyst should foster the freedom of the many and different voices, thus respecting the spontaneity of the analytic process.

Such a respect for the analytic process is vividly portrayed in the work of Bion, who emphasized the ability to tolerate not knowing by eliminating memory and desire from the analyst's mind in order to be open to what may happen in the session. Nina Coltart has developed this theme in her paper 'Slouching towards Bethlehem ... Or thinking the unthinkable in psychoanalysis'(in Coltart, 1992). She describes how the analyst needs to develop the 'capacity to sit it out with a patient, often for long periods, without any real precision as to where we are, relying on our regular tools and our faith in the process to carry us through the obfuscating darkness of resistance, and the sheer unconsciousness of the unconscious' (ibid., p.3). She also emphasizes that if we are to convey 'truth, and more importantly, authenticity in our style of speech we must also master intuitive, unlaboured *spontaneity*' (ibid., p.142). She adds that this is an extremely demanding and complex requirement, which needs a combination of unselfconscious self-forgetfulness and deep self-confidence. She also describes a process of therapeutic transformation, where we 'bring thought to the unthinkable and words to the inexpressible' (ibid., p.14). The analyst may have to think the unthinkable and, I would add, feel the unfeelable.

When we come to the place of irony in psychoanalysis, I feel we are on different territory, one that can lead towards the more theoretical issues concerning the nature of analytic subjectivity. Irony refers in its simplest form to the use of words to express something other than their literal meaning. For example: 'Fine weather we're having', says one Englishman to another at a bus queue, while both are soaking wet from rain. As Stein (1985) points out, such mockery which merges into humour can be used in analysis as a defence, both adaptively and as a resistance, especially against the expression of intense affect associated with the transference.

The original use of the Greek word *eironeia* was, as Vlastos (1991) has pointed out, that of deception. Socrates was often accused by his contemporaries of not taking values seriously, of mocking everything and corrupting society by pulling everything to bits through his use of irony. Psychoanalysts, too, have often been accused of never giving a straight answer and, at least in the early days of the discipline, of being subversive.

But there is another form of irony, which Vlastos calls 'complex' irony as opposed to the other 'simple' irony. Vlastos argues that in fact Socrates introduced a new form of irony, a new form of life even, realized in himself. This irony is serious in its mockery, earnest in its playfulness: 'in complex irony, what is said is both is and isn't what is meant; its surface content is meant to be true in one sense, false in another' (Vlastos, 1991, p.31). There is in the ironic expression, as it were, a manifest and a latent meaning.

When Socrates disavows that he has any knowledge, he does and does not mean what he says. In ways that the psychoanalyst can identify with, he engaged in discourse in order to make his interlocutors aware of their ignorance, and to enable them to discover the truth for themselves. Though a man, he acts as a midwife to other's ideas. The very appearance of Socrates is ironic – he is ugly on the surface, yet beneath the manifest surface has a beautiful soul. The Greek Sileni were small images divided in half, and so constructed that they could be opened up and displayed. When closed, they represented some ridiculous ugly flute-player; but when they were opened they revealed the figure of a god. In Plato's *Symposium*, Alcibiades starts his speech on love by praising Socrates and drawing a comparison between him and the Sileni, because though he looks ugly on the surface, once he was opened out, he had a noble and lofty soul. Alcibiades wants Socrates to respond to his sexual overtures; but Socrates remains a block of ice. He will not do so, nor will he hand him answers; Alcibiades has to search for the truth for himself.

Clearly there is something quite ironic about the psychoanalytic stance. The analyst is both present and absent; reveals and conceals; is both available and is a concealed presence, living, like Socrates, behind a mask. I would suggest that this stance both reflects and takes account of the elusive nature of our subjective life. Through the dual aspect of the analyst's position, the patient, as I have already described, may experience a constant tease, which is different from a real seduction. The latter would occur in a 'positive' or 'negative' way if the analyst were only either present or only absent.

Socrates stands at the beginning of the development of subjective knowledge, the kind of knowledge we need to lead a 'good' life. When he said he was ignorant, he was nevertheless in possession of knowledge, for he had knowledge of his ignorance. As analysts we can still learn from Socrates how not to know too much.

SUBJECTIVITIES OF ANALYST AND PATIENT

I have been emphasizing how much the analytic relationship is determined by the personal or human aspects of the analyst; how much, for example, the personality of the analyst, his style of interpreting, his readiness to accept certain feelings and not others, as well as his value systems, may determine the course of the analysis, including the unfolding of the transference. I have also emphasized how various kinds of fears, endemic to psychoanalysis, may prevent the analyst from recognizing the individuality of the patient, his own unique subjective world. Much of what I have proposed seems to me to overlap with analytic thinkers from the intersubjective perspective, who also emphasize the importance of the personal presence and participation of the analyst in the analytic relationship.

Lewis Aron's paper, 'The patient's experience of the analyst's subjectivity' (1991), gives, I think, a particularly useful account of how the analyst's subjectivity is an important element of the analytic situation, and in particular how what needs to be clarified is how the patient himself experiences the analyst's subjectivity. Aron shows how recognizing the analyst as a subject brings in a new dimension into the analytic work.

Aron defines intersubjectivity as referring to the 'developmentally achieved capacity to recognize another person as a separate centre of experience' (Aron, 1991, p.31). As I shall discuss in detail in Chapter 5, this view of intersubjectivity is based on infant research and refers to what Daniel Stern calls 'intersubjective relatedness'. It differs from other notions of intersubjectivity based on, for example, the thought of Hegel, to which I have previously referred, which emphasizes the role of desire.

Aron puts forward several clinical points. He considers that 'the analytic situation is constituted by the mutual regulation of communication between patient and analyst in which both patient and analyst affect and are affected by one another' (ibid., p.47). Though I would agree in general with this statement, I also think it tends to underplay the existence of mutual antagonism, conflict and the inevitable breakdowns of communication that are part and parcel of the analytic relationship. On the other hand, Aron does emphasize that the analytic relationship may be mutual but not symmetrical.

Aron further considers that 'The analyst's subjectivity is an important element in the analytic situation, and the patient's experience of the analyst's subjectivity needs to be made conscious' (ibid.). He considers that an analytic focus on the patient's experience of the analyst's subjectivity – for example, the way that the patient may probe the analyst's professional calm and reserve, searching for information about the analyst's subjective world – may open the door to further explorations of the patient's childhood experiences of the parents' inner world and character structure.

He also makes what I consider an important distinction about the analyst's countertransference – distinguishing between the analyst as reacting to the patient and the analyst as actively responding to the patient:

> In my view, referring to the analyst's total responsiveness with the term *countertransference* is a serious mistake because it perpetuates defining the analyst's experience in terms of the subjectivity of the patient. Thinking of the analyst's experience as 'counter' or responsive to the patient's transference encourages the belief that the analyst's experience is reactive rather than subjective, emanating from the center of the analyst's psychic self ... It is not that analysts are never responsive to the pressures that the patients put on them; of course, the analyst does counter respond to the impact of the patient's behaviour. The term *countertransference*, though, obscures the recognition that the analyst is often the initiator of the interactional sequences, and therefore the term minimizes the impact of the analyst's behaviour on the transference. (ibid., p.33)

Distinguishing between the analyst as reactive and responsive does not imply that the analyst should impose himself on the patient. Aron does recommend that patients need to find the analyst as a separate subject in their own way and at their own rate (ibid., p.42). However, my impression from his approach is that he recommends a greater degree of the analyst's use of self-revelation than I would feel comfortable with. As I have argued, the analyst's subjective position involves the use of a mask; without it, there would not be an analytic relationship. The analyst's position, which includes the use of free-floating attention, also, as I have argued, involves being in a number of different positions or moorings, where chains of meaning, narrative structures or voices criss-cross, intermix, fade, dissolve or occasionally cohere. When the analyst listens to the patient in this way, I would suggest that he has engaged him as a subject. While, if the analyst himself allows himself to think in this way, he is more fully a subject.

I also feel from Aron's work, and indeed others with the intersubjective approach, that there is not enough of a distinction between a subject and a self and that their use of the term 'intersubjectivity' is a limited one, as I shall develop further in Chapter 5 which aims to look more specifically at the relations between subjects.

In conclusion, one can say that the analyst tries to judge in what ways his personality and individual reactions affect the development of the transference; but that in itself is insufficient to explain the complexities of the analytic encounter. It is not just what the patient makes of the analyst's personality and emotional states, but also what the analyst makes of them that is at issue. The analyst tries to understand not only the patient's perceptions of them but how the analyst's own personal preferences, including the preferred models of working, help to create the meaning that arises out of the analytic relationship. The analyst has to channel his personal reactions; but his personal contribution may determine or channel the unfolding of the transference. Furthermore, various fears endemic to psychoanalysis, some of which I have outlined, may prevent the analyst from recognizing the individuality of the patient, his own unique subjective world.

There is still much one does not understand about this area of psychoanalysis. After all, a good deal of the human aspect of the analyst is unconscious, however much the analyst has been analysed. The patient may use some of the analyst's real characteristics as a vehicle for projections as well as at an ordinary human level; some of the time the analyst may find himself being relatively inhuman, instead of human, by failing to respond to the patient. The struggle in the analytic encounter can often be about how to find a way to take these kinds of issues on board without simply deflecting them back to the patient, how to find a way of talking to the patient about this kind of issue without being too intrusive or too confessional; that is, in a humanely disciplined way.

5   BETWEEN SUBJECTS

SUBJECT AND OTHER

I will aim in this chapter to examine more fully how one may understand what happens between subjects, or how subjects interact in the social field. I would suggest that the evidence from infant research, group analysis and the analytic session points to the critical importance of the environment in the organization of the subject. The place of the environment around the individual is understood in various ways by different analytic thinkers. For example, for Lacan (1966) it comes in as the 'field of the other'; in infant research (Stern, 1985) there is an 'intersubjective field'; in self psychology (Wolf, 1988) 'selfobjects' play a crucial environmental role; for Bion (1970) there is the 'container' and the 'contained'; and for Winnicott (1971) there is the pivotal role of the 'transitional space' between mother and infant. This contrasts with Klein's original model of psychical organization (1946) which has often been criticized as putting too much weight on the child's own contribution. I would agree that her model is unconvincing when the environment is only relevant through the way that the infant is taken up with processes of introjection and projection aimed towards the mother. Much is left out about the reactions from the environment, initially of course in the person of the mother.

In general terms, I am proposing that the structure of the subject, or the subjective organization, requires something beyond the mere individual for its full realization. That is to say, the subjective organization needs the social field to be fully realized. I have already emphasized this aspect of the organization of the subject when, for example, discussing how a basic innate organization is built into the nervous system, which then has to be used to become fully organized. It was suggested then that this finding was compatible with a notion of the psychological subject being in possession of various functions and structures that need to be used in social interaction for their full realization; that a subjective organization comprised the individual within a social field, hungry for interaction.

This could also be put in terms of the inevitable linking of subject and other, to which I have referred on a number of occasions, for example when referring to the thought of Dewey,

Ricoeur and Sartre. Indeed, one could say that perceiving or taking account of *one's life as another*, is the essential social element required to acquire a 'full' sense of subjectivity, one that is not encapsulated in an isolated or narcissistic position. Taking account of one's life as another would probably also involve being at a 'dialogic' level with the other, along the lines I suggested in Chapter 2, when taking account of Bakhtin's thought.

Mikhail Bakhtin in his 1923 collection of essays *Art and Answerability* (Bakhtin, 1990) describes, in terms which anticipated those of Sartre (1943), how vital taking account of one's life as another was in aesthetic activity. Bakhtin provides complex descriptions of the nature of the aesthetic process, based on considering the relations between the author as subject and the hero as the other, that could be applied to other fields. Indeed, in some ways one might add that we are all potential authors and heroes. He looks at the aesthetic moment as a pivotal experience for human beings, where subjectivity is lived and created in an intense and fundamental way.

Bakhtin describes how, for an aesthetic event to take place, there have to be at least two participants present, two distinct consciousnesses, it is a social event. When author and hero coincide, so that there is no distinction between them, then the aesthetic event finishes. The author occupies a position outside the hero, to a varying extent; but the relationship between author and hero is a deeply vital and dynamic one. The author must look at himself through the eyes of another, or he must become another in relation to himself, in order to produce a work of art. This requires that one takes a stand outside oneself to some extent; but equally important is the need to *return* from outside back to oneself. Aesthetic activity begins with this return.

> Aesthetic activity proper actually begins at the point when we *return* into ourselves, when we *return* to our own place outside the suffering person, and start to form and consummate the material we derived from projecting ourselves into the other and experiencing him from within himself. (Bakhtin, 1990, p.26)

I would add here that this process of return from the position outside the person can be seen in psychoanalytic terms, particularly in relation to the Oedipal situation. I have already referred to the father's position outside the close mother–child relationship as the third position, the Other of the mother. If the subject were to remain fixed in one position; for example, only in the third position or only stuck in the close relationship to the mother, then the Oedipus Complex remains unresolved. Resolution of the Oedipal situation implies having some ability to move between positions, for example, returning back to intimacy with the mother from a more distant perspective, and then back again. But by resolution of the Oedipus Complex I do not mean that it is dissolved or no longer active; but that the subject can take a position within the Oedipal triangle with regard to sexual desire, so that he can assume his sexual organization. A successful resolution of the Oedipus Complex is thus a complicated affair, involving some fixing of the subject's identifications, but also some mobility with regard to his position within the Oedipal triangle. Failure to stand outside oneself and to see oneself as another implies in particular becoming fixed in a narcissistic position, with an empty kind of subjectivity, and with little capacity to make the return to intimacy. As Bakhtin put it, in relation to the aesthetic experience:

> Let us suppose, for the moment, that I *could* physically stand outside myself, that I am given the possibility, the physical possibility, of giving form to myself from outside. Nevertheless, if I fail to take a stand *outside* my entire life as a whole, if I fail to perceive it as the life of *another*, I shall still find that I lack any *inwardly* convincing principle for giving form to myself from outside, for sculpting my own outward appearance, for consummating myself aesthetically ... [A]n utterance *about* my own life through the lips of another is indispensable for producing an artistic whole. (ibid., p.86)

For Bakhtin, in the aesthetic event, there is a meeting of two consciousnesses – that of the author, the *I*, and that of the hero, the *other*. 'In the aesthetic event, we have to do with a *meeting* of two consciousnesses which are in principle distinct from each other, and where the author's consciousness, moreover, relates to the hero's consciousness not from the standpoint of its objective makeup, its validity as an object, but from the standpoint of its subjectively *lived* unity (ibid., p.89).

Bakhtin emphasizes the need in aesthetic experience to find a lived experience, which involves a meeting of the other as *other*, the essence of the subjectively lived standpoint. If I am confined to inner self-reflection, if I remain without that fundamental element of otherness, if I fail to let the other's words call me to myself, I remain trapped in what he calls a 'spurious' form of subjectivity. And he describes how it is in meeting with otherness that form is given to the soul (ibid., p.101). Thus subjectivity is spurious if lived only from within; to become a subject, otherness is required.

Interestingly, Bakhtin takes us back to the origins of the aesthetic experience when he describes how it is in the relationship at a bodily and verbal level with the mother and those close to him, who 'sculpt' the infant, that one first meets otherness and also the first forms of subjective awareness:

> The plastic value of my outer body has been as it were sculpted for me by the manifold acts of other people in relation to me, acts performed intermittently throughout my life: acts of concern for me, acts of love, acts that recognize my value. In fact as soon as a human being begins to experience himself from within, he at once meets with acts of recognition and love that come to him from outside – from his mother, from others who are close to him. The child receives all initial determinations of himself and of his body from his mother's lips and from the lips of those who are close to him. It is from their lips, in the emotional-volitional tones of their love, that the child hears and begins to acknowledge his own *proper name* and the names of all the features pertaining to his body and to his inner states and experiences. The words of a loving human being are the first and most authoritative words about him; they are the words that for the first time determine his personality *from outside*, the words that *come to meet* his distinct inner sensation of himself, giving it a form and a name in which, for the first time, he finds himself and becomes aware of himself as a *something* ... This love that shapes a human being from outside throughout his life – his mother's love and the love of others around him – this love gives body to his inner body ... it ... makes him the possessor of that body's potential value – a value capable of being actualised only by another human being. (ibid., pp.49–51)

Bakhtin's vivid descriptions of the early foundations of the subject's life lead on to considering evidence about the relationship between subject and other from infant research. This evidence shows that from the beginning of life the infant is oriented to his environment, and that he learns through relating to others in what infant researchers call an 'intersubjective' perspective. This implies that the infant gradually emerges as a subject, with an increasing awareness of his own and other people's subjective experiences, as he develops what Stern calls 'an organising subjective perspective' (Stern, 1985, p.135). The latter is built up through the relationship with the caretakers and through interaction around significant social everyday events. Stern considers that 'episodic memory' is crucial for understanding how the subjective perspective is organized. Episodic memory is:

memory for real-life experiences occurring in real time. These episodes of lived experience range from the trivial – what happened at breakfast this morning, what I ate, in what order, where I was sitting – to the more psychological meaningful – what I experienced when they told me my father had a stroke. Episodic memory has the great advantage ... of being able to include actions, perceptions and affects as the main ingredients of attributes of a remembered episode ... The basic memorial unit is the episode, a small but coherent chunk of lived experience. (ibid., pp.94–5)

Stern basically operates on the assumption that the world of the infant is usually constituted from the ordinary events of the day, not from the exceptional ones. Exceptional moments are probably no more than 'superb yet slightly atypical examples of the ordinary' (ibid., p.192).

This focus on the social subjective event or experience as proving the basic framework for the subjective world of the infant corresponds to my own notion, based on working with disorganized families, of the role of what I have called the 'work of the day' (Kennedy et al., 1987; Kennedy, 1997) as providing the basic organising structure or template for daily living. This concept does not refer to everything that happens in the day, but refers only to those events which are significant in some way, or have precipitated some kind of thought process and/or action. Thus it would include unsolved problems, major worries, overwhelming experiences, undigested thoughts, forbidden or unsolved thoughts, what has been rejected and suppressed and what has been set in motion in the unconscious by the activity of the preconscious and consciousness. It refers to all the significant, and at times deceptively indifferent, thoughts, feelings and experiences that have occupied us during the day, and provide the raw material for thinking and dreaming. The work of the day is what gives material for thought and provides the basic framework for living together.

Much of this work carries on automatically, without the subject being particularly aware of its regular occurrence, or of its 'everydayness'. It is normally taken for granted, yet it is far from simple, as one can see from working with disturbed families, when such work breaks down. The work of the day is normally focused around essential activities and events such as eating, sleeping and working. Normally one performs the activities of the day without thinking about their basic structure; but in many people who come for treatment, including those in psychoanalysis, the things that most people do without thinking are charged with emotion and conflict, and this involves a breakdown in the continuity and consistency of daily life, or what Winnicott called the 'holding environment'.

The work of the day requires a constant amount of organization in order for it to be maintained; that is, ongoing maintenance activity. Furthermore, the work of the day provides 'contact points' for subjects, where they may encounter one another, however briefly and fleetingly.

Following the building up of the early psychic organization, Stern describes the next development as a 'quantum leap', when the infant discovers that he has a mind and that other people have minds. It is at this point, at around six months of age, that one can begin to think of the infant having a developed sense of relatedness with others, and the beginnings of the capacity to share experiences with the other. He describes how the infant enters into a new domain of 'intersubjective relatedness' (Stern, 1985, p.125).

Trevarthan and Hubley (1978) defined intersubjectivity as a 'deliberate sought sharing of experiences about events and things'. Though they were influenced by philosophical thinking, in particular that of Hegel's notion of the development of self-consciousness, it should be said that their concept of intersubjectivity is quite different from that of Hegel. In particular they do not develop the role of desire, which is an essential element of Hegel's thought. Indeed, one could say that the term 'intersubjective' is used by a variety of thinkers in a variety of different ways, depending on the model of a subject used and the way that the social field is, or is not, taken into consideration.

The infant researchers are essentially describing empirical evidence for intersubjective relatedness, where the infant is shown to be immediately oriented towards the other, making discriminations between self and other from the beginning. It does not develop a sense of self and then relate to the other; rather, a pattern of self relating to other is built up at once, within a social context of ordinary significant events. Intersubjective in this context refers to the capacity to share experiences with the other, and to have some notion that the other has a mind of his own with which experiences can be shared. This forms the basis for the notion of intersubjectivity put forward by intersubjective psychoanalytic thinkers such as Atwood, Mitchell, Ogden and Stolorow. Their general approach is different from, for example, that of Lacan whose notion of intersubjectivity is very much linked to Hegel's thought as interpreted by Kojève. It is different again from the notion of intersubjectivity described by the social thought of Alfred Schutz, to which I shall turn later, who extends the sociological thought of Weber. Schutz points towards a much more complex notion of intersubjectivity than is implied in considering it as merely concerned with the sharing of experiences. He describes, for example, how one needs to examine, in any intersubjective relation, the contexts of meaning surrounding the relation, as well as the relationship between one's subjective understanding of the other person's experiences and one's own experiences, the nature of the orientation to the other, how one understands the other and is affected by the other, and the nature of the social world. Such a comprehensive view of intersubjective understanding can be applied to the psychoanalytic situation, where there is a complex interaction between the different subjective positions of analyst and patient.

There are obviously similarities between different views of inter-subjectivity. But before considering the issue further, I think it important to examine more formally and in detail the nature of social structure, which underpins the relations between subjects, and which, in my view, has often been neglected in psychoanalytic thinking. In order to do this I have made a selection of various thinkers on sociology, social anthropology and social psychology. Despite their different perspectives, I hope to indicate that there is some common ground between them. My examination of the social field will culminate in the thought of Mead, who, together with Dewey, offered, in my view, a radical picture of the human subject. As I shall discuss towards the end of the chapter, of psychoanalytic thinkers, it is only Winnicott who approaches similar territory. Mead's thought will lead on to consideration of the location of the human subject, first examined at the beginning of the book.

SOCIAL STRUCTURE

In adult life, what may be critical for the subject is where they are placed in the social field, what position they take up at any moment, or, as Lévi-Strauss put it, 'men ... are distributed among different segments of society, each occupying a particular position in the social structure' (Lévi-Strauss, 1962, p.77). At the very least, social structure provides a sort of scaffolding for the subject. Obviously, family relations would seem to be fundamental in orientating the subject; that is, how they are placed within the family structure, how they position themselves with respect to Oedipal relations and how they relate to the family's present and past is fundamental in this respect. I have also suggested how the work of the day provides a framework for the day-to-day life of the subject But it is also a commonplace of institutional psychology that being part of a larger social structure, such as being on a committee or merely being part of an institution has complex effects on one's functioning. The way that an organization is structured affects the psychology of the individual. For example, if an organization has a central organising committee that keeps changing its composition, then no real change in the organization may occur, leading to all kinds of complex feelings and actions in individuals. In group therapy, the place people occupy in the room, the chairs they sit in – that is, their place in the social field or 'matrix' – is indicative of their own subjective position within the group, a kind of subjective 'marker'. One could thus see social structure as intimately involving issues to do with subjectivity.

In order to begin to clarify the role of social structure in the life of the subject, I would suggest that it is important to examine some of the many notions of social structure described by social anthropologists and sociologists. One can learn from these disciplines about the logic of the social structure, and how subjectivity comes on the one hand to be marked out and confined within social structure, and on the other hand allowed free play. I would also suggest that, in general, ideas about social structure seem to have evolved from a view that it is fairly fixed, with a fairly rigid relationship between the individual and society, to more recent postmodern views, and beyond, where there is a much more 'fluid' and 'playful' relationship between the individual and society. It is also my contention that in the thought of Durkheim, as in that of Freud, one can see both the fixed and more fluid relationship between the individual and the social.

Social structure can be defined in a number of ways, though, as Lévi-Strauss emphasized (1958, p.277), the term refers to a group of problems with a wide scope and imprecise definition, while at the same time there exist very different interpretations of these problems among different thinkers. Edmund Leach defines social structure as an expression

> used by social and cultural anthropologists in a variety of senses. British social anthropologists ordinarily follow Radcliffe-Brown. The society as a whole is envisaged as a kind of organism in which the various institutions are articulated together to form a functioning whole. The social structure is the persisting framework of such a self-perpetuating system. An approximate analogy is that the relationship between the social structure and the society as a whole is comparable to the relationship between the bony skeleton of a living mammal and its total bodily form. This use of the word 'structure' has very little in common with the ... 'structure' of Lévi-Strauss, which is concerned with the abstract (mathematical) ordering of patterns rather then their concrete manifestations. (Leach, 1982, p.237)

Lévi-Strauss himself, being a rationalist and not an empiricist, considered that, in contrast to Radcliffe-Brown's ideas, social structure had nothing to do with empirical reality (Lévi-Strauss, 1958, p.279). He distinguished between social structure and social relations, the latter consisting of the actual network of relations between people, while structure referred to a more abstract level of understanding, involving the way that elements of a system interrelated. A structural model for Lévi-Strauss should be constituted so as to make immediately intelligible all the observed facts, but the social structures are not observable elements as such; they are unconscious and are inferred, abstract elements such as binary oppositions between elements. The task of anthropology for him is not to look for conscious phenomena but to study their unconscious infrastructure.

Lévi-Strauss' many works are rich with elaborate explanatory schemes for understanding social organizations. He shows how so-called 'primitive' men have elaborated complicated ways of understanding the world, on a par with anything so-called 'civilized' men have thought up. The heterogeneous beliefs and customs once arbitrarily collected together under the heading of 'totemism' concerning, for example, myths and kinship systems, are linked to classificatory schemes which allow the natural and social worlds (or 'nature and culture') to be grasped as an organized whole.

What appears central to Lévi-Strauss' conception of the 'savage mind' is how the sociological field is organized as a system of differentiating features. Primitive societies, in his view, classify the world by using a particular kind of logic based on elaborate systems of significant differences and binary oppositions, such as differences between the raw and the cooked, birth and death, the individual and the collective, one kind of flower as opposed to another which may represent different sections of a social grouping, one set of colours as opposed to another set, etc.

> [T]he practico-theoretical logics governing the life and thought of so-called primitive societies are shaped by the insistence of differentiation ... [O]n the theoretical as well as the practical plane, the existence of differentiating features is of much greater importance than their content. Once in evidence, they form a system which can be employed as a grid used to decipher a text, whose original unintelligibility gives it the appearance of an uninterrupted flow. The grid makes it possible to introduce divisions and contrasts, in other words the formal conditions necessary for a significant message to be conveyed ... [A]ny system of differentiating features, provided that it is a system, permits the organization

of a sociological field which historical and demographic evolution are transforming and which is hence composed of a theoretically unlimited series of different contents.

The logical principle is always to be *able* to oppose terms ... [T]he systems of naming and classifying ... are codes suitable for conveying messages which can be transposed into other codes. (Lévi-Strauss, 1962, p.75).

The function of the system is 'to guarantee the convertibility of ideas between different levels of social reality' (ibid., p.76).

All the various elements of the social structure can be seen as comprising a vast group or 'system of transformations' between different elements and levels. Conceptual schemes made up of groups of differentiating features form the basic 'structures' which make up the whole system. While concerned to elaborate the various elementary and complex structures which make up the social organization, Lévi-Strauss, rather similar here to the thought of Talcott Parsons, also emphasized that what was in question was a total system, which ethnologists in the past had artificially tried to pull to pieces, in order tc conform to their own world view.

Lévi-Strauss further describes a form of activity, or the 'science of the concrete', which underpins the way that primitive man goes about making sense of the world, a form of thinking and creating that remains with us. He describes this as 'bricolage', a kind of rough and ready way of using anything that comes to hand in order to build up structures. Bricolage is, as it were, the more rough and playful counterpart to Lévi-Strauss' severe intellectual approach to his field of study. The 'bricoleur' is

> adept at performing a large number of diverse tasks; but, unlike the engineer, he does not subordinate each of them to the availability of raw materials and tools conceived and procured for the purpose of the project. His universe of instruments is closed and the rules of the game are always to make do with 'whatever is at hand', that is to say with a set of tools and materials which is always finite and is also heterogeneous. (ibid., p.17)

Lévi-Strauss' classificatory scheme comprising an elaborate system of differences and oppositions, brought together by whatever is at hand, contrasts with the empirical approach to the field, which would, for example, look at the way a society is built up into an organization by taking the basic unit of structure as the family group, and then relations between families, tribes, etc. Lévi-Strauss, while not ignoring these groupings, would put them within a wider model of more general relationships, or rather into a basic logical scheme; for, in his approach, he claims to be looking for what he would consider as the universal elements of the human mind. For example, he writes about 'atoms of kinship', unconscious social structures, rather than, say, family units, as basic elements of the social system.

Lévi-Strauss was of course greatly influenced by structural linguistics. His emphasis on the role of systems of differences and oppositions in organising the social field is linked to the way that structural linguistics emphasizes, for example, the way that the language system is built up of a network of differences between signs. Moreover, for Lévi-Strauss, structural linguistics 'shifts from the study of *conscious* linguistic phenomena to study of their *unconscious* infrastructure ... it does not treat *terms* as independent entities, taking instead as its basis of analysis the *relations* between terms ... it introduces the concept of *system* ... [and it] aims at discovering general laws' (Lévi-Strauss, 1958, p.33).

Edmund Leach (1982, p.113) extends the thought of Lévi-Strauss from primitive societies to our own, when, for example, he proposes that all human interactions can be broken down into elements of binary exchange, that is into paired oppositions, such as dirt/purity, sickness/holiness, potency/impotence, etc. One could add here from psychoanalytic thought oppositions such as subject/other, identity/ difference, and conscious/unconscious.*

Defining the term 'structure' in general terms and in relation to the conceptual scheme I have outlined, Lévi-Strauss suggests that:

> First, the structure exhibits the characteristics of a system. It is made up of ... several elements, none of which can undergo a change without effecting changes in all the other elements.
>
> Second, for any given model there should be a possibility of ordering a series of transformations resulting in a group of models of the same type.
>
> Third, the above properties make it possible to predict how the model will react if one or more of its elements are submitted to certain modifications.
>
> Finally, the model should be constituted so as to make immediately intelligible all the observed facts. (Lévi-Strauss, 1958, pp.279–80)

---

* Matte-Blanco has discussed the role of binary logic in psychoanalysis, as described lucidly by Rayner (1995).

Lévi-Strauss' emphasis on how unconscious social structures regulate social relations using the binary laws of language is similar to the thought of Lacan, when he describes how chains of meaning cut across the subject in symbolic circuits. Lacan emphasizes how the subject-to-be already has a place in the kinship structure before he is born. He is already situated as an element in a complicated, mostly unconscious, network of symbols, the 'symbolic order'. It is therefore important to understand the fundamental family relationships that structure the union of the analytic patient's parents, the family constellation, what one could call the subject's pre-history, which help to shape his destiny and with which he has to deal.

I think it important to add in this context how Enid Balint described that elements of the subject's pre-history can be unconsciously communicated across generations. Such a form of communication is most commonly seen in the children and grandchildren of Holocaust victims, but can also be seen in other situations. Balint showed how certain symptoms of one of her patients were related to the patient's mother's traumatic history of being abandoned as a baby, and this had been unconsciously communicated to the patient. Balint shows how there are times when a set of experiences is unconsciously communicated to the child as an alien formation, a piece of the mother's experiences, or her own mother's experiences, that have not been metabolized. The child then has these experiences by proxy, as it were; but, as they do not belong to them, they are not connected to the rest of their experiences and they may then form a nucleus of symptoms, which becomes 'like a foreign body inside the ego or superego. This foreign body may have to remain in place until it can be dealt with by its "host" when he or she is strong enough to do what the original recipient of the trauma could not do ... Such a chain of events means that one generation has to resolve traumata that another generation has failed to' (Balint, 1993, pp.117–18).

One can thus see how unconscious communication can occur in subtle ways between parents and between generations, and that chains of meaning can keep circulating in the social structure, as it were, until they are dealt with.

Derrida interprets Lévi-Strauss' notion of structure as consisting of a fundamental and radical shift in how one understands the human sciences, one which allows a considerable amount of 'play'. Derrida considers that Lévi-Strauss' concept of structure breaks with the traditional notion of structure underpinning western thought. Derrida's essay in fact takes one back to the issue concerning the centre of the subject, or the lack of a centre, tackled in Chapter 1.

Derrida describes how in traditional western thought, the function
of the 'centre' was used as a reference point in order to

> orient, balance, and organize the structure – one cannot in fact
> conceive of an unorganized structure – but above all to make sure
> that the organising principle of the structure would limit what we
> might call the *play* of the structure. By orienting and organising the
> coherence of the system, the centre of a structure permits the play
> of its elements inside the total form. And even today the notion of
> a structure lacking any centre represents the unthinkable itself.
> Nevertheless, the centre also closes off the play which it opens up
> and makes possible ... The concept of centred structure is in fact
> the concept of a play based on a fundamental ground, a play
> constituted on the basis of a fundamental immobility and a
> reassuring certitude, which itself is beyond the reach of play.
> (Derrida, 1967, pp.278–9)

With the thought of Nietzsche, Freud and Heidegger in particular,
Derrida points to a 'rupture', and a 'disruption' in the notion of a
centralized structure, a process of 'decentring' began to take place, and
with it a new form of discoursing about the world (ibid., p.280).

> Where and how does this decentering, this thinking the structurality
> of structure, occur? It would be somewhat naive to refer to an event, a
> doctrine, or an author in order to designate this occurrence. It is no
> doubt part of the totality of our era, our own, but still it has always
> already begun to proclaim itself and begun to work. Nevertheless, if
> we wished to choose several 'names', as indications only, and to recall
> those authors in whose discourse this occurrence has kept most
> closely to its most radical formulation, we doubtless would have to
> cite the Nietzschean critique of metaphysics, the critique of the con-
> cepts of Being and truth, for which were substituted the concepts of
> play, interpretation, and sign (sign without present truth); the Freud-
> ian critique of self-presence, that is the critique of consciousness, of
> the subject, of self-identity and of self-proximity or self-possession;
> and, more radically, the Heideggerean destruction of metaphysics, of
> onto-theology, of the determination of Being as presence. (ibid.)

Derrida then uses Lévi-Strauss, who highlights the issue of the
changed nature of structure in a particularly cogent way, to illustrate
how this new form of discourse takes shape. Lévi-Strauss' use of
bricolage results in a form of decentred discourse on myths which is
itself a myth. As Derrida writes:

Lévi-Strauss's remarkable endeavour does not simply consist in proposing ... a structural science of myths, and of mythological activity.
His endeavour also appears ... to have the status which he accords to
his own discourse on myths, to what he calls his 'mythologicals'
[mythologiques]. It is here that his discourse on the myth reflects on
itself and criticizes itself. And this moment, this critical period, is
evidently of concern to all the languages which share the field of the
human sciences. What does Lévi-Strauss say of his 'mythologicals'? It
is here that we rediscover the mythopoetical virtue of bricolage. In
effect, what appears most fascinating in this critical search for a new
status of discourse is the stated abandonment of all reference to a
centre, to a subject, to a privileged reference, to an origin, or to an
absolute archia. (ibid., p.286)

Derrida then cites as evidence for his interpretation of Lévi-Strauss
the way that he uses, in his book The Raw and the Cooked, one key
myth, the Bororo myth, simply as a way of discoursing about myths.

From the very start, Lévi-Strauss recognizes that the Bororo myth
which he employs in his book as the 'reference myth' does not
merit this name and this treatment. The name is specious and the
use of the myth improper. This myth deserves no more than any
other its referential privilege: 'In fact, [quoting Lévi-Strauss] the
Bororo myth, which I shall refer to from now on as the key myth,
is, as I shall try to show, simply a transformation, to a greater or
lesser extent, of other myths originating either in the same society
or in a neighbouring or remote societies. I could, therefore, have
legitimately taken as my starting point any one representative
myth of the group. From this point of view, the key myth is
interesting not because it is typical, but rather because of its
irregular position within the group.' (ibid.)

Derrida then points out how there is no unity or absolute source
of this myth; and how this structural discourse on myth is itself
'mythomorphic'. There is no hidden central unity behind this kind
of discourse, once the analysis of the myths has taken place. If there
is any myth it is that of the existence of an underlying centre. In
Derrida's view, this form of discourse, without the restraining
influence of the centre, opens up the field of the human science to
play, seen as a 'field of infinite substitutions' (ibid., p.289).
    With this new concept of interpreting the nature of structure,
Derrida also argues that the appearance of new structures is to be
understood in a new way, as a kind of rupture with the past. To

illustrate this view, Derrida cites how Lévi-Strauss considered that the birth of language must have happened as one sudden rupture with the past, what one might call a qualitative rather than a quantitative leap:

> Whatever may have been the moment and the circumstances of its appearance on the scale of animal life, language could only have been born in one fell swoop. Things could not have set about acquiring signification progressively. Following a transformation the study of which is not the concern of the social sciences, but rather of biology and psychology, a transition came about from a stage where nothing had a meaning to another where everything possessed it. (Lévi-Strauss, 1950, p. xivi)

Such a view of how structures change or come into being is paralleled by Foucault's study of history (Foucault, 1969), also based on the notion of a decentred subject. Foucault sees history in terms of its discontinuities, ruptures, breaks, mutations and transformations, rather than the traditional view of history as looking for succession, synthesis and continuities.

Thus one can see how the notion of social structure developed by Lévi-Strauss and interpreted by Derrida is one where there is no fixed centre, nor is the relation between the individual and the social order a fixed one. There is, one might say, a looseness in the social bond. On the one hand, Lévi-Strauss puts forward a comprehensive structural analysis of social life, yet relations between elements of the system are constantly shifting, changing, and being transformed. This model of social structure would seem to link up with what has been proposed about how subjects interact in the social field; how, for example, identities can merge and shift in various symbolic circuits, in a constant play of subjects.

The question of the looseness of the social bond is developed even further in more recent postmodern thought, such as that of Lyotard in his seminal book *The Postmodern Condition* (1979), which is heavily influenced by Wittgenstein's notion of language games. Lyotard's main concern is to examine the condition of knowledge in the most highly developed societies. He uses the word 'postmodern' to describe that condition. It

> designates the state of our culture following the transformations which, since the end of the nineteenth century, have altered the game rules for science, literature, and the arts ... [His] study will place these transformations in the context of the crisis of narratives. (Lyotard, 1979, p.xxiii)

His working hypothesis is that the status of knowledge is altered as societies enter the post-industrial age and cultures enter the postmodern age, with the extensive use of the media and new technologies as the predominant means of communication.

In order to discuss knowledge in contemporary society, he examines, rather briefly and at times cursorily, some previous modernist attempts to look at society's functioning. He uses the term 'modern'

> to designate any science which designates itself with reference to a metadiscourse ... making an explicit appeal to some grand narrative, such as the dialectics of the Spirit, the hermeneutics of meaning, the emancipation of the rational or working subject, or the creation of wealth. (ibid.)

In place of 'grand narratives' he will propose the use of 'little narratives', networks of language games. His critique of modern thought focuses on two main paradigms – the thought which looks at society as a whole system, as suggested by that of Talcott Parsons and then developed by systems theorists, and that which sees society as divided in two, such as Marxist thought.

Parsons conceived society as a whole self-regulating system. His early thought was based on a reading of the classics of sociology, such as Durkheim, Weber and Pareto, from whom he evolved a theory of 'social action', how the individual acted in the social field. He defines this theory in, for example, an essay on 'Psychoanalysis and the social structure', where he sees psychoanalysis, like his own theory, as a theory of action which accounts for human motivation and meaning:

> This theory [of action] conceives the behaving individual or actor as operating in a situation which is given independently of his goals and wishes, but, within the limits of that situation and using those potentialities which are subject to his control, actively oriented to the attainment of a system of goals and wishes. Studying the processes of action, the scheme takes the point of view of the meaning of the various elements of the system to the actor. (Parsons, 1954, p.125)

Subsequently influenced by, for example, cybernetics, as well as the thought of Durkheim, which emphasized the separateness of social facts, Parsons developed an increasingly elaborate theory of how the whole social system functioned. This notion of the role of the system differs from that of, for example, Lévi-Strauss, by putting much more emphasis on issues of motivation, regulation and synthesis; that is, it is a kind of theory still based on the old notion of a centre. As Parsons wrote, in the same essay from which I have just quoted:

> It is essential from the point of view of social science to treat the social system as a distinct and independent entity which must be studied and analyzed on its own level, not as a composite resultant of the actions of the component individuals alone ... In treating the social system as a system, structural categories have proved to be essential in the same sense as in the biological sciences, and presumably also in psychology ... [W]hat is meant by social structure is a system of patterned expectations of the behavior of individuals who occupy particular statuses in the social system. Such a system of patterned legitimate expectations is called by sociologists a system of roles. In so far as a cluster of such roles is of strategic significance to the social system, the complex of patterns which define expected behavior in them may be referred to as an institution. For example, in so far as the behavior of spouses in their mutual relationships is governed by socially sanctioned legitimate expectations in such a sense that departure from these patterns will call forth reactions of moral disapproval or overt sanctions, we speak of the institution of marriage. Institutional structures in this sense are the fundamental element of the structure of the social system. They constitute relatively stable crystallizations of behavioral forces in such a way that action can be sufficiently regularized so as to be able to be comparable with the functional requirements of a society. (ibid., pp.126–7)

Lyotard criticizes the Parsonian emphasis on the regulation of the whole system, as well as those such as Luhmann (1984) who have developed a systems theory based on that of Parsons, as being too 'optimistic' and too obsessed with the performance of the whole 'rational' system at the expense of individuals and groups, for

> it corresponds to the stabilization of the growth economics and societies of abundance under the aegis of the moderate welfare state. In the work of contemporary German theorists, *systemtheorie* is technocratic, even cynical not to mention despairing: the harmony between the needs and hopes of individuals or groups and the functions guaranteed by the system is now only a secondary component of its functioning. The true goal of the system, the reason it programs itself like a computer, is the optimization of the global relationship between input and output – in other words, performativity. (Lyotard, 1979, p.11)

Lyotard also criticizes the Marxist explanations of how society functions and the function of the knowledge that can be produced by society and acquired from it. 'This model was born of the struggles accompanying the process of capitalism's encroachment upon traditional civil societies ... in countries with liberal or advanced liberal management, the struggles and their instruments have been translated into regulators of the system; in communist countries, the totalizing model and its totalitarian effect have made a comeback in the name of Marxism itself, and the struggles in question have simply been deprived of the right to exist' (ibid., p.13).

Lyotard considers that even the more recent developments of Marxist thought, such as critical theory, lost the basic social foundation by blurring the principle of division and class struggle to the point of losing its radicality.

However, I think it is worth emphasizing that Marx did provide one of the earliest and most powerful models of social structure, one which has considerably influenced many sociologists, including Durkheim and Weber, and which, in my view, cannot be so easily dismissed. Thus, in *The German Ideology* of 1846, which laid the basis for the subsequent Marxist theory of society, Marx and Engels, prefiguring Wittgenstein's notion of 'forms of life', laid down the foundations for a 'materialist conception of history', based on how individuals' lives are organized around the production of their means of subsistence.

The mode of production ... is a definite form of activity of these individuals, a definite form of expressing their life, a definite *mode of life* on their part. What they are ... coincides with their production, both with *what* they produce and with how they produce. Hence what individuals are depends on the material conditions of their production. (Marx and Engels, 1846, pp.31-2).

Individuals who are productively active in a definite way enter into definite social and political relations. Production is connected to the social and political structure:

The social structure and the state are continually evolving out of the life-process of definite individuals, however, of these individuals, not as they may appear in their own or other people's imagination, but as they *actually* are, i.e. as they act, produce materially, and hence as they work under definite material limits, presuppositions and conditions independent of their will ... The production of ideas, of conceptions, of consciousness, is at first directly interwoven with the material activity and the material intercourse of men – the language of real life ... Men are the producers of their conceptions, ideas, etc., that is, real, active men, as they are conditioned by a definite development of their productive forces and of the intercourse corresponding to these. (ibid., p. 36)

Human thought is thus founded in human social activity. But, as Marx and Engels argue, man becomes alienated from the products of his social activity in capitalist society, they belong to 'another', the capitalist. Being alienated from his productive activity, man becomes both alienated from his own self, and also alienated from his fellow men in his community. As Marx develops both in *The German Ideology*, his previous earlier writings, and later in *Das Kapital*, instead of men having fulfilling human social relationships in their community, the result of the capitalist social structure is that men have relationships with each other through commodities, inanimate objects. This world of objects through which men now relate produces a 'fetishistic' form of social relationship; it as if, by 'magic', the objects rule the producers, not vice versa.

A commodity is ... a mysterious thing, simply because in it the social character of men's labour appears to them as an objective character stamped upon the product of that labour; because the relation of the producers to the sum total of their own labour is presented to them as a social relation, existing not between themselves, but between the products of their labour. (Marx, 1867, p.7)

Such passages from the thought of Marx are of course open to many kinds of interpretation. It is not my aim here to offer a detailed critique of Marxist theory; however, I would suggest as relevant to my argument that Marx is pointing towards how subjective life is both dependent on social structure and can be transformed in various ways by that structure. In particular, he shows how man as subject can be transformed into a mere object or commodity when he is cut off from his own products, an issue to which I shall return when considering the relation between subject and object relations. Marxist theory is thus in part a theory about the loss of subjectivity. Of course, incorporated into it is a utopian solution to that loss, through revolution, etc., which is of less concern to my theme.

To return to Lyotard, having pointed to how modernist theories of the social bond as being no longer relevant to contemporary society, he puts forward his own postmodernist interpretation of social relations, which takes account of the new forms of communication, involving computers and the media, which have transformed who has access to information.

Each self now

> exists in a fabric of relations that is now more complex and mobile
> than ever before. Young or old, man or woman, rich or poor, a person
> is always located at 'nodal points' of specific communication circuits,
> however tiny these may be. Or better, one is always located at a post
> through which various kinds of messages pass. No one, not even the
> least privileged among us, is ever entirely powerless over the mean-
> ings that traverse and position him at the post of sender, addressee, or
> referent. One's mobility in relation to these language games effects
> (language games, of course, are what this is all about) is tolerable, at
> least within certain limits. (Lyotard, 1979, p.15)

He uses language games as his general methodological approach,
though he does not claim that the entirety of social relations are of this
sort. But he does claim that

> language games are the minimum required for society to exist: even
> before he is born, if only by virtue of the name he is given, the human
> child is already positioned as the referent in the story recounted by
> those around him, in relation to which he will inevitably chart his
> course. Or more simply still, the question of the social bond, insofar
> as it is a question, is itself a language game, the game of inquiry. It
> immediately positions the person who asks, as well as the addressee
> and the referent asked about: it is already the social bond. (ibid.)

This view resembles Lacan's emphasis on how the signifier forms
symbolic circuits cutting across the subject; and how the child, the
subject-to-be, already has a place, sometimes a name, before he is
born. It also resembles the thought of, for example, Ricoeur where he
emphasizes the role of narratives in organising one's subjective life.
However, Lyotard takes further than Lacan, Lévi-Strauss and Ricoeur
the way that the social field is 'atomized' into flexible networks of
language games. Narrative knowledge becomes the key form of
knowledge. 'The social subject itself seems to dissolve in [the]
dissemination of language games. The social bond is linguistic, but it
is not woven into a single thread. It is a fabric formed by the
intersection of at least two (and in reality an indeterminate number) of
language games, obeying different rules' (ibid., p.40).
On the one hand, it would seem to me that Lyotard's analysis of
contemporary social structure is accurate with regard to its description
of how the social field is now atomized, or fragmented, into multiple
networks. It has been argued earlier that the mind itself is a kind of

amalgamation of many fragments, narrative threads and voices, with no central and controlling narrative. However, that does not necessarily imply that there is no place for some kind unification or integration of narratives, where, for example, subjects encounter one another in the social field. To eliminate modernist thought and grand narrative at the expense of the little narrative, would seem to imply only retaining the 'Many' at the expense of the 'One'. As argued previously, following Habermas, one needs to avoid a polarization of viewpoints between the one and the many. Instead of invoking plural histories and forms of life as opposed to a singular world history and life-world, and language games, or multiple narratives as opposed to univocally fixed meanings, one needs to look at both aspects of the one and the many, or at the interplay between the grand and the little narratives. Looking at this sort of interplay may help to avoid the danger that comes with Lyotard's approach, that any narrative is as good as any other and that one is left merely with many fragments of knowledge with no possibility of bringing them together in any way. Furthermore, I would suggest that Lyotard's approach also leaves confused the issue of how and where the individual is differentiated from others in the social field. I would agree that the individual can be located at 'nodal points' of narrative circuits, but if there is too much atomization, there seems little place for any sense of identity, any sense of organization of the subject; in this model of social relations, the relation between the individual and the social structure would seem to be too fluid.

In order to rescue some sense of organization of social relations, and to provide further foundation to my own concept of a subjective organization, I will look at some sociological thinkers to whom, at least in *The Postmodern Condition*, Lyotard pays little attention, beginning with one of the founders of modern sociology, Durkheim.

THE INDIVIDUAL AND THE COLLECTIVE

One of Durkheim's consistent preoccupations was with the nature of the relationship between the individual and the collective, starting with his early work, *The Division of Labour in Society* (1893). This book laid down the basis for much of his subsequent sociological thought. In his last major work, *The Elementary Forms of Religious Life* (1912), he returned to the relationship between the individual and collective, elaborating on his earlier thought. Though he emphasized that the realm of the social has its own laws, in my view he did not underestimate the intimate relationship between the individual and society, how society and the individual intermingle. I suspect that there has been insufficient attention paid to this aspect of Durkheim's thought.

In *The Division of Labour*, Durkheim states that his aim is to 'penetrate certain facts of social structure profound enough to be objects of the understanding and consequently of science ... The question that has been the starting point for our study has been that of the connection between the individual personality and social solidarity. How does it come about that the individual, whilst becoming more autonomous, depends ever more closely upon society? How can he become at the same time more of an individual and yet more linked to society?' (Durkheim, 1893, pp.xxix–xxx).

Already in this early work, as Giddens (1972, p.6) has emphasized, Durkheim was concerned about the development of the individual, or the process of the growth of individuation and how it is linked to changes in society. Social solidarity, the linking up of people with one another, can be seen in various areas, such as in marriage, the professions and in the wider social field. While Durkheim sees solidarity as a social fact, it is dependent on the constitution of the individuals who make up society, and also how these individuals relate to one another. The book is concerned to distinguish between two basic forms of solidarity – mechanical solidarity, or solidarity which unites people through similarities, and which formed the basis of early societies; and organic solidarity, arising from the division of labour, which assumes that people are different from one another and which is the basis of the modern, differentiated social order.

Each form of solidarity involves a different relationship between the individual and the collective. Thus, in mechanical solidarity the collective envelops individuals; in addition, societies dominated by this form of solidarity have a primitive form of social structure made up of similar segments, which keeps the individual more firmly in the grip of the collective. That is, the social structure corresponding to mechanical solidarity is made up of homogeneous segments similar to one another, like liquids merging into one another. As societies develop and as the division of labour arises, with increasing specialization, they gradually lose this segmentary form of structure and become increasingly organized and differentiated. With organic solidarity, the collective leaves uncovered a larger part of the individual's own territory, who thus becomes increasingly differentiated as an individual:

> The solidarity that arises from similarities is at its *maximum* when the collective consciousness completely envelops our total consciousness, coinciding with it at every point. At that moment our individuality is zero. That individuality cannot arise until the

community fills us less completely. Here there are two opposing forces, the one centripetal, the other centrifugal, which cannot increase at the same time. We cannot ourselves develop simultaneously in two so opposing directions. If we have a strong inclination to think and act for ourselves we cannot be strongly inclined to think and act like other people. If the ideal is to create for ourselves a special, personal image, this cannot mean to be like everyone else. Moreover, at the very moment when this solidarity exerts its effect, our personality, it may be said by definition, disappears, for we are no longer ourselves, but a collective being.

The social molecules that can only cohere in this one manner cannot therefore move as a unity in so far as they lack any movement of their own, as do the molecules of inorganic bodies. This is why we suggest that this kind of solidarity should be called mechanical. The word does not mean that the solidarity is produced by mechanical and artificial means. We only use this term for it by analogy with the cohesion that links together the elements of raw materials, in contrast with that which encompasses the unity of living organisms. What finally justifies the use of this term is the fact that the bond that thus unites the individual with society is completely analogous to that which links the thing to the person. The individual consciousness, considered from this viewpoint, is simply a dependency of the collective type, and follows all its motions, just as the object possessed follows those which its owner imposes upon it. In societies where this solidarity is highly developed the individual ... does not belong to himself; he is literally a thing at the disposal of society. (Durkheim, 1893, pp.84–5).

This form of solidarity contrasts with organic solidarity, where, due to the division of labour which creates ties of cooperation between individuals and occupational interdependence, the individuals are distinguished from one another. With organic solidarity, there is increasing individuation; individuals are not so absorbed into the life of the collective, and there is more room for the free play of individuality and initiative.

Society becomes more effective in moving in concert, at the same time as each of its elements has more movements that are peculiarly its own. This solidarity resembles that observed in the higher animals. In fact each organ has its own special characteristics and autonomy, yet the greater the unity of the organism, the more marked the individualisation of its parts. Using this analogy, we propose to call 'organic' the solidarity that is due to the division of labour. (ibid., p.85)

It can be seen that in order to define the way that the individual relates to society, Durkheim makes a distinction between two forms of consciousness, which runs through the whole of the book and much of his subsequent thought, and is developed further in *The Elementary Forms of Religious Life*. First of all, he writes that:

> The totality of beliefs and sentiments common to the average members of a society forms a determinate system with a life of its own. It can be termed the collective or common consciousness. Undoubtedly the substratum of this consciousness does not consist of a single organ. By definition it is diffused over society as a whole, but nonetheless possesses specific characteristics that make it a distinctive reality. In fact it is independent of the particular conditions in which individuals find themselves. (ibid., p.39)

He illustrates the existence of the collective consciousness by describing the collective reaction of groups of individuals to criminal wrongdoing, which causes people to react strongly, together and in unison. In his view, crime consists essentially of an act contrary to strong, well-defined states of the collective consciousness, where people are brought together in a strong and primitive way by sharing similar states of consciousness. The rules sanctioned by punishment are the expression of essential social similarities. The penal law thus symbolizes mechanical solidarity. With societies determined by organic solidarity, on the other hand, the law is more cooperative and does not just function at the more primitive level revealed by penal law. Contracts, for example, regulate relationships and symbolize cooperation between parties.

Durkheim further distinguishes the two forms of consciousness as existing within us:

> the one comprises only states that are personal to each of us, characteristic of us as individuals, whilst the other comprises states that are common to the whole of society. The former represents only our individual personality, which it constitutes; the latter represents the collective type and consequently the society without which it would not exist ... Now, although distinct, these two consciousnesses are linked to one another, since in the end they constitute only one entity, for both have one and the same organic basis. Thus they are solidly joined together. (ibid., p.61)

Furthermore, 'these two consciousnesses are not regions of ourselves that are "geographically" distinct, for they interpenetrate each other at every point' (ibid., p.86, fn.14).

One could say that what I have called the 'many voices of consciousness' reflects the multiplicity of the collective organization. If consciousness has a multiple type of structure, perhaps this developed during the course of evolution in order to take account of multiple social realities.

Durkheim does consider that the primal basis of all individuality is inalienable, a bedrock and does not depend upon the social condition:

> [T]here is a sphere of psychological life which, no matter how developed the collective type may be, varies from one person to another and belongs by right to each individual. It is that part which is made up of representations, feelings and tendencies that relate to the organism and states of the organism; it is the world of internal and external sensations and those movements directly linked to them. (ibid., p.145)

This could be seen as the area traditionally examined by the psychoanalyst, that is the subject's 'inner world' of thoughts, feelings and bodily sensations. Yet at the same time, Durkheim also emphasizes that:

> Collective life did not arise form individual life; on the contrary, it is the latter that emerged from the former. On this condition alone can we explain how the personal individuality of social units was able to form and grow without causing society to disintegrate. Indeed, since in this case it developed from within a preexisting social environment, it necessarily bears its stamp. It is constituted in such a way as not to ruin that collective order to which it is solidly linked. It remains adapted to it, without detaching itself from it. It is not the absolute personality of the monad, sufficient unto itself, and able to do without the rest of the world, but that of an organ or part of an organ that has its own definite function, but that cannot, without running a mortal risk, separate itself from the rest of the organism. (ibid., p.221)

Thus the individual is intimately related to the collective, as the individual and collective consciousnesses are intertwined within the individual. The individual has his own area of personal freedom, but he is also constantly being transformed by social relationships. At the same time, as the individual is transformed by society, society in turn is transformed by the changed individuals. Durkheim's thought here resembles that of Freud, referred to in Chapter 1, when the latter maintained that social psychology and individual psychology merged into one another. In this sense, the psychoanalyst cannot ignore the social aspects of the individual, the nature of his attachments to others.

Durkheim also emphasizes how in modern society the relationship between the individual and the collective can become pathological. Instead of producing social solidarity, the division of labour may, for example, produce alienation or what Durkheim calls 'anomie', where individuals feel a lack of contact with one another and with the collective. People become too distant from one another and are unaware of the bonds that unite them. A state of anomie may arise when, for example, a worker may feel like a mere lifeless cog in a vast machine of industry. It can also arise as a result of the increasing merging of world markets into conglomerate markets. As Durkheim describes, in terms which resemble those of Marx, and which are perhaps also of particular relevance today:

> As the market becomes more extensive, large-scale industry appears. The effect of it is to transform the relationship between employers and workers. The greater fatigue occasioned to the nervous system, linked to the contagious influence of the large urban areas, causes the needs of the workers to increase. Machine work replaces that of the man, manufacturing that of the small workshop. The worker is regimented, removed for the whole day from his family. He lives ever more apart from the person who employs him. (ibid., p.306)

As Giddens has suggested (Giddens, 1972, p.11), what distinguishes this view from that of Marx is that the latter thought that the division of labour and the growth of the world market inevitably produced alienation; however, Durkheim asserted that this was a consequence of an incomplete development of the division of labour. In order to counterbalance the harmful effects of the division of labour it was necessary to introduce economic and moral regulation, which would reduce social inequalities. Furthermore, he envisaged that the channels of communication between various elements of society needed to be opened up, so that individuals would not be isolated from the collectivity.

For Durkheim, then, the individual and the collective are in constant interaction, the individual and collective consciousnesses interpenetrate. When there are obstacles to a flexible or what he calls 'spontaneous' relationship between the individual and society (Durkheim, 1893, p.312), and where the channels of communication between the individual and society close up, anomie may develop.

Following some of Durkheim's thought, I would suggest that the subjective organization belongs on the one hand to the individual subject. Yet it is a dual organization, arising within a relationship to another, within, that is, a social context. And it is revealed within such a context, for example in the psychoanalytic encounter between analyst and patient. It is difficult to say where the subjective organization is individual and where it is collective; just as the individual and collective consciousnesses of Durkheim interpenetrate, so the individual subjective organization merges at various points with that of others in the social field. There is the organization belonging to the individual subject, made up of purely individual subjective phenomena, the world of individual feelings, perceptions etc., and the organization of the collective, made up of other subjects, experiencing different subjective phenomena. These two different organizations intermingle. They come together at various points; for example, around essential social activities such as eating together, working and being part of family life. Such social events, or what I have called the 'work of the day', provide the basic structure for the subjective organization, the scaffolding onto which the individual and collective organizations are built up. What I have called a subjective organization is made up of both individual and collective elements. Psychoanalysis is particularly concerned with the ways that the channels of communication between the individual and others may become obstructed or interfered with in various ways.

It is in Durkheim's *Elementary Forms of Religious Life* that one can see how and where the individual and collective come together at various contact points. He also clarifies the nature of subjective states belonging to the collective. As Giddens has described: 'The *Elementary Forms* provides a penetrating analysis of two basic features of the functioning of mechanical solidarity which was left aside in the former work [*The Division of Labour*]: the origins of the symbolic content of the *conscience collective*; and the institutional framework – of ritual and ceremonial – which creates and recreates these symbols' (Giddens, 1972, p.24).

This book is a vast tome, and I do not intend to provide a detailed commentary on it. I just want to pick out a few points relevant to my theme. Durkheim is essentially researching into the elementary forms of society. By examining primitive religions, he hopes to understand the basis of religious thought, but at the same time he is hoping to shed light on fundamental aspects of human reality, both the nature of thought and the nature of society. Or, as Talcott Parsons put it in his commentary on Durkheim's thought, 'Theoretically there are two different though intertwined elements in the *Formes élémentaires*, a theory of religion and an epistemology' (Parsons, 1937, p.411).

Durkheim's general conclusion is that: '[R]eligion is an eminently social thing. Religious representations are collective representations that express collective realities; rites are ways of acting that are born only in the midst of assembled groups and whose purpose is to evoke, maintain, or recreate certain mental states of those groups' (Durkheim, 1912, p.9).

He develops further the nature of the relationship between individual and collective representations. There are individual states that are explained by the psychic nature of the individual. But there are collective states that 'depend upon the way in which the collectivity is organized, upon its morphology, its religious, moral, and economic institutions, and so on' (ibid., p.15). At the same time, he suggests there is probably no case in which these two sorts of elements, the individual and the collective, are not found closely bound up together.

The representations that express society have a different content from the purely individual representations. 'The manner in which both kinds of representations are formed brings about their differentiation. Collective representations are the product of an immense cooperation that extends not only through space but also through time; to make them, a multitude of different minds have associated, intermixed, and combined their ideas and feelings ... [M]an is double. In him are two beings: an individual being that has its basis in the body and whose sphere of action is strictly limited by this fact, and a social being that represents within us the highest reality in the intellectual and moral realm that is knowable through observation: I mean society' (ibid., pp.15–16).

Society for Durkheim has both a constraining *and* a stimulating effect on individuals. It constrains us through its moral authority over us, which of course in psychoanalytical terms can be seen in terms of the individual's super-ego:

Precisely because society has its own specific nature that is different from our nature as individuals, it pursues ends that are also specifically its own; but because it can achieve those ends only by working through us, it categorically demands our cooperation. Society requires us to make ourselves its servants, forgetful of our own interests. And it subjects us to all sorts of restraints, privations and sacrifices without which social life would be impossible ...

[T]he hold society has over consciousness owes far less to the prerogative its physical superiority gives it than to the moral authority with which it is invested ... An individual or collective subject is said to inspire respect when the representation that expresses it in consciousness has such power that it calls forth or inhibits conduct automatically ... The ways of acting to which society is strongly enough attached to impose them on its members are ... marked with a distinguishing sign that calls forth respect. Because these ways of acting have been worked out in common, the intensity with which they are thought in each individual mind finds resonance in all the others, and vice versa. The representations that translate them within each of us thereby gains an intensity that mere private states of consciousness can in no way match. Those ways of acting gather strength from the countless individual representations that have served to form each of them. It is society that speaks through the mouths who affirm then in our presence; it is society that we hear when we hear them; and the voice of all itself has a tone that an individual voice cannot have. (ibid., pp.209–10)

Durkheim considers, like Freud, that the force of the collective is not wholly external, it does not move us entirely from the outside. 'Indeed, because society can exist only in and by means of individual minds, it must enter into us and become organized within us. That force thus becomes an integral part of our being and, by the same stroke, uplifts it and brings it to maturity' (ibid., p.211).

Durkheim also describes how the stimulating and invigorating effect of society can be seen in certain circumstances. It is worth emphasizing here that Durkheim did not only consider that society has a restraining influence, for him it was also potentially liberating; indeed, for him the liberty of the individual can only be achieved through his dependence on society, on the fact that he is fundamentally related to others.

Durkheim describes how intermittent states of stimulation occur when groups of people congregate together in crowds and assemblies of various kinds. While there may be more long-lasting effects at particular historical periods, such as during revolutions or creative epochs. Basing himself on the religious life of primitive societies, he describes how the act of congregating together 'is an exceptionally powerful stimulant. Once the individuals are gathered together, a sort of electricity is generated from their closeness and quickly launches them to an extraordinary height of exaltation. Every emotion expressed resonates without interference in consciousnesses that are wide open to external impressions, each one echoing the others' (ibid., pp.217–18).

But these intense social feelings would be quite unstable without the existence of symbols that provide a structure on which they can fix. For example, 'an emblem can be useful as a rallying point ... By expressing the social unit tangibly, it makes the unit itself more tangible to all' (ibid., p.231). I would add that it is not only symbols that provide a supporting structure for these representations but also structured events such as rituals, rites and, in ordinary life, the work of the day. Furthermore, collective representations 'presuppose that consciousnesses are acting and reacting on each other; they result from actions and reactions that are possible only with the help of tangible intermediaries' (ibid., p.232). That is, the collective feeling needs a tangible object to fix on in order to become conscious. Collective assemblies, such as those involved in religious practices, constantly renew the collective feeling and hence the moral bonds binding people together. Without such collective events, the bonds of society begin to fall apart.

In studying religions, one can thus see how and when the collective interacts with the individual through assemblies, rites and rituals. This occurs at particular differentiated or symbolic moments. I would suggest that it is as if each individual is incomplete as a subject in himself; or, as Durkheim put it when considering the nature of the soul in religions (ibid., p.267), each individual is only a portion, or a fragment, of the group's collective soul. The individual has his own identity and sphere of action, but it is only when individuals come together in some sort of collective structure, however small, that they fully come alive, that they encounter one another in their *dual* being, as individual and as other. Using Durkheim's terms, one could say that the subjective organization is a dual structure made up of individual and collective representations united or interpenetrating in some way.

As Giddens has described, for Durkheim it is only within the framework of the collective that the individual can be raised up above the level of mere sensory experience, or can become less elusive. It is only in his participation in the collective that introduces a stable order into the universe. Furthermore, though there have been successive changes in society, what remains constant is the fact that the collective exerts a transformative effect on the life of the individual, the transformation of social ties:

> What is universal, what does persist through the successive forms assumed by societies in the course of their development, is the transformative effect of the collectivity upon individual experience.

Although shown in its most 'elementary' and therefore in its most direct and vital manifestation in primitive religion, this is the condition of everything which elevates man above an animal existence. (Giddens, 1972, p.27)

Though Durkheim was concerned with the nature of individuation, he only made an occasional passing reference to the nature of subjective experience as such. However, he did make a distinction, in *The Elementary Forms of Religious Life*, between the personal, or what I would call the subjective, and the individual. Thus:

What we have from society we have in common with our fellow men, so it is far from true that the more individualized we are, the more personal we are. The two terms are by no means synonymous. In a sense, they oppose more than they imply one another. Passion individualizes and yet enslaves. Our sensations are in their essence individual. But the more emancipated we are from the senses, and the more capable we are of thinking and acting conceptually, the more we are persons [or I would say subjects]. Those who emphasize all that is social in the individual do not mean to deny or denigrate personhood. They simply refuse to confound it with the fact of individuation. (Durkheim, 1912, pp.274–5)

The social thought of Weber, in contrast to that of Durkheim, begins with basic assumptions openly incorporating the subjective element. This thought, as interpreted by Alfred Schutz, can provide a rigorous framework for conceptualizing intersubjective understanding, which can be directly applied to the psychoanalytic situation.

SUBJECTIVE UNDERSTANDING

Weber considered that sociology was a science concerned with the interpretative understanding of social action; where action refers to the way that an acting individual attaches a subjective meaning to his behaviour. Action is social when its subjective meaning takes account of the behaviour of, and is oriented to, others. Weber pointed out that human action is in fact very complex, not all of it can be understood as meaningful and much remains irrational. However, he tried to make this complex field intelligible by studying what can be rationally understood about human action. Unlike Durkheim, Weber saw the subjective interpretation of collective action in terms of the 'resultants and modes of organization of particular acts of individuals, since these alone can be treated as agents in a course of subjectively understandable action' (Weber, 1956, p.13). Durkheim, in contrast, saw collective action to be understandable as a phenomenon in its own right, though, as I have emphasized, he also pointed out that there was a complex interrelationship between individual and collective elements.

Understanding (*Verstehen*) for Weber is of two kinds: first of all there is 'direct observational understanding' of the subjective meaning of a given act as such, including verbal communications and the direct reading of facial expressions. Then there is 'explanatory understanding', which looks at motives, placing an act in an intelligible and more inclusive context of meaning. Action is not to be understood here as a question of looking at physical or biochemical phenomena in an 'objective' fashion, but instead in the sense of subjectively understandable orientation of behaviour of one or more individual human beings. However, such subjective understanding has a somewhat fragmentary character.

In order to encompass the fragmentary character of social phenomena, Weber constructed what he called 'ideal types'. It is difficult to be precise about what he meant by ideal types. When one uses terms such as 'bureaucrat', 'capitalist', 'charismatic leader', these are all generalized descriptions of ideal types. They were Weber's way of trying to delineate uniformities in social phenomena, despite the fact that 'In the great majority of cases actual action goes on in a state of inarticulate half-consciousness or actual unconsciousness of its subjective meaning' (ibid., p.21).

Parsons wrote that the ideal type is a generalized theoretical concept; as Weber used it, it was:

> both abstract and general. It does not describe a concrete course of action, but a normatively ideal course, assuming certain ends and modes of normative orientation as 'binding' on the actors. It does not describe an individual course of action, but a 'typical' one – it is a generalized rubric within which an indefinite number of particular cases may be classified. (Parsons, 1947, p.13)

One can see how Weber's method works in practice, not only in his monumental posthumously published *Economy and Society* (1956) which looks at many aspects of society, including the law, religion and politics, but also in a more digestible form in his classic study *The Protestant Ethic and the Spirit of Capitalism* (1904/5). In the latter book, Weber attempted to look at the psychological conditions which made possible the modern development of capitalism. He showed how the 'spirit' of capitalism consists of, for example, a sense of duty, a calling and a particular kind of work ethic which encourages the rational seeking of profits. He outlined the ideal type of the capitalist entrepreneur whose manner of life is adapted to hard work and making money. He showed how the code of economic conduct that arose under capitalism, and which broke with the conventions of the past, owed a lot to the rise of Protestant religious life, with its emphasis on the rational ordering of moral life; the calling, which imposed obligations upon the individual by his position in the world; and the need to live an ascetic, frugal, prudent and industrious life.

I think that my own notion of a subjective organization can be seen as a kind of ideal type, a construct aimed at trying to make sense of subjective life, taking into account both individual and social aspects of the human subject; it is an attempt to provide a way of making sense of subjective phenomena. The subjective organization, like the 'spirit' of capitalism, is a term covering a range of phenomena, a complex cluster of attitudes.

Though Weber was able to make important contributions to sociological thought, Alfred Schutz, in his classic book *The Phenomenology of the Social World* (1932), showed how limited were Weber's concepts about subjective understanding and how much they needed to be extended in order to provide a more comprehensive model of the social world. While agreeing with Weber that the function of sociology was essentially to be interpretive, Schutz considered that he had failed to state clearly the essential nature of understanding, subjective meaning and action. Schutz, influenced by Husserl and Bergson, defined more clearly the dilemmas of trying to understand another person's subjective point of view or vantage point, or what I would call their subjective position. For example, understanding the other person's subjective experience for Schutz is based on our own subjective experiences of him. Schutz provides a comprehensive and subtle analysis of the dilemmas of subjective and intersubjective understanding, which can be applied to the psychoanalytic situation.

Schutz describes how in a conversation one can understand another person's words, their objective meaning, the meaning which they have regardless of who is speaking. Similarly one can be aware of the other's objective characteristics, their shape and other bodily characteristics. One can observe a man chopping wood with an axe in a direct way, observing his activity from the outside as it were. This is to apply direct observational understanding to the other, as defined by Weber. But one does not have live contact with the other in this way. In order to have this, there is another way of understanding the other, which is to use Weber's explanatory or motivational understanding, in which the other is seen in a context, in an understandable sequence of motivation. Thus the woodcutter may be chopping wood to make a house, or be part of a lumberjack business; alternatively, he may be cutting wood in order to vent his rage with someone. Indeed, it is virtually impossible to take an action out of a social context.

However, there is a kind of leap in the way one moves from using the objective to the subjective context of meaning or subjective position. When one uses the subjective position, one begins to grasp the other person's point of view; he is seen as an other, as a person (or a subject) in a context, oriented to others and being affected by others in the social world. I would add, in addition, that while the observational attitude consists in, for example, observing and attending to one's experiences of the other, a subjective position involves allowing such experiences to penetrate and interpenetrate one's consciousness, in the way that Durkheim outlined.

Schutz defines meaning as 'a certain way of directing one's gaze at an item of one's own experience' (Schutz, 1932, p.42). This item is selected out and made discrete by a reflexive act. Looking first of all from the point of view of the solitary subject, the 'I' or the 'Ich' meaning indicates a particular attitude of the I toward the flow of its own duration. Lived experiences are meaningful only when one has selected one or more of them out of the flow of experience. Remembering lifts experience out of the stream of duration. If one merely lives within the flow of duration there is only an undifferentiated living from moment to moment. In order to retain memories and have some sense of continuity one requires an act of reflection, and a marking out of experiences by an act of attention. Meaning does not lie in the experience but in the way that the I regards its experience, in the attitude of the I to that part of the stream of consciousness that has already flown by. The meaning of a lived experience undergoes modifications depending on the particular kind of attention the I gives to that lived experience.

Action is a spontaneous activity oriented towards the future (ibid., pp.57 ff.), involving the I anticipating in advance what may happen. Action is carried out in accordance with some kind of plan more or less implicitly preconceived. An action always has the nature of a 'project' and thus involves the activity of the subject. Every projection of action is a phantasying of the subject's spontaneous activity, of what may happen. Thus for Schutz, action is a lived experience which is guided by a plan or project arising from the subject's spontaneous activity, and distinguished from all other lived experiences by a particular act of attention.

Schutz then takes account of the sphere of social meaning and the existence of other subjects and describes what he calls the ambiguities in the ordinary notion of understanding the other person. First of all, one can say that each person's stream of consciousness is unique to them and is built up of a complicated sequence of experiences. In one sense it remains inaccessible to others:

> It might seem that these conclusions would lead to the denial of the possibility of an interpretive sociology and even more to the denial that one can ever understand another person's experience. But this is by no means the case. We are asserting neither that your lived experiences remain in principle inaccessible to me nor that they are meaningless to me. Rather, the point is that the meaning I give to your experiences cannot be precisely the same as the meaning you give to them when you proceed to interpret them. (ibid., p.99)

There are, then, two types of meaning involved; that is, between self-explication and interpretation of another person's experience. However, I would add that there are also meanings which only arise out of the encounter between oneself and another. Indeed, for Schutz, while I can generally observe my own lived experiences only after they are over and done with, I can observe the other's as they actually take place. 'This in turn implies that you and I are in a specific sense "simultaneous," that we "coexist," that our respective streams of consciousness intersect ... I see, then, my own stream of consciousness and yours in a single intentional Act which embraces them both' (ibid., pp.103–4).

However, Schutz adds that,

> The simultaneity of our two streams of consciousness, however, does not mean that the same experiences are given to each of us. My lived experience of you, as well as the environment I ascribe to you, bears the mark of my own subjective Here and Now and not the mark of yours ... [Y]our whole stream of lived experience is *not* open to me. To be sure, your stream of lived experience is also a continuum, but I can catch sight of only disconnected segments of it ... When I become aware of a segment of your lived experience, I arrange what I see within my own meaning-context. But meanwhile you have arranged it in yours. Thus I am always interpreting your lived experience from my own standpoint. (ibid., p.106)

Schutz, then, proposes what I would call the 'basic frame' for understanding another person – that one can only interpret lived experiences belonging to other people in terms of one's own experiences of them, how one's own lived experience connects up with the other's experiences. This could be seen as the basis for the analyst's use of the countertransference, which can be understood as the analyst observing his own experience of the other's lived experience.

However, it is not enough to merely attend to one's experiences of the other person if one wants to genuinely understand him. Something additional is required for this to happen, a shift in one's subjective position. In order to clarify this shift, Schutz describes again how one can understand the activity of a woodcutter. There is the observational understanding, looking at the woodcutter's activity as an external event, watching the changes in his body as the wood is cut. But genuine understanding means that the centre of attention is the woodcutter's own lived experiences as an actor. One may then ask if this man is acting spontaneously according to a project he had previously formulated, and if so what is this project? One will want to know his motives and the context of his actions:

These questions are concerned with neither the facticity of the situation as such nor the bodily movements as such. Rather, the outward facts and bodily movements are understood as indications of the lived experiences of the person being observed. The attention of the observer is focused not on the indications but on what lies behind them. This is *genuine understanding of the other person.* (ibid., p.111).

In order to achieve genuine understanding of the other person, one needs to move from an observing attitude, in which one is ordering and classifying one's experiences of him as if he were merely a natural object in the world, to a fully subjective attitude. The latter involves first of all paying attention to the subjective context of meaning, the motives and projects of the person. However, this is still not enough for a genuine understanding of the other, because it basically assumes that the other person is merely another 'I' like oneself, a mere mirror image. Instead, the other is a 'Thou', an other as other, not a reflection of one's own self. What I would call a fully subjective position requires that the existence of the Thou is assumed; once this has occurred one has entered the realm of intersubjectivity; the world is now experienced by the individual as shared by his fellows, that is as a social world (ibid., p.139).

In this social world the subject is 'oriented' to the other, that is the other is first of all assumed to be both conscious and experiencing, he is a Thou, living and enduring and having lived experiences. This, however, is still not enough for intersubjective communication. One can be 'Other-oriented' while reading a book or rehearsing another's train of thoughts (ibid., p.150), but not yet in communication with another person. In order to achieve such communication, one needs to be 'affected' by, and 'affecting', the other. Social interaction, or full intersubjective communication occurs when motives actually bring about conscious (or I would add unconscious) experiences in the other. This kind of communication presupposes Other-orientation. Schutz distinguishes between a social relationship where each partner is oriented towards the other, and social interaction where each actually affects the other.

One is Thou-oriented from the 'moment that I recognize an entity which I directly experience as a fellow man (as a Thou), attributing life and consciousness to him. However, we must be quite clear that we are not here dealing with a conscious *judgment*. This is a prepredicative experience in which I become aware of a fellow human being as a *person* [or I would say a *subject*] (ibid., p.164).

Furthermore, Schutz argues that when the Thou-orientation is reciprocal, if subject and other are mutually aware of one another, that is if each is Thou-oriented to the other, then there is a directly experienced social relationship, which he calls a 'face-to-face relationship' (ibid.). The face-to-face relationship in which the partners are aware of each other and sympathetically participate in each other's life, he calls the 'We-relationship'. The world of the We-relationship is not private to either of us but is our world, the one common intersubjective relationship which is right there in front of us. Moreover:

> The basic We-relationship is already given to me by the mere fact that I am born into the world of directly experienced social reality. From this basic relationship is derived the original validity of all my direct experiences of particular fellow men and also that there is a larger world of my contemporaries whom I am not now experiencing directly ... To explain how our experiences of the Thou are rooted in the We-relationship, let us take conversation as an example. Suppose you are speaking to me and I am understanding what you are saying. As we have already seen, there are two senses of this understanding. First of all I grasp the 'objective meaning' of your words, the meaning which they would have had, had they been spoken by you or anyone else. But second, of course, there is the subjective meaning, namely what is going on in your mind as you speak. In order to get to your subjective meaning, I must picture to myself your stream of consciousness as flowing side by side with my own. Within this picture I must interpret and

construct your intentional Acts as you choose your words. To the extent that you and I can mutually experience this simultaneity, growing older together for a time, to the extent that we can live in it together, to that extent we can live in each other's subjective contexts of meaning ... I get to your subjective meaning ... by starting out with your spoken words as given and then by asking how you came to use those words. But this question of mine would make no sense if I did not already assume an actual or at least potential We-relationship between us. For it is only within the We-relationship that I can concretely experience you at a particular moment of your life. To put the point in terms of a formula: I can live in your subjective meaning-contexts only to the extent that I directly experience you within an actualised content-filled We-relationship. (ibid., pp.165–6)

There are several different kinds of We-relationship. For example, the partner may be experienced with different degrees of immediacy, intensity or intimacy. Or he may be experienced within the centre of attention or at its periphery (ibid., p.168). Also, the way that each partner attends to their experiences is modified by the relationship. 'If I know that you and I are in a face-to-face relationship, I also know something about the manner in which each of us is attuned to his conscious experiences, in other words, the "attentional modifications" of each of us. This means that the way we attend to our conscious experiences is actually modified by our relationship to each other' (ibid., p.171).

Schutz thus provides a complex account of how one may understand the other person. Such understanding is not merely making sense of the other's words or observing their behaviour, nor is it merely a question of sharing experiences with the other. Rather, there needs to be a shift to the subjective position, with orientation to the other, and the allowing of social interaction or being affected by the other. While the basic frame for understanding the other is the understanding of one's own experiences of the other and how they connect up with his lived experiences, we are both living in a common world of directly experienced social reality. For Schutz, the We-relationship defines a fully intersubjective relationship, with each attending to the experiences of the other.

However, Schutz gives no account of the role of desire, affects, nor that of unconscious communication. Also, his use of the notion of the stream of consciousness and how different streams may connect has a somewhat dated ring, influenced as it was by the now unfashionable thought of Bergson. One may similarly criticize Durkheim for using the model of consciousness that was available in his time for understanding individual and collective phenomena. However, I would suggest such thought may still have a useful place in trying to make sense of what are complex and puzzling phenomena.

Schutz's model of relatedness does tend to veer towards being Cartesian in its approach, in the sense that his notion of the other seems more like a reflection of the I than a genuine other. This is perhaps not surprising since his thought in *The Phenomenology of the Social World* was heavily influenced by the *Cartesian Meditations* of Husserl (1929), where others are seen basically as other egos, other solitary consciousnesses, however much they may strive to be oriented to one another. Husserl later tried to overcome this limitation about his view of others in his *Crisis of European Sciences*, as mentioned in Chapter 1. Despite the Cartesian tendency, Schutz does also tend in his early work to see that consciousness of the I always entails a sense of the other; and certainly later in his thought (Schutz, 1973), he make this more specific.

One of the main criticisms that one can make about Schutz's thought is that it concentrates too much on the *understanding* of another person and not enough on the emotional elements of human relationships, including the role of desire and the drives, not to mention unconscious communication.

Though in the psychoanalytic relationship there are elements of a social relationship and even of a We-relationship, it would perhaps be inaccurate to describe it as intersubjective in the full sense, due to the different and asymmetrical subjective positions occupied by analyst and patient. In this sense, Schutz's descriptions of the dilemmas of understanding the other person are clarifying. One could say that the analyst has available three different and overlapping areas of experience – his own experiences of himself, his experiences of the other as they are arising and his own experiences arising out of the other's lived experiences. The analyst's scrutiny of his subjective experiences of the other's lived experiences would seem to be the useful area of countertransference, while his experiences of the other as they are arising is more like the transference.

Schutz's thought is valuable in alerting one to the complexities and ambiguities of understanding another person. Intersubjective understanding from his perspective is not some simple sharing of experiences, but has to take account of more complex subjective dilemmas. While Schutz pays attention to the way that understanding can take place between subjects, the subjects are in a sense given or taken for granted; he does not seem to pay much attention to the way that subjects are constructed. The thought of Mead would seem to take more account of the construction of the subject as well as giving more consideration to the other as a separate phenomenon in its own right. This can lead on to a more sustainable and, I would suggest, radical model of subjectivity, which is the basis for my own notion of a subjective organization.

THE 'I' AND THE 'ME'

Mead described social psychology as studying the activity of the individual as it lies within the social process. Like Freud, he did not draw a sharp line between individual and social psychology; minds and selves were essentially social products. While not ignoring the inner experience of the individual, Mead maintained that the behaviour of the individual could be understood only in terms of the whole social group of which he was a member, 'since his individual acts are involved in larger social acts which go beyond himself and which implicate the other members of that group' (Mead, 1934, pp.6–7).

Mead looked closely at individuals acting within the social field. He saw the social act as a complex process that had to be taken as a dynamic whole, consisting of a circuit involving and, I would add, transforming the experiences of the individual and interactions with others; mind was not something that belonged merely to the individual human organism. As mentioned in Chapter 2, mind for Mead could only come into existence in terms of the social environment. The field of the mind for him included all the components of the field of the social process; that field could not be bounded by the skin of the individual organism.

Mead saw the patterns which one finds in the central nervous system as essentially patterns of action, oriented to the social field, not of contemplation. Experience was not located at any point in the nervous system, or in the head. Instead of assuming that the experienced world as such was inside of a head, located at that point at which certain nervous disturbances are going on, Mead related the world of experience to the whole act of the organism, taking the complete act as a unit, a unit of action. The unit of action involved the individual and others (ibid., p.111). In this sense, one could also call it a unit of relatedness. What goes on only in the brain are mainly the physiological processes whereby we lose and gain consciousness.

It is absurd to look at the mind from the standpoint of the individual human organism; for, although it has its focus there, it is essentially a social phenomenon; even its biological functions are primarily social. The subjective experience of the individual must be brought into relation with the natural, socio-biological activities of the brain in order to render an acceptable account of mind possible at all; and this can be done only if the social nature of mind is recognized. The meagerness of individual experience in isolation from the processes of social experience – in isolation from its social environment – should, moreover, be apparent. We must regard mind, then, as arising and developing within the social process, within the empirical matrix of social interactions. We must, that is, get an inner individual experience from the stand-point of social acts which include the experiences of separate individuals in a social context wherein those individuals interact. The processes of experience which the human brain makes possible are made possible only for a group of interacting individuals: only for individual organisms which are members of a society; not for the individual organism in isolation from other individual organisms. (ibid., p.133)

Mead's views about the location of human experience are thus consistent with the arguments first presented in Chapter 1 and developed subsequently, that human subjectivity was not located merely within the individual but that it involved the individual and social fields. As Habermas described in his commentary on Mead's theory of subjectivity, Mead developed a model of mind as not something purely inward, 'but as forming itself on the path from without to within, through the symbolically mediated relationship to a partner in interaction' (Habermas, 1992, p.177).

One could thus understand subjective experience as taking place along a path or circuit, leading from the social field to the individual and back again, along the lines already indicated in Chapter 3 on the transformations of the subject. One can see such a circuit in psychoanalytic terms by taking account of the transference. A clinical example will provide a brief illustration of this point. Mr W kept repeating relationships at work and at home which could be understood as creating a situation in which a father failed him. This was made clear when this situation was repeated with me in the transference. There was, as he put it, a constant 'loop' involved, in which he would set the other up as an authority figure, with knowledge and experience which he wanted and also envied. This then left him feeling inside like a little boy who could not get what he wanted. This was related to his relationship with his own father, a distant man, whom he felt would not give him what he wanted and needed. This resulted in Mr W feeling resentful, and also with the feeling that he could not face confrontation and communication with this other who was not going to give him what he wanted. The other for him would always fail him, and in turn Mr W constantly felt a failure, as a result of a constant loop or circuit involving his relationship with the other. As a result of understanding this situation, he was more able to step outside that particular closed circuit in his social interactions.

In locating experience as a circuit, or what I would call a transformational circuit, involving social interactions, Mead was very much influenced by the thought of Dewey, who emphasized how meaning arises out of communication. In Chapter 1 I provided an outline of how Dewey emphasized the world of social interaction and human communication in understanding human experience. Human cooperation, discourse, shared experience and sociability were the cornerstones of his thinking and not the isolated knowing subject looking out at the separate objective world of things. Dewey considered that social interaction and institutions had been treated as the products of a ready-made specific physical or mental endowment of a self-sufficient, isolated individual rather than as emerging out of social communication.

> The modern discovery of inner experience, of a realm of purely personal events that are always at the individual's command, and that are his exclusively as well as inexpensively for refuge, consolation and thrill is also a great and liberating discovery. It implies a new worth and sense of dignity in human individuality, a sense that an individual is not a mere property of nature, set in place according to a scheme independent of him, as an article is put in its place in a cabinet, but that he adds something, that he makes a contribution. It is the counterpart of what distinguishes modern science, experimental, hypothetical; a logic of discovery having therefore opportunity for individual temperament, ingenuity, invention. It is the counterpart of modern politics, art, religion and industry where individuality is given room and movement, in contrast to the ancient scheme of experience, which held individuality tightly within a given order subordinated to its structure and patterns. But here also a distortion entered in. Failure to recognize that this world of inner experience is dependent upon an extension of language which is a social product and operation led to the subjectivist, solipistic and egotistic strain in modern thought. (Dewey, 1929, p.143)

Language for Dewey is about 'communication; the establishment of cooperation in an activity in which there are partners, and in which the activity of each is modified and regulated by partnership' (ibid., p.148). A word gains meaning 'when its use establishes a genuine community of action ... Language is specifically a mode of interaction of at least two beings, a speaker and a hearer; it presupposes an organized group to which these creatures belong, and from whom they have acquired their habits of speech. It is therefore a relationship' (ibid., p.153). Communication 'is a means of establishing cooperation, domination and order. Shared experience is the greatest of human goods' (ibid., p.167). Finally, 'sociability, communication are just as immediate traits of the concrete individual as is the privacy of the closet of consciousness' (ibid., p.199).

In order to understand the origin of communication, Mead considered the primitive situation both in animals and man as involving a 'conversation of gestures'. The primitive situation 'is that of the social act which involves the interaction of different forms, which involves, therefore, the adjustment of the conduct of these different forms to each other, in carrying out the social process. Within that process one finds what we term the gestures, those phases of the act which bring about the adjustment of the response of the other form' (Mead, 1934, p.45). While, 'Mind arises through communication by a conversation of gestures in a social process or context of experience – not communication through mind' (ibid., p.50).

Gestures can become what Mead called 'significant symbols' when they arouse, in an individual making them, the same kind of response in the others to whom they are addressed. When gestures stand for a particular act or response, then they are significant symbols. 'Only in terms of gestures as significant symbols is the existence of mind or intelligence possible; for only in terms of gestures which are significant symbols can thinking – which is simply an internalization or implicit conversation of the individual with himself by means of such gestures – take place. The internalization in our experience of the external conversation of gestures which we carry on with other individual in the social process is the essence of thinking' (ibid., p.47).

Meaning for Mead arises and lies within the field of the relations between reciprocal gestures. If a gesture from one individual indicates to the other the subsequent behaviour of that individual, then it has meaning. 'In other words, the relationship between a given stimulus – as a gesture – and the later phases of the social act of which it is an early ... phase constitutes the field within which meaning originates and exists. Meaning is thus a development of something objectively there as a relation between certain phases of the social act; it is not a psychical addition to that act and it is not an "idea" as traditionally conceived' (ibid., p.76).

The interpretation of meanings is thus not a process going on merely in the mind as such; it is, as Dewey described, an external, overt process going on in the actual field of social experience. Furthermore, 'Meaning can be described, accounted for, or stated in terms of symbols or language at its highest and most complex stage of development (the stage it reaches in human experience), but language simply lifts out of the social process a situation which is logically or implicitly there already' (ibid., p.79).

The significant gesture or symbol presupposes for its significance the social field in which it arises, 'or, as the logicians say, a universe of discourse is always implied as the context in terms of which, or as the field within which, significant gestures or symbols do in fact have a significance. This universe of discourse is constituted by a group of individuals carrying on and participating in a common social process of experience and behavior, within which these gestures or symbols have the same common meaning for all members of that group ... A universe of discourse is simply a system of common or social meanings' (ibid., pp.90–1).

When the individual takes the attitudes of others toward himself and he finally crystallizes all these particular attitudes into a single, communal attitude or standpoint, Mead called the latter the attitude of the 'generalized other'.

Mead further developed the relationship between the individual and others in defining his notion of the self, which he saw as something that is different from the given physiological organization, that is not initially there at birth but has a development and is essentially a social structure arising in social experience and activity. The self for him was distinguished from the body, as unlike the latter it is an object to itself. 'This characteristic is represented in the word "self", which is a reflexive, and indicates that which can be both subject and object. This type of object is essentially different from other objects' (ibid., pp.136–7).

Mead considered that the essential psychological problem of selfhood was how an individual could get outside himself experientially in such a way as to become an object to himself. The solution was to be found by referring to the process of social conduct or activity in which the person is implicated, when he responds to his self as another responds to it, in a reflexive way, from the outside, rather on the lines of Bakhtin's thought; or in psychoanalytic terms, one could link the taking oneself as another to the process of identification with the other. For Mead, the reflexive social process involved 'taking part in conversation with others, being aware of what one is saying and using that awareness of what one is saying to determine what one is going to say thereafter' (ibid., p.140). That is, the individual is an object to himself through communication, through the linguistic process.

The self develops in two stages, involving different kinds of organization of attitudes:

> At the first of these stages, the individual's self is constituted simply by an organization of the particular attitudes of other individuals towards himself and toward one another in the specific social acts in which he participates with them. But at the second stage in the full development of the individual's self that self is constituted not only by an organization of these particular individual attitudes, but also by an organization of the social attitudes of the generalized other or the social group as a whole to which he belongs. (ibid., p.158)

The generalized other in this context is the organized community or social group which gives to the individual his unity of self. 'Thus, for example, in the case of such a social group as a ball team, the team is the generalized other in so far as it enters – as an organized process or social activity – into the experience of any one of the individual members of it' (ibid., p.154).

Mead distinguished between the area of the self, which involved social interaction, and the private or merely subjective area of the individual, what was private to him. The self involved interaction with individuals engaged in some sort of cooperative activity. The subject for Mead referred, in a rather Cartesian manner and unlike the rest of his thought, to the mere consciousness of objects. I would consider that it is not possible to make such a clear distinction between the self and the subjective. On the contrary, I have argued throughout that the subject appears at various points in the circuit between the individual and the social field, and that the notion of a subject is not merely attached to what is private in the solitary individual's consciousness. Mead himself emphasized that one cannot look at the mind merely from the individual point of view and that the subjective experience of the individual must be brought into relation with the social nature of the mind. Furthermore, one can see in his fascinating description of two aspects of the self, the 'I' and the 'me', a more open view of the subject.

> The 'I' is the response of the organism to the attitudes of the others; the 'me' is the organized attitudes of others which one himself assumes ... He can throw the ball to some other member

because of the demand made upon him from some other members of the team. That is the self that immediately exists for him in his consciousness. He has their attitudes, knows what they want and what the consequences of any act of his will be, and he has assumed responsibility for the situation. Now, it is the presence of those organized sets of attitudes that constitutes the 'me' to which he as an 'I' is responding. But what the response will be he does not know and nobody else knows. Perhaps he will make a brilliant play or an error. The response to that situation as it appears in his immediate experience is uncertain, and it is that which constitutes the 'I'. (ibid., p.175)

The 'I' is something which responds to the social situation and is within the experience of the individual, it gives the sense of freedom and initiative. It is never entirely calculable. The 'me' represents a definite organization of the community in our own attitudes, to which the individual responds as an 'I'. The 'I' and the 'me' are separated but belong together; taken together, they constitute the self. The self is constituted by the 'conversation of the "I" and the "me"' (ibid., p.179).

In summary, Mead presented 'the self and the mind in terms of a social process, as the importation of the conversation of gestures into the conduct of the individual organism, so that the individual organism takes these organized attitudes of the others called out by its own attitude, in the form of its gestures, and in reacting to that response calls out other organized attitudes in the others in the community to which the individual belongs. This process can be characterized in a certain sense in terms of the "I" and the "me", the "me" being that group of organized attitudes to which the individual responds as an "I"' (ibid., p.186).

Both aspects of the self, the 'I' and the 'me' are essential to what Mead calls the full expression of the self, or what one could call the full realization of the subject. One must take the attitude of others in a group in order to belong to a community. But, each individual has their own organization of the 'I' and the 'me'. Both the 'I' and the 'me' are involved in the self and each supports the other. There is a constant interrelationship between the two elements.

Mead's notions of the mind and self can thus be seen to support the assertion that the individual needs the social field for his full realization, that the individual is hungry for social interaction from the beginning. Also, one can see in his thought how social structure, through the organization of the 'me', provides the scaffolding for the individual. Mead addresses the essential problem of subject relations, which is how I can constitute in myself another person, how I experience what is in me as other than me. His solution to this problem is in terms of the interrelationship, or the conversation, between the self's dual structure of 'I' and 'me'. His thought thus supports the notion of an organization embracing the individual within the social field, or what I have called a subjective organization. The area covered by the term 'subject of' is perhaps similar to that covered by the 'I', while the term 'subject to' is similar to the 'me'. However, Mead left out of his model the role of desire, and he only made passing reference to unconscious communication as prior to conscious communication (ibid., p.179, fn.). In addition, Mead's model of how a self comes to be organized is somewhat optimistic; there is rather little conflict, communication is basically possible and not problematic, as the psychoanalytic experience tends to reveal. Mead's self is not an elusive organization, as I have suggested it is indicative of that of the subjective organization, as the subject weaves its way through interactions with other subjects.

SUBJECT AND OBJECT RELATIONS

For most of this chapter I have emphasized the importance of considering social structure in the life of the subject, an area which I have suggested has often been neglected in psychoanalytic theory. One may then ask how psychical structure, the contribution of the individual, interacts with social structure. I have just described how Mead saw that there was an intimate relationship between the individual and social structure, through the dual structure of the 'I' and the 'me', and that it does not make much sense to separate the two fields as such. Much psychoanalytic thought, however, focuses more specifically on psychic structure, leaving the contribution of the social element rather vague; it may be referred to as the 'external world', but it is often not developed much further. At this point, I have reached what one could call the issue of how subject and object relations interconnect; or how the subject's dual being as individual and other relates to the theory of object relations.

This issue was touched upon in Chapter 1 in philosophical terms, when there was a description of Sartre's interplay between the Other-as-object and the Other-as-subject. As outlined there, Sartre points out that the Other can be seen as an object and the Other can see me as an object. This is an important element of the relation between self and Other, but I am denied my true being as a subject, which for Sartre is my freedom. While the Other can freeze me with a look, and the self can become alienated by the act of being merely looked at; at another level the Other can potentially be encountered as a subject. We may try to know the Other, and we can as an object in one sense; yet the Other-as-object cannot be encountered in a full way. When we try to fully encounter the Other, we are taken away from the Other-as-subject to the Other-as-object, and we are perpetually moving between these two positions. From Sartre's dialectic, one could thus imagine that there is a constant interplay between subject and object relationships.

There was also an outline of the thought of Kojève (1947, p. 116 ff.), on how the knowing subject only finds a particular kind of knowledge, that of the object. To find the subject, desire is needed; the desiring subject is the human subject. Kojève proposes that what distinguishes the human from the animal is that human desire is not just directed towards other objects but towards other desires. Desire is only human if one desires the desire of the other, if one wants to possess or assimilate the other's desire. Desire is only human to the extent that it is mediated by the desire of another directed towards the same object. An object perfectly useless from the biological point of view, such as a medal or an enemy's flag, can be desired because it is the object of other desires. An object from this viewpoint, then, is an object of desire.

There is also a detailed description in this chapter of the thought of Schutz, who distinguishes understanding of the physical world of objects from subjective understanding of the other, with all the complexities that that involves.

One may ask how these philosophical ideas relate to psychoanalytic thought, if at all. One of the difficulties about the word 'object' is that it has now been so often used and in such a variety of ways that unless one is careful it may begin to lose its value as a term. Also, one may lose something essentially human if one thinks of the object without taking into account the subjective experience as such. Using the term 'object' can too easily fall into taking an objective stance rather than take account of the subjective point of view, as outlined in Chapter 1.

In looking at the term 'object' there is first of all the ordinary use of the word to describe a physical object – a ball, a tree, a body part. Such physical objects can be used in various ways; for example, to communicate with others through play. Next, there is the use of the term 'object' to describe people or aspects of a person; the object in this sense is equivalent to the 'Other'. The Other, as Sartre described, can be experienced like a physical object in the sense of being objectified or dehumanized, or can be experienced as a subject with a life of its own. There is the technical use, in classical psychoanalytic theory, of 'object' to describe the object of the drive, which can be a physical object, including a part of the body. The object of fantasy, wish or desire merges with the notion of an 'internal' representation of an 'external' object, the latter being either another person or a physical object. The notion of 'internal objects' and a 'world' of internal objects or representations comes into the picture at this point and leads to theories of object relations.

Bollas, as quoted in Chapter 1, defined object relations as the forming and projecting of internal mental representations, as opposed to subject relations which attends to the interplay of two human idioms or sensibilities. However, this is a difficult area to be precise about, if only because there are a number of different theories of object relations.

Meir Perlow has written a particularly clear review of the various psychoanalytic theories of how individuals perceive and relate to their objects, *Understanding Mental Objects* (1995). He uses the term 'mental object' to refer to a whole group of concepts 'which have been used in the psychoanalytic literature to refer to various mental organizations, structures, processes and capacities in an individual which relate his or her perception, attitude, relationship with and memories of other people (commonly referred to, in the psychoanalytic literature, as "objects"). Some of the prominent members of this group are: object images, internal objects, part-objects, object representations, introjects, identifications, transitional objects, selfobjects, psychic presences and object constancy' (Perlow, 1995, p.1).

He points out that each of these concepts, which he studies under the rubric of mental objects, is embedded in a number of different theories of mental functioning – representations or schemas, phantasies, and developmental capacities and deficits. He reviews the major psychoanalytic theories of mental objects, and then discusses several major theoretical issues that arise from these theories, in terms of the status and the origins of the mental object, the mental object and motivation, the mental object as a developmental capacity and the position of the mental object with regard to the self. His book provides remarkably clear and useful descriptions of the various theories. However, in my view, he does disguise some of the obscurities of what one means by a mental object; it is simply taken for granted in his basic acceptance of the Cartesian model of the mind. There is, also perhaps not surprisingly, no consideration of the nature of desire, nor any mention of Lacan.

I cannot do justice to all Perlow's elaborate descriptions, but I will use some of his work as a guide to my argument. He points out that Freud had a developing notion of the mental object, which

Perlow describes as occurring in four stages. He began with the notion of a mental image of the parents as guiding later object choice, moved to more complex functions of mental images of objects in the functioning of phantasy, and then, through the notion of introjection based on his work on the mourning process, eventually developed the notion of the super-ego as a structure and a mental or internal object.

The question of the origins of the super-ego's severity is particularly relevant to a number of other psychoanalytic theories. It is clear that the severity of the super-ego was not necessarily related to the behaviour of the actual parents whose images were supposed to have been introjected. Perlow suggests that Freud solved this problem first of all by explaining the severity of the super-ego as an expression of the individual's own aggressive impulses, not a reflection of the parents' behaviour. However, Perlow mentions that Freud later considered that the reality of the parents' behaviour, that is external factors, also had a part to play. Perlow goes on throughout his book to show how the issue of the balance between internal and external factors in the origin and nature of mental objects continued to be played out between different analytic thinkers. For example, Klein very much emphasized the role of innate factors in the origin of the super-ego, while Fairbairn and Ferenczi favoured the role of external factors. My own preference is to follow Freud's emphasis on the dual nature of mental structures, as involving and needing both internal and external (or individual and social) factors for their origin, structure and their subsequent functioning.

I would suggest that one can see such a dual approach in Freud's consideration of the origin of the sense of guilt and of the super-ego in *Civilization and its Discontents* (1930). He points out there that before the formation of the super-ego, the child begins to distinguish what is good from bad by means of external influences, as a result of the parents' restrictions, punishment and so on. But, he asks, what is the motive for yielding to the parents' influence and not wishing to have all their drives satisfied? Freud suggests that 'Such a motive is easily discovered in his helplessness and his dependence on other people, and it can best be designated as fear of loss of love. If he loses the love of another person upon whom he is dependent, he also ceases to be protected from a variety of dangers. Above all, he is exposed to the danger that his stronger person will show his superiority in the form of punishment. At the beginning, therefore, what is bad is whatever causes one to be threatened with loss of love. For fear of that loss, one must avoid it' (Freud, 1930, p.124).

A change then arises when the authority is internalized through the establishment of the structured super-ego. 'The phenomena of conscience then reach a higher stage. Actually, it is not until now that we should speak of conscience or a sense of guilt. At this point, too, the fear of being found out comes to an end; the distinction, moreover, between doing something bad and wishing to do it disappears entirely, since nothing can be hidden from the super-ego' (ibid., p.125).

Thus, there are two origins for the sense of guilt – the early fear of an authority, and the later fear of the super-ego. First there is renunciation of drives owing to fear of aggression and loss of love by the external authority; and then comes the later erection of an internal authority, the super-ego, and renunciation of drives through fear of it. The process involved in internalization seems to be that the child, by means of identification, takes the external authority into himself. 'The authority now turns into his super-ego and enters into possession of all the aggressiveness which the child would have liked to exercise against it ... the original severity of the super-ego ... does not ... represent the original severity which one has experienced from ... the object, or which one attributes to it; it represents one's own aggressiveness to it' (ibid., pp.129–30).

Although Freud, like Klein, emphasizes that the harshness of the super-ego is not necessarily related to the reality of a harsh parent, he does suggest that a harsh upbringing exerts a strong influence on the formation of the child's super-ego. Not only will the child identify with a harsh parent, but his own innate aggressiveness will not be appropriately modified by adequate caring and love. The normal suppression of considerable amounts of aggressiveness will not take place, and the whole process of internalization and super-ego forma-tion will be distorted, as they have had real experiences of loss of love. Thus Freud describes an intricate interrelationship between the drives and the reality of the parent in the formation of the super-ego.

Klein's theory of internal objects has continued to be influential and in widespread use, as well as a source of controversy from its inception. As Perlow points out, Klein's use of the term 'object' is ubiquitous; there is little attempt to distinguish between different meanings in which it is used. The internal object is first of all a body phantasy and very much influenced by the drives; it is located inside the child's body; for example, as shown when a child fears attacks by the internalized persecuting parent-figures which form the cruel part of the super-ego. Perlow (1995, p.42) describes how Klein blurred the distinctions between internal object and perceptions, memories and realistic images. Contents of the mind are seen as derivatives of the body phantasies. Mental life as a whole is seen almost exclusively in terms of interactions between internal objects and with the ego.

In some ways, one could see the theory of internal objects as directly based on subjective experience in quite a concrete way. For example, feelings of being persecuted or attacked from within are directly translated into a theory that there is conflict between internal objects. Theory and experience are thus intimately connected. However, there is little attempt, at least by Klein, to take account of the role of the environment, including relationships with others. By being so concrete, the relationships between objects can have the appearance of what Schafer called a 'demonology', in which the mind is seen to be populated by numerous objects doing battle with each other (Perlow, 1995, p.100).

In my view, another problem with the theory of internal objects (and indeed with the majority of psychoanalytic theories of the mind) is that it is based on what is now an outdated model of the mind, the Cartesian model; its status is hence problematical, though its value as a vivid way of viewing and making sense of clinical material is undoubted. Indeed, I myself use this way of thinking as one element of my own clinical work. This issue was discussed in detail in Chapter 2. In summary, to consider the mind as made up of internal objects means using the old Cartesian model of the mind, where the latter is a private theatre where we inspect our thoughts and feelings, and which in some way is a reflection or copy of the external world. This is also the 'representative' model of the mind, in which knowledge is built up of an assembly of representations. It is a model that many of the early pioneers of psychoanalysis, notably Klein, adhered to, though as I have suggested Freud's model is more ambiguous and complex. The main problem with this model, to put it simply, is that one may ask who looks at the internal theatre and who observes the observer? I discussed how recent attacks on the old private inner world model follow from the thought of the late Wittgenstein. Early in his thinking, he used an essentially representational model of the mind, with 'essences' or 'objects' lying behind the world, which language reflected in its propositions. But in his later thinking, this model was completely abandoned in favour of a model in which knowledge is no longer a matter of presenting thoughts to the knower, but of understanding the use of words in context, in social situations in which one finds oneself.

Sandler is an example of a thinker, very much favoured by Perlow, who has developed a complex model of internal objects under the influence of both Klein and ego psychology, and who has essentially stuck to the Cartesian model of the mind. He thinks it more appropriate to use the term 'internal object' 'to refer to the psychological *structures* that lie outside the realm of subjective experience and not to use the term for conscious or unconscious self- and object *images*' (Sandler, 1990, p.871). In addition to their role in analytic theory, he considers that internal objects can be used as 'clinically appropriate *organising constructs in the mind of the analyst*' (ibid., p.874).

Whereas Klein considered that internal objects were experienced as such, Sandler considers that they are outside the realm of subjective experience. However, wherever they may or may not be located, and I do personally find it difficult to see how one can make a clear distinction between experiential and non-experiential realms in this way, Sandler is guilty, like Klein, of the Cartesian error. He even talks quite directly of ghost-like structures in the mind, along the lines criticized by Ryle and his description of the 'ghost in the machine'. Thus:

> So I want to suggest that the world of internal objects in the nonexperiential realm be considered as *giving rise* to a phantasy and thought, to a (largely unconscious) phantom world in which we live at the same time as we live in the *real* world. This inner world is a world of unconscious ghost object images which we have constructed during the course of development. (ibid., p.877)

Some analytic thinkers, such as Bion, Fairbairn, Ferenczi, Kohut and Winnicott, seemed vaguely aware of the dilemma of the internal model, and have struggled to find a place for the environment. While Klein considered that internal objects were built up as a result of inborn instincts, Fairbairn, as Perlow has described (ibid., pp.56 ff.), considered that the establishment of internalized objects occurred as a result of the influence of interpersonal interactions with emotionally significant people, especially the mother. It was the nature of the real object, in interaction with the individual, that led to internalization and to the establishment of what Fairbairn called 'dynamic structures'. His internal objects were not to be thought of as phantasies in the Kleinian sense but as basic organizations of the personality, stable and persistent over time, and capable of acting as independent agencies with their own motivational system. Fairbairn aimed to avoid the 'demonology' of Klein by proposing a theory of internal objects which was more theoretically consistent with regard to issues of motivation. As he wrote:

> in the interests of consistency, I must now draw the logical conclusion of my theory of dynamic structures and acknowledge that, since internal objects are structures, they must necessarily be,

in some measure at least, dynamic. In drawing this conclusion and making this acknowledgement, I shall not only be here following the precedent of Freud, but also, it would seem, conforming to the demands of such psychological facts as are revealed, e.g. in dreams and the phenomena of paranoia. This further step will enhance the explanatory value of my theory of mental structures by introducing additional possibilities into the endopsychic situation by way of permutation and combination. It must be recognized, however, that, in practice, it is very difficult to differentiate between the activity of internalized objects and the activity of the ego structures with which they are associated; and, with a view to avoiding any appearance of demonology, it seems wise to err, if anything, on the side of overweighting the activity of the ego structures rather than otherwise. It remains true, nevertheless, that under certain conditions internalized objects may acquire a dynamic independence which cannot be ignored. It is doubtless in this direction that we must look for an explanation of the fundamental animism of human beings, which is none the less persistent under the surface even when it is hidden under the veneers of civilization and science, but which significantly betrays itself even in the most sophisticated forms of art. (Fairbairn, 1952, p.132)

Fairbairn, though putting forward a complex model of dynamic structures, emphasized that their origin was not internal but that the structures were established as a defensive reaction to emotionally frustrating experiences in the environment, particularly with regard to the mother–child relationship. The internal world represents a kind of withdrawal from the environment and interpersonal relations. However, he did not develop in detail how the internal structures and the environment interrelated. But, reflecting on Fairbairn's theory as one which involves some kind of intimate relation between mental structure and the environment, it may well be that not everything about the early relationships is internalized. Though there may be some basic innate mental structure, rather as the child is born with a basic visual organization that has to be used in order to function effectively, then perhaps these mental structures can only be activated and then organized in active and ongoing interrelationship with others. In addition, there is a constant need to continue to relate in order that the structures are maintained. Such a view may be more compatible with the non-Cartesian model of the mind.

Bion's uses the term 'object' in a particular way to describe primitive states of mind, mainly in psychotic or borderline patients, and avoids confusion with the many other uses of the term. He chose the term 'object',

> partly because it is sufficiently abstract to allow us to invest it with special meaning. Yet this special meaning is difficult to convey. The patient uses a word, but his word does not name the same thing as is named by the same word used by the analyst ... He appears to feel that the word is not the phenomenon ... but is identical with the thing-in-itself. Unfortunately, this is further complicated by the fact that the thing-in-itself seems to be regarded by the patient with the same expectation that we entertain for an idea. Thus, if someone moves a table, it is to him as if someone had interfered with his mind. It is for the word thus used that I reserve the term 'object'. (Bion, 1992, pp.157–8)

Objects so described can be understood as 'unassimilated sense impressions' (ibid., p.160), and cannot be articulated as words are ordinarily articulated. Thus, Bion reserved the term 'object' for quite specific uses, for trying to grasp the way that psychotic patients communicate; this avoids confusion with other uses of the term, though clearly this is a very individual way of conceptualizing the object.

Subjectivity, if one follows the thought of the later Wittgenstein, no longer arises from the private world of the individual but is a product of relating to others in the social field. Subject relations, one might say, occurs through interaction with other subjects in the social field. If the object as such enters into consideration, it is first of all as physical object in the intersubjective field. If one follows Bion's definition of the object, it may be more accurate to confine the use of other kinds of object to the field of psychotic subject relations, where the subject experiences states of fragmentation and can feel as if they were decomposed into bits, which Bion described for convenience as objects. But really, these are the basic elements that make up the individual side of the subjective organization, elements which interact with one another and are normally experienced as belonging somehow or other to the subject. The psychotic subject has a precarious subjective organization, made up of 'loose' elements that can fall apart and can be experienced then as physical objects. Perhaps one could pay more attention to the details of what holds the elements together, the psychical 'glue', so to speak; and what gives coherence to the subject and also what may push subjective organizations into breakdown.

In psychotic states, the elements of the subject are felt acutely to be subject 'to' outside forces. Instead of being part of the subjective organization, the social field is then experienced as outside the subject, and often then the place where projections are located. If one did talk of an inner world in the traditional sense, it could more accurately refer to what has already been referred to as a kind of unconscious storehouse of rules and sensory elements out of which the subject creates pictures of the world. This storehouse may correspond to the organization of Bion's alpha elements. These latter 'may be presumed to be mental and individual, subjective, to a high degree personal, particular and unequivocally belonging to the domain of epistemology in a particular person' (ibid., p.181). Alpha elements are more elemental than objects, and are involved in the transformation of raw sense experience into visual images that can be stored and registered, enabling thinking, and I would add desiring and hence subjective experience, to take place. Perhaps they are the building blocks out of which the subject is formed.

Perlow puts Winnicott and Kohut together as they both gave more emphasis than many other analytic thinkers to the 'actual roles played by the emotionally important people surrounding the individual, and their influence on the development of the self' (Perlow, 1995, p.141).

Winnicott, though Perlow does not suggest this, perhaps came closest of all the previous thinkers to a theory of the subject and to a subject relations theory. As Ogden put it, 'Winnicott's work represents a major advance in the development of the psychoanalytic conception of the subject ... At the heart of Winnicott's thinking is the notion that the living, experiencing subject exists neither in reality nor in fantasy, but in a potential space between the two. The Winnicottian subject is not at the beginning (and never entirely becomes) coincident with the psyche of the individual' (Ogden, 1994, p.49).

With his notion of a transitional object, the infant's first 'not-me' possession, Winnicott described a form of object relationship where the object is experienced simultaneously as created by the infant and as discovered by him. The transitional object comes from without from our, or the mother's point of view, but not so from he point of view of the baby. Nor does it come from within; it is not an internal object along the lines developed by Klein. The essential feature of the transitional object and transitional phenomena 'is *the paradox, and the acceptance of the paradox*: the baby creates the object, but the object was there waiting to be created' (Winnicott, 1971, p.89).

Furthermore, 'Transitional objects and phenomena belong to the realm of illusion which is at the basis of initiation of experience. This early stage in development is made possible by the mother's special capacity for making adaptation to the needs of the infant, thus allowing the infant the illusion that what the infant creates really exists' (ibid., p.14).

Thus a new area of experience, the transitional area, is brought into being by the meeting, or coming together, of two different viewpoints focused around the needs of the baby. The transitional object never 'goes inside', nor is it forgotten or mourned; it just gradually loses meaning because 'the transitional phenomena have become diffused, have become spread out over the whole intermediate territory between "inner psychic reality" and the "external world as perceived by two persons in common", that is to say, over the whole cultural field' (ibid., p.5).

Clearly, Winnicott considered that he was pointing to a fundamental kind of relationship between baby and mother, and one that also becomes vital in later life. It is not described in terms of some simple relationship between self and other, or subject and object; it is more subtle, complex and 'paradoxical'. The subject for Winnicott seems to go beyond the individual into the intermediate or transitional area; the subjectivity of the infant certainly seems to unfold within the transitional space. Based on the early transitional form of relationship, cultural experience for Winnicott, or what one could also call intense or focused subjective experience, is located in the 'potential space' between the individual and the environment, (ibid., p.100).

One could thus say that the location of the subject for Winnicott lies in the space between the individual and the social fields, not merely within the individual. This radical view of human subjectivity marks out Winnicott's ideas as quite different from most other psychoanalytic thinkers, and more in line with recent philosophical and neurophysiological thought, as well some of the sociological thought described above, which disposes of the old model of the mind as being only an internal phenomenon. In this sense, I would see Winnicott as providing the basis for a new kind of psychoanalytic theory, based on the complexities of the relations between subjects.

In his complex paper, 'The use of an object' (in Winnicott, 1971, pp.86–94), Winnicott describes what could be seen as an outline of a theory of subject relations. He first of all describes 'object-relating', which refers to when the subject is an isolate, it can be described in terms of the individual subject. The individual subject at this level functions at an omnipotent level. Winnicott describes a more mature level of functioning where the subject can use an object. First of all there is object-relating and then object-use. In between, however, 'is the most difficult thing, perhaps, in human development; or the most irksome of all the early failures that come for mending. This thing that there is in between relating and use is the placing of the object outside the area of the subject's omnipotent control; that is, the subject's perception of the object as an external phenomenon, not as a projective entity, in fact recognition of it as an entity in its own right' (ibid., p.89).

The change from relating to using involves a particular process in which the subject destroys the object, but the object survives the destruction. He uses the word 'destruction' 'not because of the baby's impulse to destroy, but because of the object's liability not to survive' (ibid., p.93). Once the object has survived – and this, then, may not necessarily happen – then the subject moves into a new kind of position where he can start to 'live a life in the world of objects' (ibid., p.90). The subject enters into a world where objects can be used, and where he can have live contact with others. I would suggest that in these descriptions of the way that the subject changes from an isolated individual to being in contact with others, one has the beginnings of what could become a fully developed theory of subject relations. For this reason, I would see Winnicott's thinking as taking us essentially into new territory, which we have only just begun to explore.

6   SUMMARY: CAPTURING
THE SUBJECT

Throughout the book it has been emphasized that the psychoanalytic encounter is more about striving to become a subject than about having objects. Freud's discoveries were very much about bringing back into the realm of the subject elements of the mind such as dreams and fantasies which had been devalued as mere objects of some kind of objective knowledge or as of no consequence. The analytic setting itself, with the analyst sitting behind the patient demonstrates literally that the analytic relationship is not about an object relationship, at least not in the usual sense, for the analyst is out of reach and out of sight. Arguments have been presented to show that, with the analyst not being available as an object, the analytic setting sets in motion a complex search for the human subject.

In the first chapter there were two images used to attempt to capture the nature of this elusive subject – that of a ploughed field and a description of Paul Klee's pictures. The ploughed field, with a number of furrows, is like the human subject, with criss-crossing paths available for multiple use, and with the owner of the field coming and going in order to attend to it. The field of the subject comprises many paths, no one path is central as such. In a late Klee picture, every point of arrival at once becomes a point of departure; it moves away from the traditional central point of focus towards many-faceted and unending points of departure. This description matches that of the analytic search for the human subject, when we try and look intimately into our own and other people's subjective lives. As was emphasized at the beginning, my own exploration of this field of inquiry has proceeded along a number of different paths, borrowing from, and making excursions into, other disciplines, in order to do justice to the complexity of the task. Where possible, I have tried to link up my thought with clinical work. However, I am also aware that much goes on in the analytic encounter that need not necessarily be defined, for it might interfere with the spontaneity of the work. Yet there is also a place to define, explore and question the very basis of the work. This may even ultimately help the patient.

I am aware, however, that what I have put forward is still only some of the foundations of a theory of subject relations, and that much needs to be developed further. I hope that I have laid the basis for such further developments.

In order to highlight what has been proposed, I shall pick out some of the key points in my argument, leaving out much of the explanation and elaboration. In order to put this outline into some sort of perspective, I would summarize my concept of subject relations in terms of the following points.

The term 'subject' captures a basic aspect of the human situation, that we are both subject 'of' and subject 'to' various phenomena. Subject relations involves interactions with other subjects in the social field. The subject weaves his way through the individual and the social fields in complex interactions. Taking account of one's life as an other is the essential social element required to achieve a 'full' sense of subjectivity. This includes the movement between subject and other in a constant search for recognition of their desires. Desire is the element of otherness essential to the subject. Analytic subjectivity comprises an openness to the unconscious, incorporating ambiguity, paradox and uncertainty; in exploring subjectivity in the psychoanalytic encounter, one is dealing with multiple processes of cohesion and dissemination. Psychoanalytic subjectivity also implies being in several different positions in relation to others. Subject relations includes being oriented to the other, being affected by the other, and dialogue between subjects. In addition, subject relations is concerned with how subjective experience takes place along a path or circuit, a transformational circuit, leading from the social field to the individual (including their drives) and back again. Subject relations needs to take account of where the subject is placed in the social field; the social subjective event provides the framework for the individual's subjective world.

In order to capture the nature of the human subject I have suggested the use of the term 'subjective organization'. This description, a kind of 'ideal type', along the lines used by Weber, refers to the organizing principle involved in one's sense of I-ness as well as that involved in the way that the subject is organized in the social field. The subjective organization belongs on the one hand to the individual subject, yet is it also a dual organization, arising within a relationship to the other in a social context. It is difficult to say where the subjective is individual and where it is collective; just as the individual and collective consciousnesses in Durkheim's thought interpenetrate, so the individual subjective organization merges at various points with that of the collective, both within the individual and at contact points with other subjective organizations in the social field. There is the organization belonging to the individual subject, made up of purely individual feelings, perceptions, etc., and the organization of the collective, made up of other subjects experiencing different subjective phenomena. These two different organizations intermingle. They may come together at various points; for example, around essential social activities. Such social events, which I have called the work of the day, provide the basic structure for the subjective organization.

One could say that each individual is incomplete as a subject in himself. The individual has his own identity and sphere of action, but it is only when individuals come together in some sort of collective structure, however small, that they fully encounter one another in their dual being, as individual and as other. The subjective organization is a dual structure made up of individual and collective elements united or interpenetrating in some way. Furthermore, I have proposed that any theory of subject relations would need to take account of how the subject shifts and moves between positions within the subjective organization, as well as between different kinds of organization.

I shall now proceed with a summary of the key points put forward as they evolved in the text.

Chapter 1 gradually built up a picture of the human subject made up of interacting elements with no privileged place where the elements all come together, no central place where meaning and truth are located.

The term 'subject' as a functioning structure is not one that can only be applied to 'internal' states belonging to a single individual, but it merges with what has been traditionally called the social, a point of view shared with Freud, whose own position was that social psychology and individual psychology merged into one another.

The issue of psychical locality, central to the book, concerns whether or not it makes sense to locate the subject in the individual, in the social field, somewhere between, or, as proposed, in some shifting position, involving both individual and social fields. My overall emphasis is that in trying to make sense of the complex issue of human subjectivity it is necessary to have a pluralistic model, one which takes account of multiple streams or processes, consisting of many elements with varying degrees of connectedness. Though there is complexity in this way of thinking, it can also leave room for a consideration of how the many elements may cohere by means of various amounts of organization.

The image of the ploughed field is put forward as a model of the human subject, with criss-crossing paths and furrows, available for multiple use and with the farmer, the owner of the field, coming and going in order to attend to it. There is no centre in the field as such, at least not in a functional sense; it has a different kind of structure, a network of traces of activity, with varying degrees of organization. Thomas Nagel has a similar description of the world as 'centreless', full of many different points of view, in his book *The View from Nowhere*.

The old quest for the human 'centre' is reminiscent of the search for the location of the 'soul', or the place where consciousness resides, or where memory or language resides in the brain. These quests have proved fruitless until the search for a centre has been abandoned in favour of an 'interactional' model, where a function is produced as a result of interaction between many elements, many paths as it were. Such a model was integral to Freud's early work on aphasia, where he saw language as a property of the whole language system in the brain rather than only a property of individual areas. Freud continued to use this interactional approach. However, at times he also stuck to the traditional Cartesian model of the individual mind isolated from other minds; but there was often a pull towards another kind of thinking, which takes account of the fleeting and ambiguous nature of our subjective life as it exists in relation to a world of other subjects, and which cannot be tied down to the centralized and solitary ego.

Freud's overturning of the central place of conscious reason in the life of the subject in favour of the unconscious, or the 'decentring' of the subject, has often been compared to the Copernican revolution. But there is a further development of this revolution: the individual is no longer even the centre of his own world; instead, the individual subject belongs to a wider structure, one which involves the network of other subjects. There is no one centre in this network; rather, there are a series of 'contact points' where subjects meet one another. The organization that involves the subject, or the 'subjective organization', goes beyond that of the individual as such and involves the realm of the social; it cuts into what has been seen mistakenly as two separate realms. The term 'subjective organization' is intentionally rather a loose term, an 'ideal type', which aims to cover a fairly wide field of subjective phenomena, ranging from what could be considered as the merely individual to what takes place between subjects in the social field, where subjects meet others in the network of other subjects. Whatever we have individually in our minds is effectively organized in interaction in the social field.

When the life of the subject is looked at, it is inevitable that another subject comes into view. Subject relations concerns how subjects interact with other subjects. Bollas describes how 'The concepts of interplay, interrelating, intersubjectivity, have as much use in a subject relations theory as in an object relations theory' (Bollas, 1989, p.109).

Analytic subjectivity incorporates openness to the unconscious, ambiguity, paradox and uncertainty. Husserl described the paradox of human subjectivity as the fact that the human being is both a subject for the world and at the same time an object in the world (Husserl, 1954, p.178).

It is suggested that there are three basic ways of looking at the subjective/objective distinction: first, to eliminate the distinction, as, for example, Husserl and Dewey attempted; second, to focus more on the subjective understanding, as for example Kierkegaard and Sartre proposed; and third, to attempt to find a place for both the subjective and objective realms, as Thomas Nagel has suggested.

Dewey argued against the setting up of a hard and fast wall between the experiencing subject and nature. The task for the existing subject is, for Kierkegaard, to become subjective and move away from objectivity. Sartre describes a complex interplay between the Other-as-subject and the Other-as-object. When we try to fully encounter the Other, we are taken away from the Other-as-subject to the Other-as-object, and we are perpetually moving between these two positions. One could interpret Sartre as indicating a model of the human subject with no centre, rather as comprising an essential absence, a negativity, something unknown, within its structure; and that the subject is constantly moving between positions rather than fixed in one position. Freud, too, considered that there was always a point where we reached the unknown in the human subject. It is suggested that there is indeed always something unknown and irreducible in the human subject, and hence something about us that is essentially difficult to describe.

Too much objectivity as well as too much subjectivity can become a clinical problem. An important task of therapy can be to help the schizoid patient emerge into subjectivity away from objectivity. But there is also a need for some objectivity to help keep the patient grounded. In this sense, Nagel's use of both subjective and objective points of view is helpful.

The picture of the human subject as made up of interacting elements with no privileged centre is consistent with recent neurophysiological research on the nature of consciousness. Chapter 2 argues that a fuller understanding of consciousness may help us to understand more about how we lose a sense of who we are, as well as to enable us to gain more of a subjective life.

A common theme that runs through many of Freud's descriptions of the psychical apparatus was how he saw it as a whole system with various interacting parts and functions. This approach was already in evidence in his monograph *On Aphasia*. His model of the speech apparatus is one involving a whole organization: a representation is not localized in one place as it always immediately involved associations, links with other places. It is argued that Freud puts forward in this monograph an important model of the relation between the psychical and physiological realms as a dual structure. One could consider that drives transform the subject, while the drives themselves are transformed by different subjective positions. This proposal is put forward in more detail in Chapter 3.

As in Freud's model of the psychical apparatus, its functions take place as a result of interactions between parts or systems, the apparatus is particularly susceptible to problems where the links between parts of the system are interfered with, such as in aphasia or psychotic states.

Dennett argues that there is no evidence for a special place in the brain where consciousness takes place or where it all comes together for presentation to consciousness. He argues that there is no single point or boundary line in the brain where all representations are united and where we can read off the results. There is no 'theatre' where representations are projected onto a screen where they are read off by an internal observer, or by the 'ghost in the machine'. In place of this kind of Cartesian model of the mind, Dennett puts forward a 'multiple drafts' model of consciousness, in which all varieties of mental activity are accomplished by multitrack processes of interpretation and elaboration. There are multiple drafts of narrative fragments at various stages of editing in various places in the brain. Consciousness is distributed around the brain, and no moment can count as the precise moment at which conscious events occur. There is not a single narrative thread that comprises consciousness, not a single 'defile', but multiple fragments of narrative, some of which are more lasting than others. There is no 'central meaner' or organizer, but consciousness is just what goes on in the brain. Each act of discrimination is registered in many places. There is, in Freudian terms, a sort of 'over-determination' written into the brain.

Dennett's model seems to reflect the experience of the psychoanalytic encounter in that we deal with narrative fragments, with bits of story, past and present; with elaborations, projections and confusions. We allow bits of the patient's story to come to light, and we may help clear the clutter and allow the unconscious meanings to come through to consciousness.

Bakhtin, in his commentary on Dostoevsky, points towards a subject relations approach to psychoanalysis by focusing on dialogue, and by contrasting the dialogic approach to communication based on interaction between subjects with a monologic approach based on the cognitive subject relating to objects of cognition. The idea in Dostoevsky's novels is a live event, played out at the point of dialogic meeting between two of several consciousnesses.

One could assert that Bakhtin's view of communication involves communion between what one could call the 'many voices of consciousness', both within the individual and between individuals. Consciousness has many streams or voices or drafts. Through dialogue, in the social field, the themes of these voices may become more or less coherent. In the analytic encounter, one could say that the patient moves from having a single or reduced stream of consciousness, with one or few voices, to the capacity to experience many voices, allowing them to interpenetrate and overlap.

The model of the Cartesian Theatre that Dennett dismissed and that Ryle called the 'ghost in the machine', implies that there is an inner private world or space where we inspect our thoughts and feelings, and that this is in some way a reflection or copy of the external world. Descartes first put forward the concept of the mind as a single inner space, or what Rorty called the 'glassy essence', with an isolated subject only certain of his own thoughts and with a mind and body somehow separate though interconnected. Since then, the problem of the mind and consciousness has become central to western thought and Descartes' model has become central to most psychoanalytical thinking.

However, I presented arguments from several thinkers, including Wittgenstein, Ryle, Rorty and Cavell, who attack this now outdated model of the mind. The traditional model of the mind, the representational model, is contrasted with one where mental events are dependent on social interactions. Wittgenstein emphasized the idea of a language system made up of elements being used in a social context, in what he called 'situations', in human customs and institutions. He denied that the picture of an inner process and hence of a private inner space was an accurate description of what takes place when we speak. There were not 'meanings' going through the mind in addition to words. The words simply expressed the thought. Instead of there being internal mental objects that become translated into meanings, meanings arise out of the use of words in a social context, the language games. Intentions are embedded in human institutions, or in 'forms of life'. Knowledge is no longer a matter of presenting thoughts to consciousness but of understanding the use of words in context, in social situations, where we find ourselves as 'living human beings'.

From this view of the mind it follows that subjective experience is not so much an issue about individual minds or about an inner process, but has to include the social field. While introspection gives us a certain amount of information about what we think and say when we turn our attention to some of our streams of thought, it is only one aspect of the human situation. It is only in an encounter with the other that matters become interesting and that true dialogic understanding can happen.

Perhaps it would be more accurate or useful to talk about our 'subjective world' rather than our inner world. That way, we leave in suspense the philosophical problem of inner and outer and whether or not there are mental representations and what they are. We have instead to consider what we have to deal with every day in the analytic relationship – what it is like to be a person, and how subjective experience is made up of many elements, some coming from ourselves and some from others, in a complex network, a unique subjective world.

In Chapter 3, it was proposed that the term 'subject' captures a basic dual aspect of the human situation, that we are both subject 'of' and subject 'to' various phenomena. That is, the term refers both to our sense of 'I-ness', who we are, that we can be the authors of our actions and our history; while at the same time it also indicates that we are subject to various forces outside of the orbit of the 'I' who speaks, forces which arise both from the individual and from the environment. The term 'subject' encompasses both the sense of positive identity and the sense of a threat to identity, some force opposing subjectivity.

Freud conceived of the psychical apparatus as a whole system, with various interacting parts and functions; there is a dynamic play between the various elements of the system. The apparatus is made up of a system of relations between elements, the functions of the psyche take place as a result of interactions between parts or subsystems. No one place is the privileged seat of the soul or psyche. But there still remains a fundamental issue for psychoanalytic theories – how much the elements of the whole system are brought together and how much they are kept separate, even when interacting; that is, how much and how the elements are organized.

From the thought of Lacan, one can say that each subject is caught up in a network of other subjects; there is an intersubjective field, made up of criss-crossing chains of meaning, a network of unconscious social structures. This model seems to correspond to the analytic experience, where one may be listening for the way that chains of meaning, narrative structures or 'voices' criss-cross, intermix, fade, dissolve or occasionally cohere. Though Lacan was against any unity in the way that the subject is organized, his thought does highlight the issue of how the subject may or may not cohere.

In Klein's theory, integration is part of a duality. There is a movement away from and towards the possibility of some kind of integrating organization, which corresponds more faithfully to what we see in the session and what can be observed in babies' experiences.

Study of the visual organization reveals what one could call a basic principle of the nervous system – that use leads to increasing organization. There is a basic innate organization built into the visual cortex, but the presence of the social field is required for the organization to develop in complexity, the visual system has to be used to become fully organized. This finding is perhaps compatible with the suggestion that the subject is in possession of various functions and structures that need to be used in social interaction for their full realization. It is in this sense that a subjective organization is conceived as comprising the individual within the social field, hungry for interaction.

From the work of Luria and Vygotsky, one can say that the structural organization of human mental life involves and requires interaction between people, social interaction.

Lichtenstein formulates how psychic structures are related to one another by avoiding conceiving them as related to the whole person. Instead, he defines the self as the sum total of the transformations which are possible functions of an early-formed invariant correlation of the various basic elements of the nervous system. The invariant element involved in human identity is the primary relationship to the mother, which is a thematic configuration, arising in the earliest contact of the infant with the mother. There is a basic identity theme with variations.

Developmentally early psychical organizations are probably in part based on sensations and body zones which require the continuous care of the mothering adult for their establishment. One could imagine that there are particularly intense early experiences, such as moments of engagement between mother and baby, which can form the basis for a fully subjective life, and could be seen as the template for an early subjective organization. One could describe the baby as already a proto-subject, one that is beginning to form meaning as it elicits care from the caretaker. The early parent–baby relationship presumably forms the matrix for the subsequent more sophisticated subjective organization.

The subjective organization is a habitual way of organizing subjective experience.

Bollas points to the pivotal existence in mental life, brought out in psychoanalysis by the use of free association, of a fundamental and creative process of fragmentation or disorganization, or what he calls 'dissemination' or 'cracking up'. Bollas seems to be describing the use of a radical process of dissemination in the way that the subject discovers their own truth and elaborates their personal idiom. He points towards a notion of multiple processes of cohesion and dissemination with no actual centre in the psychic organization.

It is suggested that it is worthwhile to focus on the nature of the psychic organization, how its elements are organized, how the subject is built up and how the organization is experienced in the analytic situation. Any theory of subject relations would need to take account of how the subject shifts and moves between positions or between different kinds of organization. These movements will in turn affect the way that the subject relates to other subjects, the way that others impact on the subject and the orientation of the subject to objects.

Being a subject involves some capacity to take up different positions without their becoming fixed in a kind of frozen state of being. The analyst may have to bear being in a number of different subjective positions in the session, rather than allow himself to become fixed in one place; though at any moment, he may find himself 'moored' in one place more favoured than another. The analyst's free-floating attention consists of a subjective oscillation between different positions or moorings or placements. This may mean having to tolerate a considerable amount of ambiguity, uncertainty and paradox. In this sense, the analyst is poised at the point at which the paradox of human subjectivity arises.

The importance of the relationship between the subject and the drives is emphasized. The drive is seen as having a dual nature, being both attached to the physiological organization and yet also touching on the developing subject's psychological organization. Freud's theory of the drives points towards ways that the subject may become organized or disorganized, through the way that the partial drives are unified or fragmented at adolescence around the primacy of the genitals. Freud seems to be describing an elaborate relationship between the subject and drives, where the subject appears and disappears at various points in a complicated 'circuit' or 'route' of the drive. Fundamental to the vicissitudes of the drive, or how it is transformed, is the position taken by the subject in relation to other subjects. The drive can be seen as involving a process, or a complicated pathway, capable of transforming the subject; while the drive itself can be transformed by the different positions taken up by the subject. Involved along the way in the perverse pathway is the loss of subjectivity, usually by the subject desiring to control the other, using them as an object in the sense of someone whose only function is to elicit sexual pleasure for the other; so that one could say that in this process, one subject is replaced by another subject.

Desire is put forward as the essential psychical element involved both in the drive and in the structure of the subject. Kojève emphasized that the person who contemplates and is absorbed by what he contemplates, that is the 'knowing subject', only finds a particular kind of knowledge, knowledge of the object. To find the subject, desire is needed. The desiring subject is the human subject. As Kojève described, what distinguishes the human from the animal is the fact that human desire is not just directed towards other objects but towards other desires. The mutual desire for recognition plays a fundamental role in structuring human relationships. The doubling of self-consciousness is the essential dynamic structure of relations between subjects, in which there is simultaneously activity by the individual and activity of the other, a dynamic which one could call 'intersubjective'. The movement between the subject and the other in a constant search for recognition of their desires constitutes human reality, what is truly intersubjective. Desire is the element of otherness essential to the subject, a notion which leads on to consider the elusive nature of human identity, of who and what we are, how we may appear or disappear as subjects, where subject and other come together or fail to connect, in what one might call a 'play' of subjects.

Shakespeare's *The Comedy of Errors* reveals some fundamental truths about ourselves, for example that human identity is an elusive and precarious entity, nothing about it can be taken for granted, and that perhaps we rely too much on things being the same for reassurance about who we are. The play also seems to emphasize how having a human identity and being identical are not the same thing. We may rely on things being the same, but identities can be easily transformed. One subject can easily turn into another subject, while appearing to remain the same. There is often in life a play of subjects. Furthermore, we are perhaps all incomplete to some extent, we need the other to feel more ourselves.

In the theatre, there is often some kind of process of masking and unmasking, which has parallels with the psychoanalytic process. The analytic subject, like a character in a play, starts from a position where various kinds of truths are concealed and then, in the course of the analytic process, are revealed. The psychoanalyst has a mask-like function. He is out of sight and is not fully known to the patient. The patient's ordinary defences are then lost and there is potentially greater access to the unconscious. The analyst wears a mask in order to help reveal the patient's truth. This is not to say that the analyst only wears a mask, for there are times when his human aspects are revealed, as discussed in detail in Chapter 4. But this takes place in a context in which he appears and disappears from behind the mask.

Further consideration of the nature of human identity, based on the thought of Locke, led Lichtenstein to develop a concept of identity as a theme with variations. The personality can be seen to be organized around certain essential configurations. This allows for the possibility of multiple themes, or narratives, or voices, becoming organized around one or two basic patterns. In addition, one can see how in some patients there is little sense of a basic and secure 'invariant' identity theme. Without this basic element, they may become too easily merged with the other, and hence either retreat into a citadel of unrelatedness, or else find themselves becoming confused with the other. There may be a variation around a theme, but if the basic theme is not grounded, the variations may become fragmented, rigid or confusing.

Ricoeur emphasizes how it is in narratives that one can find some constancy and consistency in one's life. Being affected by narrated events becomes the organizing principle of subjective life, where one may gather together one's life. Literary and personal narratives interlink and are complementary. In fiction, the connections between action and agent are often easier to perceive than in life, and so can provide for an illustration of, or a kind of imaginary experiment about, issues such as the nature of the self. Networks of narratives united in plots, involving characters in interaction, are ways of organizing the actions of agents.

One could say that for an author to write about characters in interaction, there is a fundamental need to transform himself so that he can see himself through the eyes of the other; only then can he imagine these interactions in a live way. This may require some stepping back from himself while also immersing himself in the life of the other. In this sense, the literary activity is relevant to one's understanding of subjectivity. The author makes a character, a subject, who appears to be outside himself in some way; and yet the character arises from the author himself, often unconsciously, from some 'other' place. The created literary world seems to be separate from the writer, and separate from the real, mundane world, in an imaginary space. And yet, maybe the subject of the story, the subject that is created by the author, is true to life in more than the literal way. Usually the subject of the story is seen as just fiction. But maybe this subject is a true subject. We are all subjects of a story, which is perhaps why we may like reading and can feel that a novel or a play makes us feel more alive. When we enter a story, we come into contact with something alive in us, we enter into a deep relationship with our own subjectivity, where subject and other are in an alive and 'playful' interaction. Fiction in this sense is not escape but discovery; we find ourselves, our sense of being a subject, through a play of subjects, through the playful transformation of subjects.

It follows that if psychoanalysis is fundamentally concerned with subject relations, then the subjectivity of the analyst plays an inevitable part in the analytic relationship.

Chapter 4, which was mainly concerned with clinical matters, dealt with aspects of the analyst's subjectivity, concentrating particularly on the analyst's human aspects, and using the work of John Klauber as a basis for discussion and elaboration of this theme. The analytic relationship, though an intimate one, is also a distorted one, where the subjectivities of analyst and patient are not at the same level: the patient's world is to be examined in the open, while the analyst's is essentially private, or masked, except at a few contact points with the patient. However, how the mask may be lifted, or not, may have important bearings on the conduct of an analysis. Analyst and patient do not, then, start from similar subjective positions.

The chapter discussed the human or personal aspects of the psychoanalytic relationship and how the analyst's humanity may or may not be coordinated with his analytic function. Discussion was focused around general issues about how the personality of the analyst affects his method of working. For example, how his style of interpreting, his readiness to accept certain feelings and not others, as well as his value systems, may determine the course of an analysis, including the unfolding of the transference. There was also discussion of how the fear of being seduced by the patient may motivate the attitudes of analysts in their individual work and in their institutional behaviour; and how the strain of having to be restrained with patients affects the analyst's attitudes to them. There was also discussion of three reasons why analysts may need to interpret – for intellectual, emotional and defensive reasons. There was also a discussion of the place of humour and irony in psychoanalysis. It was argued that appropriate humour is an essential accompaniment of the psychoanalytic relationship, while consideration of the place of irony leads on to the more theoretical issues concerning the nature of analytic subjectivity. There is something ironic about the analytic stance. The analyst is both present and absent, reveals and conceals, is both available and is a concealed presence. This stance both reflects and takes account of the elusive nature of our subjective life.

One could say that the analyst should try to judge in what ways his personality and individual reactions affect the development of the transference, but that in itself is insufficient to explain the complexities of the analytic encounter. It is not just what the patient makes out of the analyst's personality and emotional states but also what the analyst makes of him that is at issue. The analyst should try to understand not only the patient's perceptions of him but how the analyst's own personal preferences, including his preferred models of working, help to create the meaning that arises out of the analytic relationship. Various fears endemic to psychoanalysis may, however, prevent the analyst from recognizing the individuality of the patient, his own unique subjective world.

The analyst's position, which includes his use of free-floating attention, involves being in a number of different positions or moorings, where chains of meaning, narrative structures or voices criss-cross, intermix, fade, dissolve or occasionally cohere. When the analyst listens to the patient in this way, one has engaged him as a subject. If the analyst himself allows himself to act in this way, he is more fully a subject.

Chapter 5 dealt with the realm 'between subjects'. It was proposed that the structure of the subject, or the subjective organization, requires something beyond the mere individual for its full realization.

Subject and other are inevitably linked. One could say that perceiving or taking account of one's life as an other is the essential social element required to acquire a 'full' sense of subjectivity, one that is not encapsulated in an isolated or narcissistic position. Taking account of one's life as an other involves the dialogic element.

Bakhtin looks at how the aesthetic moment is a pivotal experience for human beings, where subjectivity is lived and created in an intense and fundamental way. An author must look at himself through the eyes of another, or he must become another in relation to himself, in order to produce a work of art. This requires that one takes a stand outside oneself to some extent, but equally important is the need to return from outside back to oneself. Resolution of the Oedipal situation implies having some ability to move between positions; for example, returning back to intimacy with the mother from a more distant perspective. Failure to stand outside oneself and see oneself as another implies being fixed in a narcissistic position, with an empty kind of subjectivity, and with little capacity to make the return to intimacy.

Bakhtin emphasizes the need in aesthetic experience to find a lived experience, which involves a meeting of the other as other, the essence of the subjectively lived standpoint. Subjectivity is spurious if only lived from within; to become a subject, otherness is required.

From the work of infant research on the development of the child, the infant is oriented to his environment from early on, he learns through relating to others in an intersubjective perspective. This implies that the infant gradually emerges as a subject, with an increasing awareness of his own and other people's subjective experiences, as it develops an organizing subjective perspective. The latter is built up through the relationship with the caretakers and through interaction around significant social everyday events. The social subjective event, or what I call the work of the day, provides the basic framework for the subjective world of the infant. The work of the day requires a constant amount of organization in order for it to be maintained; that is, ongoing maintenance activity. The work of the day provides contact points for subjects, where they may encounter one another, however briefly.

Infant researchers conceive intersubjectivity in terms of sharing experiences. The term 'intersubjective' is used by a variety of different thinkers in different ways, depending on the model of a subject used and the way that the social field is taken into consideration. Schutz has a complex notion of intersubjectivity. He describes how one needs to examine, in any intersubjective relation, the contexts of meaning surrounding the relation, the relationship between one's subjective understanding of the other person's experiences and one's own experiences, the nature of the orientation to the other, how one understands the other and is affected by the other, and the nature of the social world. Such a comprehensive view of intersubjective understanding could be applied to the psychoanalytic situation, where there is a complex interaction between the different subjective positions of analyst and patient.

In adult life, what may be critical for the subject is where they are placed in the social field, what position they take up at any moment, or which position they occupy in the social structure. In order to clarify the role of social structure in the life of the subject, a number of different notions of social structure are examined. Subjectivity comes on the one hand to be marked out and confined within social structure, and on the other hand allowed a certain amount of free play.

For Lévi-Strauss, the sociological field is organized as a system of differentiating features. All the various elements of the social structure can be seen as comprising a vast group or system of transformations between different elements and levels. Lévi-Strauss' emphasis on how unconscious social structures regulate social relations using the binary laws of language is similar to the thought of Lacan, when he described how chains of meaning cut across the subject in symbolic circuits. The subject-to-be already has a place marked out on the kinship structure before he is born. He is already situated in a complicated, unconscious network of symbols.

Enid Balint described how elements of the subject's pre-history can be unconsciously communicated across generations. Chains of meaning can be kept circulating in the social structure until they are dealt with.

The notion of social structure developed by Lévi-Strauss and interpreted by Derrida is one where there is no fixed centre, nor is the relation between the individual and the social order a fixed one. There is a looseness in the social bond. Relations between elements of the social structure are constantly shifting, changing and being transformed. This model of social structure is consistent with what has been proposed about how subjects interact in the social field; for example, how identities can merge and shift in various symbolic circuits, in a constant play of subjects.

Marx pointed towards how subjective life is both dependent on social structure and can be transformed in various ways by that structure. In particular, he showed how man as subject can be transformed into a mere object or commodity when he is cut off from his own products. Marxist theory is in part a theory about the loss of subjectivity.

For Lyotard, a person is always located at 'nodal points' of specific communication circuits. One is always located at a post through which various kinds of message pass. There are varying degrees of mobility with regard to these language games. For Lyotard, the social subject seems to dissolve in the dissemination of language games. The social field is atomized into multiple networks.

With Durkheim's thought, the individual is intimately related to the collective, as the individual and collective consciousnesses are intertwined within the individual. The individual has his own area of personal freedom, but he is also constantly being transformed by social relationships. At the same time, as the individual is transformed by society, society in turn is transformed by the changed individuals.

Following some of Durkheim's thought, it is suggested that the subjective organization belongs on the one hand to the individual subject. Yet it is a dual organization, arising within a relationship with others, and within that is a social context. It is difficult to say where the subjective organization is individual and where it is collective; just as the individual and collective consciousnesses of Durkheim interpenetrate, so the individual subjective organization merges at various points with that of others in the social field. There is the organization belonging to the individual subject, made up of purely individual subjective phenomena, and the organization of the collective, made up of other subjects. These two different organizations intermingle. They may come together at various points; for example, around essential social activities, during the work of the day. The latter provides the basic structure for the subjective organization, the scaffolding on to which the individual and collective organizations are built up.

Each individual is incomplete as a subject in himself. The individual has his own identity and sphere of action, but it is only when individuals come together in some sort of collective structure, however small, that they fully come alive, that they encounter one another in their dual being, as individual and other.

Schutz defined in detail the dilemmas of trying to understand another person's subjective point of view, or what I would call their subjective position. For example, understanding the other person's subjective experience is based on one's own subjective experience of him.

When one uses the subjective position, one begins to grasp the other's point of view; he is seen as an other, a person, or a subject, in a context, oriented to others and being affected by others in the social world. A subjective position involves allowing experiences of the other to interpenetrate one's consciousness.

Schutz proposes what I would call the 'basic frame' for understanding another person – that one can only interpret lived experiences belonging to other people in terms of one's own experiences of them, and how one's own lived experience connects up with the other's lived experiences. This could be seen as the basis for the analyst's use of the countertransference, which can be understood as the analyst observing his own experience of the other's lived experiences.

In order to achieve genuine understanding of the other person, one needs to move from a merely observing attitude, in which one is ordering and classifying one's experiences of him as if he were merely a natural object in the world, to a fully subjective attitude. The latter involves paying attention to the subjective context of meaning and the motives and projects of the subject. A fully subjective position requires that the existence of the other as Thou is assumed; that is, the other is not a mere mirror image of one's self.

Schutz proposes a complex account of how one may understand another person. Such understanding is not merely about making sense of the other's words or observing their behaviour, nor is it merely a question of sharing experiences with the other; rather, there needs to be a shift to the subjective position, with orientation to the other, and the allowing of social interaction or being affected by the other. While the basic frame for understanding the other is the understanding of one's own experiences of the other and how they connect up with his lived experiences, we are both living in a common world of directly experienced social reality. For Schutz, the We-relationship defines a fully intersubjective relationship, with each attending to the experiences of the other.

One could say that the analyst has available three different and overlapping areas of experience – his own experience of himself, his experiences of the other as they are arising, and his own experiences arising out of the other's lived experiences. The analyst's scrutiny of his subjective experience of the other's lived experiences would seem to be the useful area of countertransference, while his experiences of the other as they are arising is more like the transference.

The thought of Mead takes more fully into account than Schutz the construction of the subject, as well as giving more consideration to the other as a separate phenomenon. Mead saw minds and selves as essentially social products. He saw the social act as a complex that had to be taken as a dynamic whole, consisting of a circuit involving and, I would add, transforming the experiences of the individual and interactions with others; mind was not something that belonged merely to the individual human organism. The field of the mind included all the components of the field of the social process; that field could not be bounded by the skin of the individual organism. Mead related the world of experience to the whole act of the organism, taking the complete act as a unit, a unit of action. The unit of action involved the individual and others, and in this sense one could also call it a 'unit of relatedness'. Mead developed a model of the mind as not something purely inward, but as forming itself on a pathway between self and other.

One could thus understand subjective experience as taking place along a path or circuit, or what I would call a 'transformational circuit', leading from the social field to the individual and back again. The subject appears and disappears at various points in the circuit.

Mead presented 'the self and the mind in terms of a social process, as the importation of the conversation of gestures into the conduct of the individual organism, so that the individual organism takes these organized attitudes of the others called out by its own attitude, in the form of its gestures, and in reacting to that response calls out other organized attitudes in the others in the community to which the individual belongs. The process can be characterized in a certain sense in terms of the "I" and the "me", the "me" being that group of organized attitudes to which the individual responds as an "I"' (Mead, 1934, p.186).

Both aspects of the self for Mead, the 'I' and the 'me' are essential to its full realization.

Mead's notions of the mind and self can be seen to support the assertion that the individual needs the social field for his full realization. Also, one can see how in his thought social structure, through the organization of the 'me', provides the scaffolding for the

individual. Mead addressed the essential problem of subject relations –
how I can constitute in myself another person, how I experience what
is in me as other than me. His solution to this problem was in terms
of the interrelationship, or the conversation between the self's dual
structure of 'I' and 'me'. His thought thus supports the notion of an
organization embracing the individual within the social field, what I
have called a subjective organization.

Finally, there was consideration of how subject and object relations
interconnect, or how the subject's dual being as individual and other
relates to the theory of object relations.

Various psychoanalytic thinkers were looked at, such as Freud,
Klein, Fairbairn, Bion and Sandler. But it is argued that it is only with
Winnicott that one comes close to a theory of subject relations which
can take account of recent findings in neurophysiology, as well as
philosophy and the social sciences. Because of his notion of the
transitional space between subjects, the Winnicottian subject is not
entirely coincidental with the psyche of the individual. That is,
bringing the argument of the book back to the preoccupation of
Chapter 1, the location of the human subject for Winnicott lies in the
space between the individual and the other in the social field.
Winnicott thus provides the basis for a new kind of psychoanalytic
theory, based on the complexities of the relations between subjects. In
his descriptions of the way that the subject changes from being an
isolated subject to being in contact with others, one has the beginnings
of what could become a fully developed theory of subject relations.

To end with, I have in mind aspects of two artists, Cézanne and
Giacometti, which encapsulate aspects of the dilemmas of trying to
capture the human subject. Before a Cézanne picture, there is an
encounter between spectator and work; it appears to be 'out there', yet
the pictures often draw us in towards ourselves in a powerful way. I
know of no other artist, except perhaps Giotto, who does this quite so
effectively, so that we almost touch the objects, or they almost seem to
look at us. We are brought right up against our own sense of who we
are. It is difficult to be precise about states of mind relevant to artistic
activity. However, Cézanne himself had much to say about the
process, often emphasizing the need for the artist, and hence the
spectator too, to restrain ordinary perception and control, and allow
another, more receptive process to take place (Gasquet, 1921, p.150).

Cézanne also described the synthesizing role of the artist's 'temperament', what brings together the various fragments of sensations
and enables the artist to 'realize' his vision in the 'motif', an
essentially subjective process. Cézanne was a revolutionary because he
presented us with a new vision of the world and overturned traditional

means of representation. Instead of the old Cartesian view of the human subject looking out at the world with a little world inside him reflecting the outer world, Cézanne proposed a different way of seeing, which of course became the basis for the modernist revolution in art. Cézanne presents us with the issue of subjectivity itself, or 'temperament', as he called it. After him, art is no longer (if it ever really was) a question of simply representing what one sees in some kind of way truthful to the object out there; but instead, one may keep the object in the landscape before oneself, but represent the very encounter between the artist and the object – the artist represents what was true to the human subject.

I have been trying throughout to define an area of our work as analysts with which we constantly grapple, but often in the dark conceptually – for example, how we come to know the patient, gradually (perhaps like an artist) building up a picture of them; how we become familiar with their intimate ways of relating; how we evaluate what goes on between us and the patient. It is difficult to capture precisely what does go on between patient and analyst in writing, because by its very nature the analytic relationship is a subjective affair. Something always seems to elude us when we try to make formal descriptions of what takes place.

David Sylvester, in his book on Giacometti, tries to describe how the artist captures the elusive image of the subject in the physical objective material of the sculpture. This defines rather well the elusive area I have been trying to describe.

Our experience of the work reconstitutes the relationship between sculptor, sculpture and model. As an object, the sculpture is within our reach as it was within the sculptor's reach – indeed, it is the reverse side of his gestures, the traces of his gestures ... but the sculpture as a human figure is separate from the sculpture as an object, it is not within reach. It is detachable from the object. It can seem to move away while we are getting closer to the object until finally the figure disappears into bronze or plaster and we are left with the object only. Thus the work shows forth the dual nature of a work of art as object and image – an object that is hard and firm, flat, cold, an image that is soft, round, warm. (Sylvester, 1994, p.27)

I have been trying, however inadequately, to capture something of this human image, detachable from the physical object, not always of course soft, round and warm, but certainly elusive and endlessly fascinating.

REFERENCES

Arendt, H. (1963), *On Revolution*. Harmondsworth: Penguin, 1973.

Aron, L. (1991), 'The patient's experience of the analyst's subjectivity'. *Psychoanal. Dialogues*, 1: 29–51.

Atwood, G. and Stolorow, R. (1984), *Structures of Subjectivity*. Hillsdale, N.J.: The Analytic Press.

Bacal, H. (1985), 'Optimal responsiveness and the therapeutic process', in A. Goldberg (ed.), *Progress in Self Psychology*, New York: Guilford Press, pp.202–7.

Baker, R. (1993), 'Some reflections on humour in psychoanalysis'. *Int. J. Psychoanal.*, 74: 951–60.

Bakhtin, M. (1963), *Problems of Dostoevsky's Poetics*, trans. C. Emerson. Minneapolis: University of Minnesota Press.

—— (1990), *Art and Answerability*, trans. M. Holquist and V. Liapunov. Austin: University of Texas Press.

Balint, E. (1968), 'The mirror and the receiver', in *Comprehensive Psychiatry*, 9: 344–8. In J. Mitchell and M. Parsons (eds), *Before I was I*. London: Free Association Books, 1993, pp. 56–62

—— (1993), 'Unconscious Communication', in J. Mitchell and M. Parsons (eds), *Before I was I*. London: Free Association Books, pp. 109–18.

Benvenuto, B. and Kennedy, R. (1986), *The Works of Jacques Lacan*. London: Free Association Books.

Berger, P. and Luckmann, T. (1966), *The Social Construction of Reality*. London: Allen Lane.

Bettelheim, B. (1983), *Freud and Man's Soul*. London: Chatto and Windus.

Bion, W. (1962a), *Learning from Experience*. London: Heinemann.

—— (1962b), 'A theory of thinking'. *Int. J. Psychoanal*, 43: 306–10.

—— (1963), *Elements of Psychoanalysis*. London: Tavistock.

—— (1970), *Attention and Interpretation*. London: Tavistock.

—— (1992), *Cogitations*. London: Karnac.

Bollas, C. (1987), *The Shadow of the Object*. London: Free Association Books.

—— (1989), *Forces of Destiny*. London: Free Association Books.

—— (1995), *Cracking Up*. London: Routledge.

Brandschaft, B. and Stolorow, R. (1990), 'Varieties of therapeutic alliance'. *Annals of Psychoanal.* 18: 99–114.

Brecht, B. (1948), 'A short organum for the theatre', in J. Willett (ed.), *Brecht on Theatre*. London: Methuen, 1964.

—— (1963), *The Messingkauf Dialogues*, trans. J. Willett. London: Methuen, 1965.

Britton, R. (1989), 'The missing link: parental sexuality in the oedipus complex', in J. Steiner (ed.), *The Oedipus Complex Today*. London: Karnac, 1989, pp. 83–101.

Bromberg, P. (1993), 'Shadow and substance: a relational perspective on clinical process'. *Psychoanal. Psychology*, 10 (2): 147–68.

Brook, P. (1988), *The Shifting Point*. London: Methuen.

Buckley, P. (1988) (ed.), *Essential Papers on Psychosis*. New York and London: New York University Press.

Cavell. M. (1991), 'The subject of mind'. *Int. J. Psychoanal.* 72: 141–54.

—— (1993), *The Psychoanalytic Mind*. Cambridge, Ma. and London: Harvard University Press.

Christie, G. (1994), 'Some psychoanalytic aspects of humour'. *Int. J. Psychoanal.*, 75: 479–89.

Coen, S. (1994), 'Love between patient and analyst'. *J. Amer. Psychoanal. Assn.*, 42: 1107–35.

Coltart, N. (1992), *Slouching towards Bethlehem*. London: Free Association Books.

Crick, F. (1994), *The Astonishing Hypothesis: The Scientific Search for the Soul*. New York: Simon and Schuster.

Darwin, C. (1872), *The Expression of the Emotions in Man and Animals*. Chicago and London: Chicago University Press, 1965.

Davidson, D. (1980), *Essays on Actions and Events*. Oxford: Clarendon Press.

—— (1984), *Inquiries into Truth and Interpretation*. Oxford: Clarendon Press.

Dennett, D. (1991), *Consciousness Explained*. London: Allen Lane.

Derrida, J. (1967), *Writing and Difference*, trans. A. Bass. London: Routledge and Kegan Paul.

Dewey, J. (1929), *Experience and Nature*. La Salle, Ill.: Open Court.

Dilthey, W. (1883), *Introduction to the Human Sciences*, ed. R. Makkreel and F. Rodi. Princeton, N.J.: Princeton University Press, 1989.

Durkheim, É. (1893), *The Division of Labour in Society*, trans. W. Halls. London: Macmillan, 1984.

—— (1912), *The Elementary Forms of Religious Life*, trans. K. Fields. New York and London: Free Press, 1995.

Fairbairn, R. (1952), *Psychoanalytic Studies of the Personality*. London: Tavistock/Routledge.

Ferenczi, S. (1926), 'The problem of acceptance of unpleasant ideas', in *Further Contributions to Psychoanalysis*. London: Hogarth Press, (1926).

Foucault, M. (1969), *The Archaeology of Knowledge*, trans A. Sheridan Smith. London and New York: Routledge, 1972.

Freeman, W. (1991), 'The physiology of perception'. *Scientific American*, February: 34–41.

Freud, S. (1891), *On Aphasia*, trans. E. Sterger. New York: International Universities Press, 1953.

—— (1895a), 'Project for a scientific psychology', in James Strachey (ed.), *The Standard Edition of the Complete Pyschological Works of Sigmund Freud*, 24 vols. London: Hogarth, 1953–73, vol. 1, pp. 283–398.

—— (1985b), with J. Brener, *Studies in hysteria, S.E.* 2.

—— (1896), 'The aetiology of hysteria', *S.E.* 3: 191–221.

—— (1900), *The Interpretation of Dreams, S.E.* 4 and 5.

—— (1905a), *Three Essays on Sexuality, S.E.* 7: 135–243.

—— (1905b), *Jokes and the Unconscious, S.E.* 8.

—— (1911a), 'The handling of dream-interpretation', *S.E.* 12: 91–5.

—— (1911b), 'Formulations on the two principles of mental functioning', *S.E.* 12: 218–26.

—— (1912), 'Recommendations to physicians practising psychoanalysis', *S.E.* 12: 111–20.

—— (1913), 'On beginning the treatment', *S.E.* 12: 123–44.

—— (1915a), 'Instincts and their vicissitudes', *S.E.* 14: 117–40.

—— (1915b), 'The unconscious', *S.E.* 14: 232–5.

—— (1917), 'A metapsychological supplement to the theory of dreams', *S.E.* 14: 217–35.

—— (1920), *Beyond the Pleasure Principle, S.E.* 18: 1–64.

—— (1921), *Group Psychology and the Analysis of the Ego, S.E.* 18: 69–143.

—— (1924), 'A note on the mystic writing-pad', *S.E.* 19: 225–32.

—— (1927), 'Humour', *S.E.* 21: 161–6.

—— (1930), *Civilization and its Discontents, S.E.* 21: 64–145.

—— (1940), *An Outline of Psychoanalysis, S.E.* 23: 139–207.

Gasquet, J. (1921), *Cézanne*, trans. C. Pemberton. London: Thames and Hudson, 1991.

Giddens. A. (1972), *Émile Durkheim, Selected Writings*. Cambridge: Cambridge University Press.

Goldstein, R. (1995), 'Hughlings Jackson and Freud'. *J. Amer. Psychoanal. Assn.* 43: 495–515.

Grotstein, J. (1978), 'Inner space: its dimensions and its coordinates'. *Int. J. Psychoanal.*, 59: 55–61.

Habermas, J. (1985), *The Philosophical Discourse of Modernity*, trans. F. Lawrence. Cambridge: Polity Press, 1987.

—— (1992), *Postmetaphysical Thinking*, trans. W. Hohengarten. Cambridge: Polity Press.

Hegel, G. (1807), *Phenomenology of Spirit*, trans. A. Miller. Oxford: Clarendon Press, 1977.

Havel, V. (1986), *Living in Truth*, ed. J. Vladislav. London: Faber, 1987.

Heimann, P. (1989), *About Children and Children-no-longer*. London: Tavistock/Routledge.

Hoffman, I. (1991), 'Towards a social-constructivist view of the psychoanalytic situation'. *Psychoanal. Dialogues*, 1: 74–105.

Hume, D. (1740), *A Treatise of Human Nature*, ed. L. Selby-Bigge. Oxford: Clarendon, 1888.

Husserl, E. (1929), *Cartesian Meditations*, trans. D. Cairns. The Hague: Martinus Nijhoff, 1973.

—— (1954), *The Crisis of European Sciences*, trans. D. Carr. Evanston, Ill.: Northwestern University Press, 1970.

Joseph. E. (1987), 'The consciousness of being conscious'. *J. Amer. Psychoanal. Assn.*, 35: 5–22.

Kennedy, R. (1984), 'A dual aspect of the transference'. *Int. J. Psychoanal.*, 65: 471–83.

—— (1989) 'Starting analysis of a self-mutilating adolescent', in M. Laufer and E. Laufer (eds), *Developmental Breakdown and Psychoanalytic Treatment in Adolescence*. New Haven, Conn. and London: Yale University Press.

—— (1993), *Freedom to Relate: Psychoanalytic Explorations*. London: Free Association Books.

—— (1995), 'Aspects of consciousness: one voice or many? *Psychoanal. Dialogues*, 6: 73–96.

—— (1996), 'Bearing the unbearable: working with the abused mind'. *J. Assoc. Psychoanal. Psychotherapy*, 10: 143–54.

—— (1997), *Child Abuse, Psychotherapy and the Law*. London: Free Association Books.

—— Tischler, L. and Heymans, A. (1987), *The Family as In-Patient*. London: Free Association Books.

Kierkegaard, S. (1846), *Concluding Unscientific Postscript*, trans. D. Swenson and W. Lowrie. Princeton, N.J.: Princeton University Press, 1941.

Klauber, J. (1981), *Difficulties in the Analytic Encounter*. London and New York: Jason Aronson.

—— (1987), *Illusion and Spontaneity in Psychoanalysis*. London: Free Association Books.

Klein, M. (1946), 'Notes on some schizoid mechanisms', in *Envy and Gratitude and Other Works*. London: Hogarth, 1980.

Kojève, A. (1947), *Introduction to the Reading of Hegel*, trans. J. Nichols. Ithaca, N.Y. and London: Cornell University Press, 1980.

Lacan, J. (1956), 'Le seminaire sur La lettre Volée', *La Psychanalyse*, 2: 1–44. trans. J. Mehlmann. Yale French Studies, 1972, 48: 38–72.

—— (1966), *Ecrits*. Paris: Le Seuil.

—— (1973), *The Four Fundamental Concepts of Psychoanalysis*, trans. A. Sheridan. London: Hogarth.

—— (1978), *The Seminar of Jacques Lacan, Book 2*, trans. S. Tomaselli. Cambridge: Cambridge University Press, 1988.

Laing, R.D. (1960), *The Divided Self*. London: Tavistock.

Laufer, M. and Laufer, E. (1984), *Adolescence and Developmental Breakdown*. New Haven, Conn. and London: Yale University Press.

Leach. E. (1982), *Social Anthropology*. London: Fontana.

Lévi-Strauss, C. (1950), 'Introduction l'oevre de Marcel' in M. Mause *Sociologie et Antropologie*. Paris: Presses Universitaires de Paris.

—— (1958), *Structural Anthropology*, trans. C. Jacobsen and B. Grundfest Schoepf. Harmondsworth: Penguin, 1963.

—— (1962), *The Savage Mind*. London: Weidenfield and Nicholson, 1966.

Lichtenstein, H. (1977), *The Dilemma of Human Identity*. New York: Jason Aronson.

Locke, J. (1689), *An Essay Concerning Human Understanding*, ed. P. Nidditch. Oxford and New York: Oxford University Press, 1975.

Luhmann, N. (1984), *The Differentiation of Society*. New York: Columbia University Press.

Luria, A. (1966), *Human Brain and Psychological Processes*, trans. B. Haigh. New York: Harper and Row.

Lyotard J.-F. (1979), *The Postmodern Condition*, trans. G. Bennington and B. Massumi. Manchester: Manchester University Press.

Malcolm, N. (1986), *Wittgenstein: Nothing is Hidden*. Oxford: Blackwell.

Marx, K. (1867), *Capital*, Vol. 1. trans. S. Moore and E. Aveling. Moscow: Foreign Language Publishing House, 1961.

Marx, K. and Engels, F. (1846), *The German Ideology*. London: Lawrence and Wishart.

Mead, G. (1934), *Mind, Self, and Society*. Chicago and London: Chicago University Press.

Mitchell, S. (1991), 'Contemporary perspectives on self: Toward an integration'. *Psychoanal. Dialogues*, 1:121–47.

—— (1993), *Hope and Dread in Psychoanalysis*. New York: Basic Books.

Nagel, T. (1971), 'Brain bisection and the unity of consciousness'. *Synthese*, 22: 396–413.

—— (1974), 'What is it like to be a bat?', in *Mortal Questions*. Cambridge: Cambridge University Press, 1979.

—— (1979), *Mortal Questions*. Cambridge: Cambridge University Press.

—— (1986), *The View from Nowhere*. New York and Oxford: Oxford University Press.

Ogden, T. (1992a), 'The dialectically constituted/decentred subject of psychoanalysis. 1. The Freudian subject'. *Int. J. Psychoanal.*, 73: 517–26.

—— (1992b), 'The dialectically constituted/decentred subject of psychoanalysis. 2. The contributions of Winnicott and Klein'. *Int. J. Psychoanal.*, 73: 613–26.

—— (1994), *Subjects of Analysis*. London: Karnac.

Padel, J. (1994), 'Coming to know somebody new'. Paper presented at University College London and Independent Group Conference.

Parfit, D. (1986), *Reasons and Persons*. Oxford and New York: Oxford University Press.

Parsons. T. (1937), *The Structure of Social Action*. New York: The Free Press.

—— (1947), Introduction in Max Weber: *The Theory of Social and Economic Organization*. New York: The Free Press.

—— (1954), Psychoanalysis and the social structure, in P. Hamilton (ed.), *Readings from Talcott Parsons*. London: Chichister and Tavistock Publications, 1985.

Perlow, M. (1995), *Understanding Mental Objects*. London and New York: Routledge.

Plato (1951), *The Symposium*, trans. W. Hamilton. Harmondsworth: Penguin.

Pribram, K. (1969) (ed)., *Brain and Behaviour 1. Mood, states and mind*. Harmondsworth: Penguin.

Rayner, E. (1995), *Unconscious Logic: An Introduction to Matte-Blanco's Bi-Logic and its Uses*. London and New York: Routledge.

Ricoeur, P. (1990), *Oneself as Another*, trans. K. Blamey. Chicago and London: Chicago University Press, 1992.

Rorty, R. (1980), *Philosophy and the Mirror of Nature*. Oxford: Blackwell.

—— (1989), *Contingency, Irony and Solidarity*. Cambridge: Cambridge University Press.

—— (1991), *Objectivity, Relativism and Truth, Philosophical Papers*, Vol. 1. Cambridge: Cambridge University Press.

Ryle, G. (1949), *The Concept of Mind*. London: Hutchinson.

Sandler, J. (1960), 'On the concept of the superego'. *Psychoanalytic Study of the Child*, 15: 128–62.

—— (1990), 'Internal object relations'. *J. Amer. Psychoanal. Assn.*, 38: 859–80.

Sartre, J.-P. (1943), *Being and Nothingness*, trans. H. Barnes. London: Methuen, 1958.

Saussure, F. (1915), *Course in General Linguistics*, trans. W. Baskin. London: Peter Owen, 1960.

Schutz, A. (1932), *The Phenomenology of the Social World*, trans. G. Walshe and F. Lehnet. London: Heinemann, 1972.

—— (1973), *Collected Papers 1: The Problem of Social Reality*. The Hague: Martinus Nijhoff.

Searles, H. (1963), 'Transference psychosis in the psychotherapy of chronic schizophrenia'. *Int. J. Psychoanal.*, 44: 249–81.

Solms, M. and Saling, M. (1986), 'On psychoanalysis and neuroscience: Freud's attitude to the localizationist tradition'. *Int. J. Psychoanal.*, 67: 397–416.

Starling, E. and Lovatt Evans, C. (1962), *Principles of Human Physiology*, ed. H. Dawson and M. Grace Eggleton. London: Churchill.

Stein, M. (1985), 'Irony in psychoanalysis'. *J. Amer. Psychoanal. Assn.*, 33: 35–57.

Steiner, J. (1987), 'The interplay between pathological organizations and the paranoid-schizoid positions'. *Int. J. Psychoanal.*, 66: 69–80.

Stern, D. (1985), *The Interpersonal World of the Infant*. New York: Basic Books.

Stolorow, R. and Atwood, G. (1992), *Context of Being: The Intersubjective Foundations of Psychological Life*. New Jersey: The Analytic Press.

Stolorow, R., Brandschaft, B. and Atwood, G. (1987), *Psychoanalytic Treatment: An Intersubectivist Approach*. New Jersey: The Analytic Press.

Stolorow, R. et al. (1994) *The Intersubjective Perspective*. Northvale, NJ: Jason Aronson.

Sylvester, D. (1994), *Looking at Giacometti*. London: Chatto and Windus.

—— (1996), *About Modern Art*. London: Chatto and Windus.

Tarachow, S. (1962), 'Interpretation and reality in psychotherapy'. *Int. J. Psychoanal.*, 43: 377–87.

Taylor, C. (1989), *Sources of the Self*. Cambridge, Mass.: Harvard University Press.

Trevarthan, C. and Hubley, P. (1978), 'Secondary intersubjectivity:

Confidence, confiders and acts of meaning in the first year', in A. Lock (ed.), *Action, Gesture and Symbol*. New York: Academic Press.

Tustin, F. (1972), *Autism and Childhood Psychosis*. London: Hogarth.

Viederman, M. (1991), 'The real person of the analyst and his role in the process of psychoanalytic cure'. *J. Amer. Psychoanal. Assn.*, 39: 451–89.

Vlastos, G. (1991), *Socrates, Ironist and Moral Philosopher*. Cambridge: Cambridge University Press.

Vygotsky, L. (1960), *Development of the Higher Mental Functions*. Moscow: R.S.F.R. Academy of Pedagogic Sciences Press (Russian edn). Quoted in K. Pribram, 1969, p.49.

Weber, M. (1904/5), *The Protestant Ethic and the Spirit of Capitalism*, trans. T. Parsons. London: Unwin University Books, 1930.

—— (1956), *Economy and Society*, ed. G. Roth and C. Wittich. Berkeley, Los Angeles and London: California University Press, 1978.

Winnicott, D. (1971), *Playing and Reality*. London: Tavistock.

Wittgenstein, L. (1921), *Tractatus Logico-Philosophicus*, trans. D. Pears and B. McGuiness. London: Routledge and Kegan Paul, 1922.

—— (1953), *Philosophical Investigations*, trans. G. Anscombe. Oxford: Blackwell.

—— (1967), *Zettel*, trans. G. Anscombe. Oxford: Blackwell.

Wolf, E. (1988), *Treating the Self*. New York: Guilford Press.

Wright, K. (1991), *Vision and Separation*. London: Free Association Books.

Young, J. (1987), *Philosophy and the Brain*. Oxford and New York: Oxford University Press.

Zeki, S. (1992), 'The visual image in mind and brain'. *Scientific American*, September, 42–50.

INDEX

By the same author

CHILD ABUSE, PSYCHOTHERAPY AND THE LAW
Bearing the Unbearable
Roger Kennedy
Foreword by Dame Elizabeth Butler-Sloss
Through many detailed case studies, the author illustrates the work of the
Cassel Hospital, an internationally renowned centre for the treatment of
families with severe emotional and psychological problems whose children
are at risk and have been abused. He describes how a legal framework can
help those working in the mental health field and a psychotherapeutic
understanding of individuals, families and groups can aid lawyers and
steer families more effectively and humanely through the legal process.

FREEDOM TO RELATE - Psychoanalytic Explorations
Roger Kennedy
What is the relationship between psychoanalysis and human freedom?
Does psychoanalysis enhance it? Is it coercive? What are the limits?
*'Kennedy has a rare gift for selecting a mixture of overviews of an analytic case and
details of session material which illustrate his argument vividly. There has been too
little dialogue in the UK between psychoanalysis and philosophy; this book is a welcome addition to the small body of work. It will be read eagerly by practitioners,
teachers and students.'* **David Mayers, London Centre for Psychotherapy**

THE WORKS OF JACQUES LACAN - An Introduction
Bice Benvenuto and Roger Kennedy
*'Anyone who has attempted to read Lacan's works and has become lost in his lan-
guage and concepts will welcome this book...A book which is both enjoyable and very
stimulating.'* **The Journal of Analytical Psychology**
'Concise and readable...a useful source book.' **Changes**
The first and still the most comprehensive introduction to the works of the
French psychoanalyst and thinker.

THE FAMILY AS IN-PATIENT
Roger Kennedy
This book describes pioneering work on the psychoanalytic treatment of
families in hospital for prolonged periods. It is based on the experience of
the Cassel hospital which combines intensive psychoanalytic psychotherapy and psychosocial nursing; in-patient clinical work centres on everyday
activities.

MIDWIFERY OF THE SOUL
A Holistic Perspective on Psychoanalysis

Margaret Arden

Early on in her career, Margaret Arden became fascinated by the problem of the gap between theory and practice. She came to realise that what she relied on in her work was not the theory she had been taught but her sense of the truth of what was going on in the consulting room. The process of psychoanalysis, the work of transference and counter transference, enables the analyst to meet one of the patient's basic needs by recognising the truth of who he or she is.

This book takes the reader on an intellectual journey. Each chapter represents a stage in the exploration of ideas which have influenced the author's view of psychoanalysis. The book is remarkable for the coherance of her thinking and the clarity of presentation of ideas which connect Jung with Freud, science with religion and the emerging science of consciousness with Goethe's scientific views. Anyone who has felt the need to explore the unrealised possibility of psychoanalytic theory will find this book rewarding.

THE PSYCHOANALYTIC MYSTIC

Michael Eigen

Most psychoanalysts tend to be anti-mystical or, at least, non-mystical. Psychoanalysis is allied with science and, if anything, is capable of deconstructing mystical experience. Yet some psychoanalysts tend to be mystical or make use of the mystical experience as an intuitive model for psychoanalysis. Indeed, the greatest split in the psychodynamic movement, between Freud and Jung, partly hinged on the way in which mystical experience was to be understood.

Michael Eigen has often advocated and encouraged a return to the spiritual in psychoanalysis - what Freud called the 'oceanic feeling'. Here he expands on his call to celebrate and explore the meaning of mystical experience within psychoanalysis, illustrating his writing with the work of Bion, Milner and Winnicott.

Also published by Free Association Books

FREELY ASSOCIATED
Encounters in Psychoanalysis with Christopher Bollas, Nina Coltart, Michael Eigen, Joyce McDougall, Adam Phillips
Edited by Anthony Molino
From a series of interviews conducted over two years, this book offers a rewarding, fascinating and rare opportunity to encounter five extraordinary psychoanalysts speaking for themselves.

H.J.S. GUNTRIP - A Psychoanalytical Biography
Jeremy Hazell
'This extraordinary book does more than any ordinary biography could to rescue from the archives of the Menninger Clinic a uniquely intimate study of Harry Guntrip - the man described by John D. Sutherland as "one of the psychoanalytic immortals".
No analyst or therapist, from the newest student to the eminences grises, can fail to be absorbed by the detailed session-by-session story of two of the great figures of psycho-analysis at work in their consulting rooms. We see the theories, techniques but, more importantly, the personalities of these two Object-Relations pioneers evolving before us as we read. I was aware of a sense of privilege at being admitted to a unique event, the unfolding of the psychological history of a rare and engaging man.' **Nina Coltart**

AN INTRODUCTION TO OBJECT RELATIONS
Lavinia Gomez
'..enjoyable, stimulating and informative. I would recommend it to students of psychotherapy and counselling, and also to psychiatrists in training or in continuing professional development.' **British Journal of Psychiatry**

In this critical introduction to the subject, Lavinia Gomez presents the work of the main theorists chronologically, enabling the reader to gain a sense of how Object Relations developed, and the way in which the theorists built on, diverged from and opposed each other's ideas. A brief biography brings to life the persons behind the theory, contributing to a deeper understanding and critical appreciation of their ideas.